CONFRONTING TERROR

CONFRONTING TERROR

9/11 and the Future of American National Security

DEAN REUTER

JOHN YOO

Encounter Books *e* New York • London

First American edition published in 2011 by Encounter Books,
an activity of Encounter for Culture and Education, Inc.,
a nonprofit, tax exempt corporation.
Encounter Books website address: www.encounterbooks.com

Manufactured in the United States and printed on
acid-free paper. The paper used in this publication meets
the minimum requirements of ANSI/NISO Z39.48 1992
(R 1997) (*Permanence of Paper*).

FIRST AMERICAN EDITION

LIBRARY OF CONGRESS CATALOGING-IN-PUBLICATION DATA

Confronting terror: 9/11 and the future of American national security/edited by
John Yoo and Dean Reuter.
p. cm.
Includes bibliographical references and index.
ISBN-13: 978-1-59403-562-3 (hbk.: alk. paper)
ISBN-10: 1-59403-562-8 (hbk.: alk. paper) 1. Terrorism—United States—Preven-
tion. 2. Terrorism—Government policy—United States. 3. National security—United
States. I. Yoo, John. II. Reuter, Dean, 1960–
HV6432.C6547 2011
363.325'160973—dc23
2011024452

Dean Reuter

To Lou Anne, Taylor, and Hannah

John Yoo

In memory of Barbara K. Olson

TABLE OF CONTENTS

CONTENTS

introduction

DEAN REUTER

After the September 11, 2001, terrorist attacks, the United States went to war. With thousands of Americans killed, billions of dollars in damage, and now ten years of military and security measures in response, we are still living with the war, an uncertain future, and many unanswered questions. A change of presidential administration has not dulled the controversy over the most fundamental legal and policy issues, the strategies and tactics of the war, or the ontological issue of whether this is even a war.

This book sets the stage for a reasoned, clear, and robust discussion of the future with a collection of new essays examining the law and policy of the war on terror. The contributors include supporters and critics of the war, liberals and conservatives, commentators, scholars, and former government officials; people with very divergent viewpoints, all genuinely held.

The book begins with a stirring address by Theodore B. Olson, delivered just weeks after the attacks, when Ground Zero was still smoldering. Victor Davis Hanson then offers his critique of President Obama the apologist, and the danger that results from a President who has disclaimed the spirit of the war on terror that he inherited, yet has followed and even expanded many of his predecessor's aggressive policies. Then follows a historical account by Arthur Herman, who examines the alternating periods of interventionism and isolationism throughout American history to provide the larger context for the 9/11 attacks and America's response.

The next set of essays frames the fundamental questions, provides essential context, and suggests new ways of thinking. Several chapters touch on the peculiar nature of the enemy and the unprecedented nature of the threat: a non-state actor that has a demonstrated ability to inflict heavy damages and casualties on the United States. Former Secretary of Homeland Security Michael Chertoff argues that the binary choice between a law enforcement and military regime is false, and discusses what flows from that reality. Former Attorney General Edwin Meese and his co-author Paul Rosenzweig urge a nonpartisan approach to the war against terrorists and take a close look at the restructuring of America's intelligence operations. Judge Laurence Silberman, a senior judge on the D.C. Circuit Court of Appeals, gives an insider's account of his work as co-chairman of the Presidential Intelligence Commission, and joins Meese in his criticism of the intelligence restructuring. Renowned libertarian scholar Richard Epstein offers a provocative discussion of how to analyze the most aggressive and intrusive intelligence collection methods, the use of racial profiling, and the treatment and interrogation of detainees.

Harvard Law School Professor Alan Dershowitz argues in favor of the use of torture in carefully defined circumstances and under certain controlled conditions, including a court-issued warrant. Other contributors, including Professor Jonathan Turley, recoil from that idea. Still others such as Marc Thiessen and Andrew McCarthy cite the successes of our anti-terror strategies, including aggressive interrogation. My co-editor, John Yoo, discusses the difference between torture and the coercive interrogation methods used by the Bush administration, and the role executive power plays in wartime.

Our authors then turn to the issue of domestic civil liberties. Former Congressman Bob Barr and former U.S. Attorney General John Ashcroft, with co-author Viet Dinh, debate the virtues and vices of the USA Patriot Act. We now have the benefit of a decade-long track record and several congressional reauthorizations to inform thinking on the future of civil liberties during this war. Another former U.S. Attorney General, Michael Mukasey, and the president of the ACLU, Anthony Romero, disagree about the proper forum for the trial of terror suspects. These chapters display stark differences in thinking on the extent of the President's authority to detain, the assertion of state secrets, the limits of surveillance, the use of unmanned drones and targeted killing, whether and how to continue to prosecute the wars in Iraq and Afghanistan, and more.

Executive branch activities are necessarily a focus of the book, but the presidency is not alone in fielding its share of criticism. We have also included critiques of the judiciary from unexpected sources. The long-time former president of the ACLU, Nadine Strossen, argues that our court system is effectively being closed to terror suspects in what amounts to a fundamental denial of access to justice. Judge Raymond Randolph, a judge on the D.C. Circuit Court of Appeals, emphatically criticizes the U.S. Supreme Court for its war on terror jurisprudence. Charles Kesler completes the volume, discussing America's reaction to 9/11, focusing on the interaction between patriotism, religiosity, and the spread of democracy. In the book's conclusion, John Yoo identifies the areas of continuity between Bush and Obama administration policies, but criticizes the incentives created by the differences introduced by the Obama administration and its harmful effects for the nation's security.

I commend these contributors for having remained principled throughout the last decade. Those who criticized President Bush for what they saw as policies that were overly aggressive now criticize Obama for the same. They do not remain silently on the sidelines as women's rights proponents did when President Clinton was investigated and impeached. Likewise, contributors who defended President Bush during and after his administration have never cashed in on the easy opportunity to accuse President Obama of flip-flopping. Rather, most have at least acknowledged that he has performed well on many terrorism issues, allowing President Obama to implement what he believes to be the best policies.

Our authors collectively reveal an interesting fact. Conservatives generally disfavor centralized government on taxing, spending, and market regulation. They rely on the structural Constitution, which sets three federal branches of government against one another in a manner designed to prevent the accumulation of great power in any one branch. The Constitution then further pits the whole of the federal government against the several states to prevent the accumulation of power at the federal level. For conservatives, big government in the domestic realm is anathema. Conservatives question the very need for income redistribution and the rent-seeking that it unavoidably brings. Some conservatives might acknowledge the need for limited government oversight and standard-setting in some circumstances (think abortion, pornography, marriage, antitrust, rules prohibiting fraud), but not in the vast majority of cases. Nearly every measure of government regulation slows the engine of the free market—even when the government is able to implement the policies it intends, those policies are replete with unintended consequences that run opposite to the regulatory intent. Conservatives doubt the very competence of big government to oversee the domestic policy of the country.

In contrast, liberals consistently welcome an interventionist domestic government. They see it as essential for leveling the playing field. The faith that progressives place in centralizing the government's control over domestic matters has few limits. The liberal vision of America and a robust, redistributive, pervasive government are one and the same.

But when it comes to national security, intelligence gathering, and making war, the conservatives and liberals reverse their attitudes toward government power. In these realms, liberals are distrustful of government and jealous of their own privacy, while small-government conservatives find (or at least hope for) competence in the same large government that they distrust to implement domestic policy. Liberals, trusting and accepting of the need for big government when it comes to all things on the domestic front, oppose dearly the assertion of government power in the national security, intelligence gathering, and war powers areas.

There is a great deal of tension in these positions on both sides. Distinct parts of the government deal with domestic and national security matters. Few would argue, after all, that the U.S. Postal Service is interchangeable with the U.S. Marine Corps. There are structural and even cultural differences in the armed services, intelligence agencies, and the Departments of Education and Transportation. They certainly attract very different personnel. But these differences cannot account for the vastly different respect and criticism that they alternately enjoy and suffer. This tension may be as inexplicable as it is real.

Reading this book, you will surely find that reasonable people can differ on many of the hard questions with currency. Our authors make coherent arguments that are at once divergent and compelling. One area of agreement deserves highlighting: the war on terror policies of two very different Presidents are surprisingly similar. President Bush, a conservative President, implemented what most of our contributors would characterize as aggressive anti-terrorist policies in response to the 9/11 attacks. For this, after a short period of acclaim, he received increasingly strident criticism from the courts, Congress, the media, the international community and, notably, from a liberal presidential candidate who would become his successor.

Yet that same anti-war, liberal candidate, once in office and privy to all the intelligence available to the commander-in-chief, and with the weight of responsibility for the first time on his shoulders, has adopted some of the same positions as his predecessor. Certainly there are differences between the anti-terror policies of Presidents Bush and Obama, but there is agreement in more areas than anyone could have predicted on Inauguration Day 2009. Most of the contributors acknowledge (some with relief, others with concern rising to consternation) that President Obama's policies are in some vital respects indistinguishable from those of President Bush. There is less discussion in these pages of why President Obama arrived there—through a process of enlightenment or by force of circumstance. But there is agreement on his point of arrival.

Undoubtedly, a measure of political expediency or practical realism has motivated President Obama. His first choice was to close the Guantánamo detention center. His second choice was to try terrorists in the civilian justice system. More than one contributor criticizes the President for apologizing for perceived American foreign policy transgressions that made the environment fertile for the growth of terrorism—not a tack taken by President Bush. Other contributors question whether President Obama even fully appreciates the insidious nature of the enemy—not the mark of a hawk. Several contributors cite him for abandoning President Bush's interrogation policies, and for choosing to kill suspected terrorists through remote drones rather than capturing and interrogating them aggressively. On the other hand, he has surged troops in Afghanistan. He has defended the extension of important USA Patriot Act provisions with more vigor than some recently elected Republican members of Congress. He has pressed in the courts for a very broad state secrets privilege. He has claimed authority for indefinite detention. He ordered the successful killing of Osama bin Laden, but in doing so solidified his preference for avoiding the messy question of detention at the expense of intelligence collection. He held a detainee on a U.S. Navy warship, risking the ire of his allies in the U.S. Congress, but also of other critics when he committed to an Article III trial for that detainee.

In sum, President Obama looks a lot like a war on terror President despite his progressive political leanings—in defiance of his electoral base—and notwithstanding a successful electoral campaign based in part on an anti-war stance. The fact that two Presidents with strikingly different ideological views have arrived at similar conclusions strongly validates those policies. That both

Presidents have come to the same conclusions from such different starting points could be taken as evidence that a robust, aggressive response to the attacks was and still is the correct response.

In his 1862 annual message to Congress, President Abraham Lincoln delivered a sentiment that is relevant here: "The dogmas of the quiet past are inadequate to the stormy present. The occasion is piled high with difficulty, and we must rise with the occasion. As our case is new, so we must think anew and act anew."[1] Our legal system, constrained by the laws of armed conflict, strains at the seams as it attempts to wedge an atypical enemy and a novel form of warfare into a static set of rules. The new enemy and the new model of warfare create a number of novel issues and complex questions, particularly for our open and free society. Too many of those questions remain unanswered today. Each open question creates uncertainty for our society and for those responsible for waging the war, and each deserves a clear answer. This book identifies those open questions, and then provides a forum for their discussion.

in memory of barbara k. olson[*]

THEODORE B. OLSON

T he Federalist Society established an annual lecture series in memory of Barbara K. Olson, who was murdered in the terrorist attacks against the United States as a passenger on the hijacked American Airlines flight that was flown into the Pentagon on September 11, 2001. The Society envisions that

---

* This essay is an edited version of a speech delivered at the Federalist Society's 15th Annual National Lawyers Convention in Washington, D.C., on November 16, 2001.

the Barbara K. Olson Memorial Lecture each year will address the ideals and principles that the Federalist Society holds dear and that Barbara cherished: limited government, liberty, and freedom. I felt that it would be fitting to inaugurate this series with some words about Barbara, why she died, and how much of her life and death were interwoven with those very principles that will animate the lecture series in her name.

On September 11, 2001, Barbara Olson and thousands of other Americans were murdered. There were victims from other nations that day as well, but they were accidental casualties. Barbara and her fellow Americans were the targets; selected at random to be slaughtered that day precisely because they were Americans.

The places of their deaths were carefully chosen for what they meant to America, and to the world about Americans, and because they were unique symbols of America's vitality, prosperity, and strength. The World Trade Center towers were an emblem of America's largest and most prosperous city and an internationally recognized symbol of America's leadership in commerce, free enterprise, and international trade. The Pentagon was an even more fitting target for the perverted minds that planned this day of terror. Construction on it had begun precisely sixty years earlier, on September 11, 1941, as America was awakening to the nightmare of Adolf Hitler and Nazi terror in Europe. Since its construction, the Pentagon has stood for the power, strength, and seeming invincibility of a free people. It has been the place from which America, again and again, sent its men and women to fight and die to save not only its own citizens, but millions of others as well, from tyranny, oppression, brutality, and murder. One additional symbol of America, the U.S. Capitol, was spared that day only because the brave Americans on that fourth aircraft did what Americans instinctively do when their lives and their country are threatened: they fought. They died, but they saved the lives of countless others and averted an even greater and barely imaginable tragedy.

Barbara Olson had less time—and maybe not as many resources—as the heroes on United Flight 93, which was brought down in Pennsylvania short of its target. But the moment her flight was hijacked, she began to try to save herself and her fellow passengers. Barbara somehow managed (I think she was the only one on that flight to do so) to use a telephone in the airplane to call—not only for help from the outside, but for guidance for herself and the flight crew in the battle that she was already undertaking in her mind. She learned during those two telephone conversations that two passenger jumbo jets had already that morning been turned into instruments of mass murder at the World Trade Center. So she knew the unspeakable horror that she was facing—and I know without the slightest doubt that she died fighting—with her body, her brain, and her heart—and not for a moment entertaining the notion that she would not prevail. Barbara died therefore not only because she was an American, but as one more American who refused to surrender to the monstrous evil into whose eyes she and her fellow countrymen stared during those last hideous moments.

September 11, 2001 was unprecedented in our nation's history. Our country has been attacked before. Our soldiers and innocent citizens have been the victims of terrorism before. But never before in our history have so many civilian citizens, engaged in the routines of their daily lives—who neither individually nor collectively had done anything to provoke the savage attack that they were to experience that day—been brutally murdered for the simple reason that they were Americans, and because they stood, in their countless individual lives, for all the things that America symbolizes.

As President Bush immediately recognized, September 11 was an act of war. But, as he has also explained, it was much more than that. It was also a crime, an act of pure hatred and unmitigated evil. It was a ruthless, brutal, intentionally malignant attack on thousands of innocent persons.

Think of the sick calculation that gave birth to these acts. The victims were persons of all races, backgrounds, religions, ages, and qualities. They had one thing in common: they were Americans who believed in the values that their country stands for: liberty, democracy, freedom, and equality. Their lives were cruelly extinguished because they were the living embodiment of the aspirations of most of the world's peoples. The people who killed them, and who planned their death, hate America and Americans for that very reason. They despise America and the beacon that America holds out to people who are impoverished, enslaved, persecuted, and subjugated everywhere in the world. The men who planned the savage acts of September 11 cannot prevail; they cannot even long exist, as long as American ideals continue to inspire the very people they hope to tyrannize and enslave. Hence they have declared war, in fact they have declared hatred, on this country and the values that we hold dearest.

It is a cynical lie that the animals that killed our loved ones on 9/11 were motivated by Islam, or because this nation of ours is anti-Islamic. Among our most cherished values, enshrined in the First Amendment to our Constitution, is freedom of conscience, liberty of expression, and the free exercise of religion. This continent was populated by people who surrendered their homes and crossed a terrifying ocean to reach a rugged and inhospitable frontier in order to escape religious persecution and to seek religious freedom.

From its birth, this nation and the American people have offered sanctuary and shelter to persons of all faiths. Our Constitution—always with the support of our people—has again and again extended its embrace to the unpopular, the unusual, the unconventional, and the unorthodox. We protect not only those who will not salute our flag, but those who would spit upon it or burn it. We regularly pledge our allegiance to a constitution that shelters those who refuse to pledge their allegiance to it. Far from tyrannizing those who worship a particular God or embrace a particular religion, we protect those who worship any God—or no God. Indeed, Americans have defended with their lives persons whose religious convictions preclude them from taking up arms to defend the same constitution that gives them the right to refrain from defending it.

It is true, I suppose, that there are many in the Middle East who hate this country for its support of Israel. But how tragic and misguided for them to despise us for extending comfort and defense to a people who have so long, and so recently, been the victims of indescribable ethnic persecution. Nor has America's support for Israel ever been rooted in or manifested by hostility to the Muslim faith or those who practice it. The terrorists and their apologists have lied about these things, but what is another lie when their goals and tactics are so vastly more evil?

So, while the terrorists of September 11 invoke the name of Islam, that is simply a mask for their hate, envy, and despicable ambitions. The terrorists who seek to destroy us do so because America and Americans are everything that their hatred and motives prevent them from being. They are tyrants, so they hate democracy. They are bigots and religious zealots who persecute Christians and Jews and Hindus and Buddhists and women. So they must hate America, because America stands for tolerance and freedom and respect for all races, all religions, and all peoples, regardless of their sex, color, national origin, or accent. They are despots who will not permit children to go to school.

So they must hate the nation that commits vast resources to the education of its children, and whose Supreme Court has said that free public education cannot even be withheld from those who are in this country illegally.

These terrorists can succeed only through corruption, cruelty, and brutality. Thus they hate and must tear down America and its system of laws, which shields its people from those malevolent acts. And these terrorists can enslave the people they wish to subjugate only by keeping them poor and destitute, so they must undermine and discredit the one place in all the world that stands the most for the rule of law and individual liberty and that allows its people—and the people who flock here daily by the thousands—the opportunity to rise above all those conditions.

Abraham Lincoln was paraphrasing our Declaration of Independence when he characterized our nation as having been "conceived in liberty and dedicated to the proposition that all men are created equal." That revolutionary document set down our collective belief in unalienable human rights to liberty, freedom, and equality; to the proposition that governments derive their powers from the consent of the governed, the principle that tyrants who would oppress their people are unfit to be rulers of a free people, and the right to the pursuit of happiness. How can these terrorists ever prevail if these American ideals are not only allowed to be expressed, but to succeed so dramatically—and to inspire so many people throughout the world for so many centuries?

The answer is simple: the terrorists of September 11 cannot prevail in a world occupied by the Declaration of Independence, the U.S. Constitution and its Bill of Rights, the Emancipation Proclamation, the Gettysburg Address, the Statue of Liberty, the World Trade Center, the Pentagon, the Capitol, the Supreme Court, and the White House. They cannot coexist with these ideals, these principles, these institutions, and these symbols. They cannot survive, much less prevail, in the same world as America and its people. So they must try to destroy America, and the principles for which it stands.

We do not claim that America has been or is today without imperfections and shortcomings. Our Constitution was undeniably flawed at its origin. Implementation of our lofty ideals has never been without error, and some of our mistakes have been shameful. But the course of our history has been constant, if occasionally erratic, progress from the articulation of those lofty ideals to the extension of their reality to all our people: to those who were born here and those, from hundreds of diverse cultures, who flock to the American soil because of the principles and opportunities it promises.

Reflect on the fact that there is no segment or class of the world's peoples who have exclusive claim on the term "American," and no segment of the world's population to whom that claim has been denied. We welcome 100,000 refugees per year into this country. Over 650,000 people immigrated legally to America in the most recent year for which we have reliable statistics. Over 5 million people are in this country today who were so desperate to come here that they did so illegally.

There are more Jews in New York City than in Israel. More Poles in Chicago than any other city in the world except Warsaw. America is home to 39 million Irish-Americans, 58 million German-Americans, 39 million Hispanic-Americans, and nearly a million Japanese-Americans. And there are 7 million Muslims in America, nearly the population of New York City.

How tragic it is that the operatives of the September 11 terrorist acts were people whom we welcomed to this country, and to whom we extended all of our freedoms, the protections of all of our laws, and the opportunities this country affords to everyone to travel, work, and live. But, we welcome immigrants because nearly all of us are immigrants or descendants of immigrants who came here to enjoy America's freedoms, rights, liberties, and the opportunity, denied elsewhere, to pursue happiness and prosperity. People from all places on the globe give our country its identity, its diversity, and its strength.

Ronald Reagan often said that "every once in a while, each of us native-born Americans should make it a point to have a conversation with someone who is an American by choice. A few years back, a woman who had fled Poland wrote a letter and said: 'I love America because people accept me for what I am. They don't question my ancestry, my faith, my political beliefs. . . . I love America because America trusts me.'" President Reagan was also fond of quoting from a letter he had received from a man who wrote, "You can go to live in Turkey, but you can't become a Turk. You can't go to live in Japan and become Japanese, [and so on for Germany, France, etc.] But . . . Anyone from any corner of the world can come to America and be an American."

So it is particularly sad and a bitter irony that the nineteen savages who took the lives of thousands of Americans on September 11 were able to come here because we welcomed them, and trusted them, and allowed them to learn to fly our airplanes and the freedom to travel. And they took these precious gifts and turned them into instruments of hatred and death. How perverse and twisted. How incredibly sick they must have been— that not one of them had a moment of conscience after all that time in this beautiful and free country. Everywhere they looked they saw Americans and immigrants to America at work and at play exercising the freedoms and opportunities that this country offers unstintingly to everyone, including them. But their hatred was so intense, their malignancy so advanced, that they never, as far as we know, even for a moment, paused to reconsider the despicable, unconscionable, and evil acts they planned to inflict on the people they were walking, working, and living amongst.

It has, I suppose, always caused some resentment that we believe so passionately and so unquestioningly that freedom, equality, liberty, democracy, and the rule of law are concepts and rights that should belong to all people. But how can that be seen as arrogance, as some have called it? I simply cannot accept that. What can possibly be wrong with the aspiration that moved the founders of this country to believe that people are entitled to self-determination, the right to choose their system of government, the right to freedom within an orderly and secure society, and the maximum liberty to pursue happiness and fulfillment? We know that these are enduring values. We can debate nearly everything else, but we don't need to debate that. We know that these principles lift everyone up. And we know that these principles are only questioned by those who would seek to advance their own twisted agendas by withholding freedom, liberty, and prosperity from others.

We have now been reminded, in the most horrible way, that there are people who not only hate our principles, but who would dedicate their lives—and surrender their lives—to banish the ideals and the incentives our Founding Fathers provided for tyrannized and impoverished people everywhere in 1776. We have tragically learned again, in the most unthinkable fashion, that our values and our principles are neither self-executing nor self-sustaining, and that we must sacrifice and fight to maintain what our forebears sacrificed and fought to bequeath to us. And now the rest of the world is learning again that Americans will not flinch from that fight or tire of it. Americans will fight, they will sacrifice, and they will not give up or leave the job unfinished. This war is for all living Americans. It is for the parents, grandparents, and great-grandparents that fought and sacrificed to come here. And it is for our children and generations to come. And it is for those who choose to become Americans in the future.

America will not lose this war because we cannot tolerate, we cannot contemplate, we cannot even consider that we will lose what centuries of Americans fought to create, improve, and maintain. We cannot and we will not betray the people who gave us this glorious heritage. We cannot and will not dishonor or wash away the memories of those who somehow clawed their way out of poverty, tyranny, and persecution to come to this country because it was America, and because they were willing to risk death to become Americans, and to give their children and grandchildren the opportunity and freedom and inspiration that make this place America. Americans could no longer call themselves Americans if they could walk away from that legacy.

People who write regularly for newspapers and who offer opinions on television, or who send advice to us from other parts of the world, sometimes say that America is too rich, lazy, complacent, frightened, soft, and enervated to fight this fight. That we have no stamina, strength, will, patience, or steel; that we will collapse. They are so wrong. We will prevail for the very reason that we have been attacked. Because we are Americans. Because the values that made us free, make us strong; because the principles that made us prosperous, make us creative, resourceful, innovative, determined, and fiercely protective of our freedoms, our liberties, and our rights to be individuals and to aspire to whatever we choose to be. Those values and those characteristics will lift us and will defeat the dark forces who have assaulted our ideals, our country, and our people. The very qualities that bring immigrants and refugees to this country in the thousands every day made us vulnerable to the attack of September 11, but those are also the qualities that will make us victorious and unvanquished in the end. These dreadful, despicable people have hurt us, but they can never conquer us.

Let me return to Barbara Olson. So many people loved and admired Barbara. But whether you loved and admired her values, her spunk, her energy, her passion, her courage, her unconquerable spirit, or her incredible warmth, whether you knew it or not, underneath it all, you admired and were captivated by Barbara because she was pretty darn close to being a quintessential American.

Barbara was a Texan, from a family whose ancestors came to this country from Germany. She went to the all-American University of Texas and also a Catholic college, St. Thomas, in Houston. She became a professional ballet dancer in San Francisco and New York because of the beauty of dance, the rigor of its discipline, and because you have to be extraordinarily tough and ambitious to do it. And Barbara was extraordinarily tough and ambitious.

But she always wanted to be a lawyer and to be involved in politics. In order to afford law school, she invented a career out of whole cloth in Hollywood because that, she determined, was the fastest way to earn the money she needed. It did not matter in the slightest to Barbara that when she went to Hollywood she knew absolutely nothing about the motion picture and television industries. And, in fact, it really didn't matter because, as she later explained to the unwitting producer who gave her her first job, she was a fast learner.

And, of course, she succeeded. She turned down the last job she was offered in Hollywood because she had finally earned enough money to go to law school, and they were offering her so much money she did not want to be so tempted to forego her dream to be a lawyer.

She went to Cardozo Law School at Yeshiva University in New York, not necessarily the obvious choice for a blond Catholic girl from Texas. She was even told that she would never fit in, and that she would be miserable. But the people who told her that really did not know Barbara. She thrived at Cardozo as she had thrived at St. Thomas and in the ballet and in Hollywood. She loved the people, the classes, the professors, and she was a huge success, popping up for one reason or another with embarrassing frequency on the cover of *Jewish Weekly*.

Barbara created a Federalist Society chapter at Cardozo because she believed in the Society's principles—and it only served to goad her on that almost no one at Cardozo shared her political views. In her third year of law school, she somehow managed to finesse herself into an internship with the Office of Legal Counsel at the Department of Justice in Washington. And, as a very brassy and gutsy intern, she managed to be the only employee of the government of the United States willing, feisty, and fearless enough to personally serve the papers on the PLO mission to the United Nations in New York announcing that it was being expelled from this country—because they were terrorists. How Barbara loved to tell that story to her friends at Cardozo!

She turned down jobs with the finest law firms in New York to come to Washington where, it seems, she was always destined to be. In rapid succession, she succeeded as a lawyer in private practice, as a hot and very successful federal prosecutor, as Deputy General Counsel to the House of Representatives, and as a top congressional investigator, television personality, and lobbyist.

It was typical Barbara that when Al Regnery suggested that she write a book about Hillary Rodham Clinton, she literally jumped at the chance. She told me at the time that she wasn't sure that she was a writer, but a friend of ours told her that she didn't have to be a writer to be an author. So, with her legendary energy and limitless self-confidence, she poured herself into the book, finished it in nine months and, against seemingly insurmountable odds, without any previous experience with serious writing, climbed onto the *New York Times* bestseller list during the heaviest competitive time of the year, and stayed there for nine weeks. Ten days ago, her second book, written in about six months and finished just days before her death, opened at number two on the *New York Times* bestseller list, ahead of Bill O'Reilly, Jack Welch, and Tiger Woods. Not bad.

Barbara was everywhere in Washington. A witness for Clarence Thomas at his confirmation; a co-founder of the Independent Women's Forum; hosting Federalist Society members from all over the country in her home; at the epicenter of the travel office and Filegate investigations and the China campaign contributions investigation; as the second-most invited guest on "Larry King Live," appearing on MSNBC, FOX, "Meet the Press," "Crossfire," "Geraldo," "Politically Incorrect"—you name it. Ready to talk about any subject, ready to face down any adversary, she always had an opinion. And she always had that smile.

I could tell you Barbara stories for hours, and I think that you would be glad to listen. But, in short, Barbara partook of everything life gave her. She saw no limits in the people around her and she accepted no limits on what she could accomplish. She could be charming, tough, indefatigable, ferocious, and lovable. And all those things at once.

Barbara was Barbara because America, unlike any other place in the world, gave her the space, freedom, oxygen, encouragement, and inspiration to be whatever she wanted to be. Is there any other place on earth where someone could do all these things in forty-five years?

So, sadly, and ironically, Barbara may have been the perfect victim for these wretched, twisted, hateful people. Because she was so thoroughly and hugely an American, and such a symbol of America's values, ideals, and robust ambition. But she died as she lived: fighting, believing in herself, and determined to succeed. And, if she was the perfect victim, she is also a perfect symbol of what we are fighting for now and for why we will prevail.

I know—and she knows—that her government and the people of America will win this war, however long it takes, whatever it has to do. We will never, ever forget—or flinch. We will prevail for Barbara and all the other Americans we lost on September 11, and for the American spirit for which they stood and which their lives embodied. Most of all, we will defeat these terrorists because Barbara, all the other American casualties of September 11, our forebears, and our children would never forgive us if we did not.

the obama response to september 11

VICTOR DAVIS HANSON

The Bush administration's response to 9/11 should be acknowledged as a clear-cut success. After almost a decade there has not been a second attack of the magnitude of 9/11, but dozens of foiled radical Islamic terrorist attempts. The adage of "not a question of if, but when" concerning successive 9/11-like assaults is no longer much quoted. The Taliban remains out of power in Afghanistan. Much of the al-Qaeda leadership has been either killed or jailed, or is currently in hiding. The consensual government in Iraq is still stable, nearly eight years after the removal of Saddam Hussein—and seems to be exempt from much of the popular unrest elsewhere in the Arab world that reveals deep-seated anger at authoritarian government. Osama bin Laden's own popularity in the Middle East has been in decline since the mid-2000s.

Yet on the decade anniversary of 9/11, radical Islam still poses a threat, as it did ten years ago—be it among its extremist adherents residing in Europe and the United States, or in the Middle East among overt terrorist organizations such as Hezbollah and Hamas, or through the state of Iran and elements within the Syrian, Saudi, and Pakistani governments. A review of the three ongoing theatres of conflict explains why.

SHREDDING THE CONSTITUTION?

President Barack Obama had either previously condemned the Bush anti-terrorism protocols as assaults on constitutional freedoms or promised to curtail them in his first few months in office: renditions ("shipping prisoners away in the dead of night"), tribunals ("flawed military commission system"), the Guantánamo Bay detention facility ("al-Qaeda's recruiting tool"), predator drone attacks, preventive detentions ("detaining thousands without charge or trial"), and elements of the Patriot Act ("shoddy and dangerous"). Yet by 2010 President Obama adopted them all, and such measures have operated after January 2009 essentially as before—even as administration officials continue to offer criticism in rhetorical fashion in deference to their leftist base.

For example, Attorney General Eric Holder promised to try Khalid Sheikh Mohammed, an architect of 9/11, in a civilian court in New York—before apparently scrapping the initiative. He made loud and repetitive promises of shipping inmates from

Guantánamo to the United States—before quietly dropping that plan.

Publicly, President Obama critiques the policies that he inherited as much as he admits to feeling compelled to keep them. While the resulting political calculus broadcasts both his displeasure and private conviction of the utility of these ongoing protocols, the effect on the enemy is unclear, and may be one of sending mixed signals. Obama assured the world that Guantánamo was a prime recruiting tool for al-Qaeda; by keeping that facility open, he appears either ineffective in his inability to fulfill his vows, or cynical in suggesting that he does not believe his own prior fierce criticism of the Bush administration.

When Obama loudly denounced the waterboarding of three known terrorists in Guantánamo but simultaneously increased fourfold the Predator drone operations on the Afghan border and inside Pakistan, his message was again contradictory and confused: the United States is to be condemned by its own elites for waterboarding three *known* terrorists to elicit information that may have saved lives, but is not so culpable as judge, juror, and executioner of *suspected* terrorists in a foreign country—as well as any family members, associates, or bystanders who happen to be in the general vicinity when the missiles strike. Most ethicists might conclude that waterboarding a known terrorist in detention was a less morally conflicted decision than executing a suspected terrorist and, in some cases, causing collateral damage to others. In 2010 the United States killed on average about three suspected terrorists and/or their associates per day. Although precise figures are in dispute, general estimates about drone missions suggest that in two years the Obama administration had killed four times as many suspected terrorists and their associates as the Bush administration had in five years. Defenders of the President might argue that his liberal bona fides and rhetorical skills allow Obama to eliminate far more suspected terrorists than did George W. Bush—inasmuch as the Nobel laureate Obama is better positioned politically to exercise U.S. military options with greater immunity from criticism.

GOOD AND BAD WARS

A decade after 9/11, the same ambiguity surrounds the present policies in the once good war in Afghanistan and the formerly bad one in Iraq. When Senator Obama announced his presidential candidacy in autumn 2007, he almost immediately advocated the removal of U.S. troops by March 2008—a mandatory withdrawal date that soon proved embarrassing when it was dropped. And while candidate Obama declared that the surge "was not working" and lectured General David Petraeus in the September 2008 hearings on Iraq, President Obama quietly accepted the Bush-Petraeus schedule of troop withdrawals negotiated with the Iraqi government. The success of the surge, continuing quiet in Iraq in comparison to other parts of the Arab world, and the viability of the current Iraqi government apparently led Vice President Joe Biden—a former advocate of trisecting the country during the violent days of 2006–2007—to suggest such nation-building might become one of the Obama administration's "greatest achievements."

In any case, in 2010, 60 U.S. soldiers were lost in Iraq versus 499 in Afghanistan—an asymmetrical calculus never envisioned by candidate Obama. His promised bellicosity in Afghanistan, cheek-by-jowl with anti-war condemnation of Iraq, was predicated on the conventional wisdom that the NATO- and UN-approved multilateral effort against the Taliban was both easier and more politically acceptable than the supposed unilateral and doomed effort in Iraq. Yet that consensus proved outdated by the time Obama entered office, as the bad war in terms of violence became good and the good, bad. The result, as in the case of Guantánamo, was that one of the fiercest critics of the Bush effort in Iraq has become the most loyal custodian of Bush policies.

The Iraqi democracy held its first oil auction in June of 2009. Three facts were apparent. First, the negotiations were entirely transparent. Second, no American oil company was awarded an oil concession. Instead, Chinese, Russian, British, French, and other national oil consortia were given the contracts. Third, the new representative Iraqi government drove as hard a bargain on foreign oil interests as the corrupt autocrat Saddam Hussein had done—indeed, he had once given them sweetheart deals in exchange for international political cover.

In fact, there is hope that Iraq will prove, as once envisioned, to be a stabilizing force in the Middle East. While conventional wisdom emphasized that the removal of the anti-Iranian Saddam Hussein empowered theocratic Iran, the opposite may come to be true: a constitutional and open Iraq, and especially its Shiite majority, might prove unsettling to a population across the border yearning for the same freedom of expression and transparent elections. In any case, popular protests against the government are far more frequent in Tehran than in Baghdad.

Moreover, during the so-called Anbar Awakening of 2007–2008 that saw the surge of 30,000 combat troops, the United States and Iraqi forces killed thousands of radical Islamic terrorists and insurgents. That fact is as little discussed now as it was privately assumed to have been of enormous importance in humiliating the cause of radical Islam and effectively eliminating scores of terrorists who otherwise might have taken their operations elsewhere. For much of 2005–2006, Ayman al-Zawahiri had boasted that Iraq was the chief front in radical Islam's war against

the West ("the place for the greatest battle of Islam in this era")—
a theatre that by all accounts led to al-Qaeda's defeat.

Similar anomalies abound in the Afghan war. The once heralded and Americanized Afghan President Hamid Karzai (two
of his brothers are restaurant owners in the Washington, D.C.
area) has metamorphosed in the popular press from the recipient of the Philadelphia Liberty Medal (2004) and three honorary degrees from American universities (2006) into a supposed
manic-depressive.

When Iraq went quiet in 2008–2009 and Americans supposedly could at last quit "taking our eye off the ball" and devote the
proper attention and capital to defeating the Taliban, U.S. fatali-
ties instead spiked. Indeed, the number of Americans killed in
action in just the first two years of the Obama administration has
far exceeded the aggregate number from the first eight years of
the war. Our presence in Afghanistan has also radically expanded
under the Obama administration. Nearly 100,000 American
troops are now in the country—aided by 40,000 NATO troops—
and the cost is reaching between $100 billion and $125 billion a
year.

The Obama administration's anticipated multilateral effort
had already turned problematic by Inauguration Day 2009. That
unforeseen escalation of violence in Afghanistan prompted a
series of confusing reactions from a commander-in-chief whose
once good war had now turned bad: initial disengagement from
and eventual firing of General David McKiernan; the announcement of troop withdrawal dates, unexpectedly followed by
pledges of a 30,000 man surge; the relief of the indiscreet and
unhappy General David McChrystal, followed by the appointments of Generals Petraeus and Mattis; bifurcation of diplomatic
responsibilities between Ambassador Eikenberry and the late
Richard Holbrooke; a passive/aggressive public praise and blame

of President Karzai; massive increases in Predator drone attacks in Pakistan following earlier criticism of the Bush anti-terrorism protocols; and the bombast of an erratic Vice President Biden about alternately winning, losing, leaving and staying on. In sum, it proved hard for the newly inaugurated Obama to be against Iraq and for Afghanistan, when Iraq was nearly won and Afghanistan seemed nearly lost.

It is eerie how a number of the current prophets of doom about Afghanistan are now channeling the same pre-surge Iraq despair about another war that is supposedly "lost." We must partition Afghanistan; the war has become a quagmire; we have only empowered Pakistan; we need to stop counterinsurgency and simply bomb terrorists. And so on.

Yet for all these present problems, there are various reasons why even a corrupt Afghan government and its Western allies will probably not be defeated or expelled from the major cities. The infusion of billions of dollars in annual international aid allows Afghanis to survive the present global downturn. The Afghan security forces are slowly growing. An entire generation of American troops, veterans of Iraq and Afghanistan, has become skilled in counterinsurgency. The increase in Predator attacks has extended the vulnerability of Taliban and al-Qaeda terrorists well into Pakistan. For all the talk of quagmire, in November and December 2009 General Petraeus made real progress in securing provincial cities and killing large numbers of Taliban insurgents, often with the hammer-and-anvil aid of the Pakistani army.

Despite the disruption caused by the brief tenures of Generals McKiernan and McChrystal, the appointments of Generals Petraeus and Mattis—with their reputations as the top two combat officers in the U.S. military—are generally heralded. For now, the Democratic President has either embraced or expanded the prior Bush commitment to Afghanistan. In response, the left has abruptly muted its anti-war criticism against one of its own. Although public support wanes—America's Afghan war recently exceeded the duration of the Soviets' nine-year, fifty-day long conflict—there is, as yet, no move in either the Democratic-controlled Senate or the Republican-dominated House to cut off funds for the conflict. Most conservatives usually uncondition-ally support the President in times of controversial wars; liber-als only when the commander-in-chief is himself a liberal and there is no draft. Iraq remains quiet. And the U.S. commitment in manpower and dollars there continually diminishes, ensuring in times of lean budgets both more attention and resources for Afghanistan while ending a source of general anti-war fervor.

Nor has a popular anti-war movement arisen analogous to that of the opposition to Iraq. Hollywood is making no movies on Afghanistan similar to the anti-war *In the Valley of Elah*, *The Green Zone*, or *Lions for Lambs*. We won't see Alfred A. Knopf publish something analogous to Nicolson Baker's *Checkpoint*, or a for-eign mockumentary akin to Gabriel Range's *Death of a President* about the imagined assassination of George W. Bush. In sum, the supposedly unacceptable status quo in Afghanistan turns out, in many ways, to be tolerable—especially in comparison to the dark days in Iraq.

So a second question arises: to what degree can the Afghan government secure enough provincial territory outside the major cities to prevent Taliban and al-Qaeda enclaves from threaten-ing the Kabul government or exporting terror beyond the bor-ders of Afghanistan? Despite President Obama's talk of deadlines and troop withdrawals, the Taliban will not prevail so long as the United States maintains the status quo and continues to under-mine Taliban authority through a mixture of arms, economic assistance, and cultural change—at least enough so that the coun-try might resemble something close to the forty-year span of relative peace during the reign of Mohammed Zahir Shah between 1933 and 1973.

True, Iran and Pakistan have done their best to undermine U.S. efforts in Afghanistan; yet both face internal unrest that renders their own stability as questionable as the conditions in Afghanistan. Predator strikes have terrified much of the Taliban and al-Qaeda leadership in the borderlands, and sanctions are beginning to ossify the Iranian economy. Pakistan privately is as duplicitously working with the United States against the Taliban as it is with the Taliban against the United States. In the view of the Taliban, it has been unable to return to power for nearly a decade, during which time millions of Afghanis have grown accustomed to its absence as a governing power. If it is likely that the Karzai government will make some accommodations with some elements of the Taliban, it is unlikely that Afghanistan will return to its pre-9/11 status.

The United States—and perhaps even NATO as well—will probably not summarily withdraw from Afghanistan and leave the Taliban control of the country in a fashion akin to Saigon in 1975. To do that would doom millions of women, reformers, and allies who took the West at its word that it would prevent the return of a radical Taliban Islamization of the country and the outsourcing of its territory to al-Qaeda terrorists. In sum, Afghanistan may not look like the constitutional, pro-Western state that was once envisioned in autumn 2001, but it will not resemble the Islamic republic of 1996–2001 either.

THE IDEOLOGICAL FRONT

Yet a third theatre involves the ideological struggle against radical Islam. Here, candidate Obama likewise promised a sharp break from the Bush administration's identification of Islamic extremism as the nexus of the terrorist threat. But unlike his sudden reversals to embrace Bush-era policies in the war against terror and the wars in Afghanistan and Iraq, President Obama seems intent on forging an entirely new way of envisioning the enemy.

This Obama reset ideology manifests itself abstractly in rhetoric and nomenclature and more concretely through foreign policy initiatives. In his first interview as President on January 26, 2009, Barack Obama outlined to *al Arabiya* his new philosophy of America's relationship with Islam. Obama promised that he could resonate with the Muslim world in a way Bush did not, in part because of his own non-traditional heritage—Muslims in his family and his own prior residence in a Muslim country—and in part because of his unique willingness to admit past American culpability and error, in light of the fact that "all too often the United States begins by dictating."

The so-called "apology tours" followed. Obama offered regret for American sins ranging from past treatment of Native Americans to nineteenth-century slavery, and racial segregation to Guantánamo Bay. Apparently, such self-effacement was designed to win over the radical Muslim community on the theory that a new, repentant American was no longer deserving of retribution. The irony was lost on Obama: he offered some of his contrition while in Turkey—a nation whose past wars against Armenians, Greeks, and Kurds have bordered on the genocidal.

New nomenclature—much of it vague—was introduced by members of the Obama administration: terrorism became "man-caused disasters" and the war against it consisted of "overseas contingency operations." Formerly "rogue states" were now officially "outliers," as "enemy combatants" at Guantánamo were renamed as the more neutral-sounding "detainees." "Jihad," along with "radical Islam," simply disappeared—the American people were not to be reminded that those who sought to kill them before and since September 11 were exclusively Islamic radicals. Islamic terrorists received the message that Americans were afraid to label them for what they were, and the world's Muslim community saw that the United States was more afraid of offending its sensitivities than of accurately identifying killers intent on targeting Americans.

Often this philological correctness proved awkward when applied to the real world. Given the President's therapeutic nomenclature, we might be surprised to learn that the so-called Christmas Day bomber Umar Farouk Abdulmutallab, the Fort Hood mass murderer Nidal Hasan, and assorted terrorists who in the past two years planned to detonate explosives in a Dallas skyscraper, the New York subway system, Times Square, and in Portland, Oregon, were all united by a belief in radical Islamic doctrine. They all enjoyed a middle-class existence that belied the notion that Islamic terrorists target Americans because of their own poverty, past ill treatment from the United States, or lack of education.

Indeed, 2009 saw the most foiled terrorist attempts in any one year since 2001. In 2010, Muslim radicals continued to plan ways to kill thousands of Americans, despite presidential support for the so-called Ground Zero Mosque and the Muslim outreach missions assigned to NASA Administrator Charles Bolden by Obama. In his June 2009 Cairo speech, President Obama had claimed that the Muslim-controlled city of Cordoba taught us tolerance during the Christian-inspired Inquisition (1487)—quite a feat two-and-a-half centuries after most Muslims of Cordoba were cleansed, fled, or converted during the city's fall (1236) to Christian forces of the Reconquista. President Obama's declarations that Muslims had helped to foster the Western Renaissance and Enlightenment not only were historically unsound, but also did not appear to win over Islamic hearts and minds—at least not enough for the Muslim community to insist on zero tolerance for those who sought to use terrorism against Western interests.

We now are in a conundrum: Obama administration officials expect more attempts by radical Islamic terrorists and jihadists to kill Americans en masse, but must either sidestep using the words "terror," "jihadist," or "Islam," or begin to use accurate terminology and thus suffer the accruing wage of appearing erratic or hypocritical or both. Does the President continue to offer more Cairo-speech revisionism in hopes of convincing Muslims that his continual contrition is real? Or does he cease, in worry that such confessionals encourage terrorists who sense weakness and uncertainty rather than fear of retribution and punishment?

Abroad, the administration in early 2009 loudly announced a reset-button outreach effort to Iran. Iran then ignored warnings that it would have to cease efforts on its nuclear program before the 2009 UN General Assembly meeting in New York, the 2009 G-20 summit, the beginning of 2010, and the start of face-to-face negotiations. Worried about offending our new interlocutors in Tehran, the Obama administration had earlier voted "present" in late spring 2009 when nearly a million Iranians went out into the streets to protest the cruelty and lawlessness of Iranian theocracy. That policy of official silence came back to haunt the administration in February 2011 when the streets of Cairo erupted in mass protests against the authoritarian Mubarak regime. The President, after sending conflicting signals, demanded that Mubarak step down—just the sort of "meddling" that he eschewed in the case of the June 2009 unrest in Tehran. Such inconsistency raised troubling questions: was the United States harder on authoritarian friends than on far more repressive totalitarian enemies? Were dictators more savage to their own people than were Islamic theocrats? And why did the United States assume that street protestors in Cairo were future democrats but not their more likely counterparts in Tehran?

At the same time, the administration planned to restore diplomatic relations with Syria, despite the regime's manifest support for Hezbollah's terrorist ambitions, its new alliance with Iran, its involvement in assassination and destabilization in Lebanon, and its efforts at nuclear proliferation and weapon sales to terrorists. Again, the administration has not extended its critique of the Egyptian government's human rights violations to the even more repressive Assad regime in Syria. In contrast, the Obama administration made it clear from the outset through criticism of Israeli policies that Israel—and especially the Netanyahu government—was no longer considered the staunch ally that it had been in the past. Yet after two years of such reset diplomacy in the Middle East, there is no progress in the so-called peace process: Iran continues its efforts to obtain a nuclear bomb; wars against Israel involving Hezbollah and Hamas—and perhaps Iran and Syria—are more rather than less likely; Iran is forging new economic and/or diplomatic relationships with China, Russia, and Venezuela. President Obama's message that the United States is far more interested in becoming a neutral (presence? power?) with Israel and an interlocutor with Iran and Syria suggests that—in any future conflict—many in the Middle East will wonder to what extent the United States might remain a staunch defender of Israeli democracy.

CONCLUSION

Ten years after 9/11, the United States continues to thwart renewed attacks largely because of the continuance of anti-terrorism policies at home that make it difficult for Islamists to carry out operations, and successful wars abroad that have killed tens of thousands of jihadists, routed al-Qaeda from its bases, and made it clear that sovereign nations will be held responsible for hosting terrorists within their borders.

Will this successful interlude continue? The Obama administration has made it clear that it opposes the spirit of many of the policies it inherited yet has sometimes expanded, while reaching out to prior enemies on the assurance that America was as much at fault as were they, since "all too often the United States begins by dictating." Such ambiguity may put enemies off balance in the short term, but eventually anti-terrorism policies and wars that were adamantly opposed in the past and only reluctantly pursued in the present become unsustainable—and dangerous.

9/11 in its
historical context

ARTHUR HERMAN

Ten years is not a long time. Certainly no one who witnessed in person or on TV those terrible hours of September 11, 2001 will ever forget them—let alone those who either survived the attack or lost loved ones. Like Pearl Harbor and the assassination of JFK, 9/11 will be forever etched on the American cultural consciousness.

On the other hand, its impact on our domestic politics has faded. It led to a flurry of new legislation, including the Patriot Act and the creation of the Department of Homeland Security.

It enabled preventive measures such as the detention center at Guantánamo and so-called warrantless wiretaps. All were fiercely debated. Yet despite occasional bursts of liberal outrage regarding Gitmo and simmering frustration over TSA's long lines at airports, all are largely accepted today. Neither Democrats nor Republicans get much political leverage trying to revisit those debates.

The impact of 9/11 on America's outlook on the world has dwindled even faster. Immediately after 9/11, Americans went from a state of false security to one of hair-trigger alertness. The public overwhelmingly supported any and all resolute action against those who harbored al-Qaeda or similar terrorist groups. It strongly backed intervention in Afghanistan to root out al-Qaeda and its Taliban allies in late 2001. It firmly supported the Bush administration's invasion of Iraq to make sure no weapons of mass destruction belonging to that country became available to terrorist groups.

America was in a preemptive mood. When President George W. Bush, in his 2002 State of the Union address, described an "axis of evil" composed of North Korea, Iraq, and Iran, he was borrowing a phrase his predecessor President Bill Clinton had coined—but which now took on a new urgency.

Ten years later, the public's interest in confronting possible foreign threats such as Iran's nuclear weapons or China's steady military buildup is largely nonexistent. The two remaining components of evil's axis, Iran and North Korea, not only continue to expand their nuclear weapons programs, but are joined by other would-be members of the same nefarious club: Hugo Chavez's Venezuela and Hafez Assad's Syria. The reaction on the part of the American public, and even the current administration, has been little more than a regretful shrug. Some blame this apathy on the Bush administration's mishandling of the wars in Iraq and

Afghanistan, and rightly so. The public is gun-shy of politicians pointing to threats from abroad and demanding U.S. action. But the problem has a deeper historical dimension.

Since the founding of the republic, America's attitude toward the outside world has tended to swing pendulum-like in two different directions. One points toward a passionate, self-assertive involvement in the world, reinforced by a belief that America has a unique leadership to offer the world in terms of freedom and prosperity. Presidents Theodore Roosevelt, Harry Truman, Ronald Reagan, and George W. Bush epitomize this activist phase. The other direction points to withdrawal and a "plague on both their houses" attitude regarding the world. In the words of one of our most interventionist Presidents, Lyndon Johnson: "Why must this nation hazard its ease, its interests, and its power for the sake of a people so far away?" Here, Presidents James Monroe, Warren Harding, and Jimmy Carter rule the day. This attitude is sometimes misleadingly summed up as isolationism. It is reinforced by a fear that overreaching entanglements abroad will undermine stability and liberty at home. If the activist sees American exceptionalism imposing on us "the moral leadership of the planet," in Robert Kennedy's phrase, the isolationist sees exceptionalism best upheld by remaining disengaged from the world, unless we are faced with a direct threat like Pearl Harbor or 9/11.

This is, of course, precisely the problem. The danger of the isolationist trend is that it ignores gathering threats until it is too late to prevent disaster. The risk of activism is that it inspires unrealistic, sometimes almost messianic expectations about America's ability to change the world for the better—that is, until another disaster imposes first a sense of reality, then disillusionment, and triggers another withdrawal from the world. The War of 1812, World War I, and Vietnam all fit this category. But so did the end of the Cold War, and victory in World War II: these were not disillusioning disasters but disarming triumphs, after which Americans lost interest in order to enjoy some hard-earned peace and quiet.

The twin wars in Iraq and Afghanistan have triggered a backlash against the interventionist attitude that prevailed immediately after 9/11. They belong to a pattern that has asserted itself time and again. But what if the pendulum swings too far toward a reactive geopolitical stance once again, until that backlash takes another 9/11 to rouse us from our apathy—this time, perhaps, in the shape of a mushroom cloud?

Those who prefer that the United States take an aloof stance like to quote George Washington's Farewell Address. "Tis our true policy to steer clear of permanent alliances, with any portion of the foreign world," and to avoid "excessive partiality for one foreign nation and excessive dislike of another" he wrote. Washington urged America to keep its independence in foreign as well as national policy, while remaining strong enough that "belligerent nations, under the impossibility of making acquisitions upon us, will not lightly hazard giving us provocation . . ."[1]

But Washington also argued that "our detached and distant situation invites us to a different course" than the nations of Europe. Washington was far from calling for an American withdrawal from world affairs. "The great rule of conduct for us, in regard to Foreign Nations is in extending our commercial relations to have with them as little *political* connection as possible." That lack of connection should never be misunderstood as "patronizing infidelity to existing engagements." Instead, "let those engagements be observed in their genuine sense," even as "we may safely trust to temporary alliances for extraordinary emergencies . . ." And when faced by provocation, "we may choose peace or war, as our interest guided by justice shall counsel."

Washington's position can best be summed up as: make no entangling *permanent* alliances, but do not neglect the temporary ones, i.e., the ones that further our real interest. Seek to live in harmony with other nations, but do not expect altruism to rule the day. If the Farewell Address was, in the final analysis, a counsel for detachment and isolation, however, there was no way to uphold it. The young republic found itself hemmed in by imperialist neighbors. Even before Washington's death, America was drawn into global conflict by the French Revolution and the Napoleonic Wars.

When Great Britain asserted a right to search American vessels at sea, the young republic was forced out of its stance of official neutrality. In 1812, Congress and President James Madison declared war on Great Britain. The result was disaster and national humiliation. Americans learned their lesson. They decided to embrace their "detached and distant situation," and for the next four decades retreated into debates on internal improvements and slavery. Their attitude toward the outside world was summed up by John Quincy Adams:

> Wherever the standard of freedom and independence has been or shall be unfurled, there will [America's] heart, her benedictions and her prayers be. But she goes not abroad, in search of monsters to destroy. She is the well-wisher to the freedom and independence of all. She is the champion and vindicator only of her own.[2]

In order to keep free of entanglements with Europe, the cockpit of world power and conflict, America would rely on the 1823

Monroe Doctrine. In theory, it shut Europe out of the Western Hemisphere; in practice it shut America *in* for nearly half a century, with internal struggles of its own. The timing was lucky: during the same period that America was focused on its westward expansion and domestic problems, Europe was bogged down in internal struggles brought by nationalism and industrialization. Then, in the 1880s, a new age of imperialism arose with an extended global reach, thanks to the telegraph and steam-powered ironclad navies.

Some, like Henry Cabot Lodge, Albert Beveridge, and Theodore Roosevelt, began to call on America to emulate its more assertive European cousins by building a strong navy (in 1890 America's navy was smaller than Italy's) and an overseas empire, including annexing Hawaii. But they made little headway until the Gilded Age experienced its version of 9/11—the sinking of the USS *Maine*.

The explosion that sank the battleship in Havana harbor on February 15, 1898, killed 266 sailors and triggered a wave of popular support for freeing not only Cuba but also the Philippines from Spanish rule. It also legitimized a new, far more assertive American stance in relation to other nations. America would now act as a full-fledged Great Power, with its own spheres of influence—especially in Latin America. In 1904, President Theodore Roosevelt added a corollary to the Monroe Doctrine: a general right of intervention in Western Hemisphere affairs. He warned Congress that the "increasing interdependence and complexity of international political and economic relations" meant that in extreme cases the United States might have to exercise "an international police power" to preserve its dominance of the hemisphere—or even, presumably, to defend its interests elsewhere.[3] Two wide oceans had once provided a buffer of security. Roosevelt saw them as springboards for unilateral action.

Analysts like to draw a contrast between Teddy Roosevelt's assertive Realpolitik, "big stick" diplomacy and the altruistic globalism of his successor. Yet global activism was just as implicit in Roosevelt's calculus of America's place on the world stage as it was in Woodrow Wilson's military intervention in Mexico and in America's entry in the Great War. The shocking loss of American lives in the 1917 conflict (almost 80,000 in less than eleven months), and the sordid Great Power squabble at the Paris Peace Conference in 1919, dealt Wilson's internationalist vision a blow from which it never recovered—and set America on its next great swing toward withdrawal from outside affairs.

The 1920s–1930s period is usually described as the age of isolationism. It is important, however, to bear in mind what isolationism was *not*. For one thing, it was not a specifically Republican or even conservative phenomenon. Indeed, three Republican Presidents—Harding, Coolidge, and Hoover—offered invaluable help in settling questions of post-war reparations and rebuilding Germany. In keeping with Washington's advice, they kept America actively involved in Europe at a financial and diplomatic level. They also did not hesitate to follow Teddy Roosevelt in intervening in the Western Hemisphere.

Unfortunately, America also suffered from a weakness for multilateral treaties. America's leaders assumed formal written agreements would have the same binding impact on possible foes as they did on present friends. The ill-considered 1924 Kellogg-Briand Pact outlawed war. The Harding administration organized and signed the Washington Naval Treaty, which allowed Japan to build more battleships and aircraft carriers while the United States scuttled cruisers and destroyers and abandoned the fortification of naval bases west of Hawaii. Both would clear the way for the Japanese attack at Pearl Harbor.

The passage of the Smoot-Hawley tariff in 1930 and the election of Franklin Roosevelt in 1932 marked isolationism's high tide. The former worsened the Depression; the latter encouraged rising totalitarian dictators to think they would win the looming battle with the Western democracies. Democrats, not Republicans, were determined to kill off the ill-starred interventionist legacy of their own Woodrow Wilson. The Democratic Congress passed Neutrality Acts in 1935 and 1936, and a Democrat President signed them. The Democratic Congress perpetuated a long, slow stagnation of America's defense budget, to the point that in 1939 the U.S. Army numbered eighteenth in the world. After the Munich Agreement in October 1938, Franklin Roosevelt sent a telegram to its principal architect, Neville Chamberlain: "Good man."[4]

Not one but two disasters were required to break Americans out of their stupor. First, the 1940 collapse of France forced Roosevelt and Congress to put the nation's defense budget on a wartime footing. The second was Pearl Harbor. But even before December 7, 1941, many Americans were ready to rethink their nation's proper role in the world. Globalization, argued 1940s thinkers Nicholas Spykman and Arnold Wolfers, had changed the definition of national security.[5] It was time for America's strategic and military strength to match its economic power, or else face challenges from Europe and Asia it could not deflect or control. Once again, the significance of the two oceans had changed. Now, control over those oceans had become vital to our defense. It would allow joint action with our allies for collective security, and it would deter our enemies by allowing us to deliver the means of their defeat with overwhelming force.

Both ideas would take hold in the grand strategy of World War II, and both would be key ingredients in the Cold War consensus that formed afterward. The immediate aftermath almost triggered another swing of the pendulum. The end of fascism seemed to presage the end of great power conflicts. The sudden and massive cut in defense spending (from $556 billion in 1946 to less than $53 billion in 1947) and the possibility of sharing our most powerful weapon, the atomic bomb, with the rest of the world expressed an optimism that ignored the gathering Soviet threat. The 1950 invasion of Korea cut that optimism short—too late to save Eastern Europe and China from Communist domination, but enough to draw the future battle lines of containment.

The experience of Korea reinforced the activist swing of the pendulum. A new paradigm elevated the United States to super-power status, the primary player in a struggle with international communism. This was the golden age of realism in American foreign policy. It taught that international relations are dynamic, and that sudden shifts can reset or erode a nation's power regardless of objective strengths or weaknesses. It was these shifts and the competition for advantage—not international treaties or multi-lateral bodies like the United Nations—which determined the direction of international relations. The global nature of that conflict's boundaries demanded a strong situational awareness and engagement in the world, as well as a second-to-none military deterrent. "The international community is a world in which war is an instrument of national policy," wrote Nicholas Spykman, "and the national domain is the military base from which the state fights and prepares for war during the temporary armistice called peace."[6] It seemed a good summary of Cold War reality.

But the new paradigm also brought something from its Wilsonian and Roosevelt-era past: a New Deal humanitarianism, symbolized by Roosevelt's World War II declaration of the Four Freedoms, of which Freedom from Want was paramount. The new Cold War consensus brought an outpouring of aid, starting with the Marshall Plan. Then, it was Atoms for Peace, the Alliance for Progress, the Agency for International Development, and the Peace Corps that shaded into John F. Kennedy's push to help countries, including Vietnam, turn away from communism and toward democracy. When JFK pledged that Americans would "go anywhere and pay any price" to defend liberty, he was thinking in terms of dollars as well as blood.

Yet there lurked a fundamental tension between these twin urges for engagement. When does one undermine the other? When does the need for military action contradict our concern for promoting democracy, and when does the desire to uphold our humanitarian image interfere with our ability to conduct effective military interventions? These questions were first broached in a serious, even existential, way in Vietnam, and they tore the Cold War consensus down the middle.

On one side, Cold War realism gave way to a more calculating Realpolitik perspective, represented by Henry Kissinger. From the other side came a new emphasis on human rights and development, though this time they would advance not with our help but despite it. It was not whether America was too good for the world, as in the 1930s, but whether it was too wicked. The malign monolith was not communism; it was America's multinational corporations and its military-industrial complex. By divesting America of its "arrogance of power" and disengaging from the world, we would foster a new era of global harmony. This view in turn fed the reaction against the Vietnam War and gave the isolationist withdrawal of the Carter years its peculiar character. When OPEC's 1973 embargo quadrupled the price of oil, and when Iran suspended its oil exports in 1978–1979, the American reaction was not to send an aircraft carrier but to put on a sweater.

A new generation in the late 1970s learned the full price of disengagement, starting with the Soviet invasion of Afghanistan and continuing through the fall of the Shah and the Iranian hostage crisis. With Ronald Reagan's election, the pendulum swung back again—not to a conservative revolution in foreign affairs, as some claimed at the time, but to a re-establishment of the old principles of Cold War leadership—most importantly military deterrence. Reagan's foreign policy was pro-navy like Teddy Roosevelt's, pro-covert like Eisenhower's and Kennedy's, and opposed to unverifiable paper treaties. Containment, which had been discredited during the 1970s, gave way to deterrence as a form of leverage—most spectacularly with the Strategic Defense Initiative.

The collapse of the Soviet Union in 1991 ushered in the peace dividend of the Clinton years. Unlike his two immediate predecessors, Clinton had no coherent strategy for dealing with forces promoting global instability. But like them, he largely ignored the advance of radical Islam until it arrived catastrophically on our doorstep on 9/11. That traumatic event brought into prominence a foreign policy that moved the pendulum back in the activist direction. It is usually described—and dismissed by critics—as the work of neocons. In fact, the neoconservative persuasion sprang from retooling the old Cold War balance between humanitarianism and military deterrence for a post–Cold War world. The Cold War had shown that totalitarian dictators and terrorists made a natural fit. The same fit existed with the axis of evil. Why assume that the new threat posed by al-Qaeda and Islamic radicalism should be any different? The ultimate goal was democratic modernization and pluralist change, backed by robust Chinook diplomacy and a post–Cold War coalition of democratic allies, including those of Eastern Europe.

Where neoconservatives guessed wrong, however, was in assuming that the post–Cold War coalition, symbolized by the stunning success of the First Gulf War, would last. The coalition had fallen apart during the Clinton years in the bitterness

over Bosnia and sanctions against Iraq. Far from waiting to follow America's lead, competitors like Russia and China were now
waiting for America to fail. Through inaction and support for
those covertly fighting against us like Iran, our opponents very
nearly succeeded in Iraq. It remains to be seen how effective their
efforts in Afghanistan will be.

Where does the pendulum swing now? Iraq did not become
the Vietnam-like quagmire some predicted. It did, however,
sour Americans' taste for military action in confronting foreign
challenges and threats. Like the Great Depression, the 2008
financial meltdown and recession have turned the attention of
people and policy inward. So too, paradoxically, has the success of President Bush's war on terror. The killing of Osama
bin Laden in May 2011 only put the crown on what had been a
long and impressive string of American intelligence and operational coups against al-Qaeda. As the reality of the catastrophic
al-Qaeda attack faded, so has the impulse to confront threats:
Iran's Revolutionary Guard and its Quds Force, for example,
or terrorist networks in Pakistan and Yemen (and soon possibly in Egypt and Libya). For the Obama administration, the
occasional strike by a Predator drone seems to be enough. This
seems enough for the American public as well.

Yet problems *are* gathering, both in and outside the Middle
East. The list is long and the threats are varied: the rise of China;
the resurgence of Russia; the spread of Marxist regimes from
Venezuela to Latin America; chaos on our southern border in
Mexico; and, the possibility of a failed state, in Pakistan, armed
with nuclear weapons.

In spring 1945, a group of foreign policy scholars gathered
for a conference in Rye, New York, and declared, "The day when

the United States can take a free ride in security is over."[7] If those words had weight on the eve of victory in World War II, when the United States was unquestionably the single most prosperous and powerful nation in the world, they should have even more weight now as power and prosperity are slipping away. September 11's legacy should *not* be a fear we overreacted and a need to disengage; or alternately a belief that the world would not stand with us during the attacks and now can go to hell. We cannot be Achilles sulking in his tent. We need a mature reconsideration of our foreign policy, so that we can respond decisively to threats without losing our identity or our cool. It's time to bring the pendulum to rest.

war v. crime: breaking the chains of the old security paradigm

MICHAEL CHERTOFF

September 11 caused a tragic upheaval in the lives of thousands of families and in the United States economy. But it also caused an upheaval in the doctrine and legal architecture that govern our national security strategy. Not only did these infamous attacks expose gaps in our ability to collect and analyze intelligence, they also revealed inadequacies in our abilities to prevent and protect against future attacks. The source of these security flaws lies in an outmoded conception of the nature of modern security threats and the requirements for defeating them. In this essay, I follow a critique of the conventional, binary approach of viewing terrorism as either war or crime by sketching the outlines of a more holistic, full-spectrum response to twenty-first-century security threats.

THE "GOOD OLD DAYS"

In the last decade of the twentieth century, security problems fell neatly into two categories. Traditional national security issues were couched in the domain of warfighting—or preparation for warfighting—overseen by the military and intelligence communities. The threat of war was viewed as emanating from other nations or groups sponsored by other nations. Responsibility and authority for addressing and defeating the threat of war belonged to the Defense Department and intelligence agencies tasked with gathering information on foreign enemies. Warfighting was outward-facing.

A fundamentally different type of threat came from groups and individuals normally within the purview of local law enforcement. Murderers, drug dealers, thieves, and others who challenged our physical and economic security were classified as criminals, to be dealt with by police authorities. Because many such criminals were American citizens, law enforcement policies evolved within a civil liberties framework concerned with the desire to limit government powers over society. Even when criminals such as organized crime figures and drug traffickers were located or operating from overseas, this civil-liberties-oriented architecture was reflexively applied. And because the paradigm of law enforcement arose from an inward-facing effort, intelligence collection on criminal threats was largely undertaken through local agencies and by means of constrained methods very different from those deployed by outward-facing warfighting.

This binary classification of security threats became a comfortable default position for government agencies. On the international front, military authorities were largely confined to operations overseas, with various statutes and executive orders prohibiting intelligence agencies from either collecting or maintaining records on U.S. citizens or domestic activities or contaminating foreign records with information about Americans or domestic affairs.[1] Domestically, laws such as the Posse Comitatus Act and the Insurrection Act tightly restricted military activities that could be undertaken on American soil,[2] relieving the military of any necessity to train for or develop strong rules of engagement for domestic enforcement activities.

By the same token, in the crime-fighting domain, local law enforcement agencies operated with many more inhibitions than those felt by their military or intelligence community counterparts. Requirements of judicial supervision in investigating, prosecuting, and incarcerating criminals placed law enforcement agents under much stricter operational burdens than applied to military or intelligence operatives overseas. For example, while military personnel could properly use force against overseas enemies without resort to judicial process—such as the 1986 bombing of Libyan leader Qaddafi's headquarters in response to a terror attack against U.S. servicemen in Germany, law enforcement personnel could not order a lethal blow against those responsible for many domestic American drug-related deaths—instead they must go to court and seek to extradite Colombian drug lords. Freedom of action in the former case flowed because the threat of transnational terrorism was characterized as a nation-based security threat; by contrast, legal constraints were imposed in the latter case because the matter was treated as criminal. Whether this distinction was more apparent than real is debatable.

Perhaps the best known emblem of this binary approach to security was the establishment of the now-notorious intelligence wall that sharply restricted the integration of information collected by intelligence operatives with that collected by law enforcement investigators. As developed by the U.S. Department of Justice and the U.S. Foreign Intelligence Surveillance Court over time, this doctrine effectively prevented those involved with criminal law enforcement from having any access to foreign intelligence or counterintelligence information until intelligence activities were terminated and a prosecution was ready to begin. Similarly, once a criminal investigation was underway, intelligence officials were largely denied access to its fruits unless special permission was obtained or the information eventually became public.[3] The consequence of this radical division of security information and responsibility became manifest when the country learned that "the wall" had seriously hampered authorities' ability to detect the preparations for the September 11 hijackings.[4]

THE REALITY OF TWENTY-FIRST-CENTURY SECURITY

During the late twentieth and early twenty-first centuries, three developments undermined the neat binary conception of national security threats as either warmaking or crime: globalization, technological innovation, and the rise of ungoverned space throughout the world.

Globalization has eroded the distinction between the global reach of the nation-state and the reach of the individual or group.

The abilities to travel, communicate, and finance activities on a global basis have generated the first true international networks. These networks, whether ideological or criminal, can and do support a presence around the world in a way previously limited to national governments.

When this global reach is coupled with the destructive leverage created by technological innovation, the danger posed by a sophisticated international network begins to rival that potentially posed by all but the most powerful countries. On September 11, a globalized al-Qaeda was able to project its operatives into the United States and to exploit America's own aviation technology against itself, resulting in more loss of American civilian life by a foreign enemy than in any other single day in our history. Had al-Qaeda wielded the technological knowhow to create a biological- or cyber-weapon, similar or greater blows might have followed.

The threat distinction between nation-state actors and non-state networks is further effaced when we consider the number of geographic locations in which terrorist or criminal groups are able to create literal safe havens in which they set up recruiting centers, training camps, and laboratories to enhance their destructive capabilities. These safe havens thrive in ungoverned space—whether in the frontiers of Pakistan, Somalia, Yemen, or regions within other weak states. From the standpoint of consequence, there is little difference between the terrorist group that is granted safe haven by a nation-state and one that seizes safe haven in a territory which lacks an effective sovereign that can police within its own borders.

In the face of these developments, does the binary distinction between nation-based security threats and network- or organization-based security threats still make sense? Their global reach is often identical. Their destructive effects are often the same. Is it arbitrary, then, to classify some of these threats as war-related and others as crime-related?

A NEW SECURITY PARADIGM

Imagine that we abandon the old binary system of classifying national security threats and adopt a new paradigm—call it the relativity paradigm. Under post-Einsteinian physics, a particle does not inhabit a particular location; rather, it is capable of being in many different positions based on the relationship between it and its perceiver. By (admittedly imperfect) analogy, one might say that security threats are capable of being perceived as a number of different things along the spectrum from classic war to garden-variety crime—and addressed accordingly. Instead of calling something "war" or "crime" at the outset, the relativity paradigm directs us to define the particular set of circumstances in which we confront a certain threat. The rationale is that circumstances—and not abstract categories—should determine the tools and authorities that come into play.

To illustrate this concept, imagine a radical al-Qaeda recruiter, currently soliciting and enabling operatives to commit bombings against Americans all over the world. If we locate this extremist in the ungoverned space in the Middle East, may we use lethal force against him? Are we relegated to trying to apprehend him? If we do catch him, does he get Miranda warnings and a lawyer within forty-eight hours? What if, instead of finding him in the Middle East, we find him hidden in an apartment in New York City? Is our response different? Are our authorities different? And suppose again that we find him in a European capital—far from a battlefield but unlikely to be extradited to face justice? Finally, do these answers change if the recruiter is an American citizen?

In each of the above instances, the identity of the enemy is the same, as are his intent and the possible consequences of his threat. What differs is the set of circumstances in which we encounter him. We may decide, for good reason, that the range of permissible responses will change depending on those circumstances. This judgment should not be a matter of rigid, front-end categorization. Rather, it should reflect consideration of a variety of factors that reasonably influence the range of coercive options that we are willing to pursue in different contexts. Indeed, the most dramatic example of a pragmatic, conditions-based paradigm to counterterrorism is the recent elimination of Osama bin Laden during an operation conducted in a residential area of Pakistan. Old-style thinking would have suggested that as an indicted individual living in suburban Pakistan, bin Laden should be arrested and extradited. Instead, the Obama administration—correctly in my view—made the practical decision in light of several factors to deploy deadly force directly against bin Laden in Pakistan without host government knowledge or permission.

What are these factors? Some will depend on the nature of the individual and the network that pose the security threat. Others will depend on the time and place in which we encounter the threat. Still others will depend on our strategic and tactical objectives.

Most important, these factors should be applied flexibly to accommodate two competing and compelling goals. On the one hand, our government should have the flexibility to deploy the best adapted tools to assure our survival as a nation and our safety as citizens. On the other, our government should be constrained in using those tools in ways that would undermine our fundamental freedoms and values as Americans. Thus, the range of permissible actions should always balance the tension between the efficacy of our security and the preservation of our rights.

CHARACTERISTICS OF THE THREAT:
THE INDIVIDUAL AND HIS NETWORK

Few would have difficulty in concluding that al-Qaeda and its operatives constitute a network against which all the tools of national power ought to be deployed. But most would think that the Unabomber—a classic lone wolf—or a gang of bank robbers are not reasonable targets for launching a missile. Why?

One obvious difference is that al-Qaeda is a global network, physically rooted in ungoverned spaces in South Asia and the Horn of Africa, while domestic terrorists or violent criminals lack an international dimension. This distinction is important for two reasons: First, the international reach of a network amplifies the threat and raises the risk that the members of the network are fundamentally hostile not just to our citizens but to our existence as a nation. Any attacks by such a network would cause a greater threat to our security than the lone wolf or ordinary criminal could.

Second, the international dimension affords an important limiting principle in safeguarding our rights as Americans. Military force is less circumscribed than judicially hedged law enforcement action. By treating an international dimension as a predicate to invoking warfighting tools, we avoid the possibility that the government might short-circuit existing legal rights to harass domestic political adversaries or to make it easier to address garden-variety criminal activity.

This leads to a second important factor in considering the range of permissible actions against a terrorist: is that person an American citizen? To be sure, American citizens affiliated with international terror networks—or with enemy nations—can pose as serious a threat as non-citizens. But the limiting principle of guarding against erosion of core domestic liberties should counsel caution in applying the full range of warfighting tools against a United States citizen.[5]

A third factor to be considered is whether it should matter that the individual and network that pose the threat are motivated by ideology or more prosaic objectives, such as greed. The answer may be less obvious than appears at first blush. Although conventional wisdom discerns a meaningful difference between ideological international terrorists and international organized criminals, the distinction is less clear in practical terms. Mexican drug lords have for some years practiced the tactics of terrorism to intimidate their foes and to discourage government law enforcement. The beheadings, car bombings, and massacres of innocent civilians are no different in kind from the worst we have seen in news reports from Iraq. While these organized crime bosses have not articulated a political philosophy beyond their own rapaciousness, the effects of their tactics clearly terrorize and promote certain political objectives.

Moreover, criminal groups and terrorist groups may easily merge. The Colombian insurrectionist group, FARC, began as a left-wing revolutionary group. Eventually, however, they began to protect cocaine loads in return for weapons and money, and eventually became directly involved in narco-trafficking.[6] At this point, should we consider the FARC a terrorist group, a criminal enterprise, or both? The line between the two is permeable and ever-changing. Ideology of the network may be only marginally relevant in determining the appropriateness of warfighting, as compared with the tactics and political objectives of the group.

CIRCUMSTANCES IN CONFRONTING THE THREAT

The most salient factor that generally defines the range of permissible tactics in confronting members of a terrorist network is geography. The types of tools employed in an ungoverned region overseas may be very different from those available domestically or in a well-ordered foreign state. Law enforcement methods such as arrest and trial have little efficacy against terrorists hiding in inaccessible and ungoverned regions in South Asia or elsewhere. At the same time, the collateral damage and harm to international alliances of kinetic warmaking are high when the target is located in a European capital with its own sovereign legal requirements. These practical considerations necessarily drive whether military or civilian law enforcement processes are used in overseas areas of operation.

Domestically, other considerations come into play. Within the United States, traditional law enforcement approaches are obviously lawful and appropriate. But there is also precedent for using some of the tools of warfighting within the country, at least with regard to the process of intelligence collection and combatant detention.[7] At the same time, too ready a willingness to use military tools to combat security threats at home again raises the specter of shortcutting traditional civil rights protections in cases in which the national security threat is, arguably, marginal. A presumption—though a rebuttable one—in favor of using judicially supervised law enforcement against threats apprehended in the United States is a hedge against the gradual diminution of fundamental liberties.

What might rebut that presumption in favor of law enforcement in domestic circumstances? Another prudential factor to be weighed is the practical objectives to be served by catching a terrorist in the United States, including obtaining information about other threats and incapacitating the operative so as to end a threat. These objectives may sometimes conflict with the methods of traditional law enforcement, which include rules against the interrogation of suspects without legal representation and highly technical evidentiary requirements during the criminal trial process. However, in instances where the need for information is high and where the threat posed by the terrorist is severe, options that are customary in military theatres—such as intelligence interrogation or indefinite detention—may become more attractive, and even necessary.

This balancing is illustrated by practice under the Bush administration. Non-Americans caught overseas were put through military channels and held subject to military review panels.[8] At least one native-born American, Yaser Hamdi,[9] was detained as a combatant but not subject to trial by a military commission. John Walker Lindh, another American caught in Afghanistan, was convicted in federal court under domestic criminal laws.[10] And of those apprehended in the United States on terrorism-related charges, all but two entered the criminal justice system directly; the remaining two were held in military custody (though eventually convicted on federal charges).[11] This pattern reflects an inclination to use civilian courts for those caught domestically, but with a willingness to use military authorities if practical requirements so dictate.

TOWARD AN ARCHITECTURE FOR TWENTY-FIRST-CENTURY SECURITY

If the national security threat spectrum is now very different from the old binary division between war and crime, the architecture of our security authorities and strategy must also change. The traditional method of organizing authorities around the definition of the threat as either military or criminal no longer fits the reality of the security challenges that we face. Authorities must be designed and enacted with a view to empowering security agencies with as many tools as possible to be applied overseas and at home. While these authorities must be bounded by constitutional limits, those limits permit far more flexibility than a binary system allows.

Fundamentally, security means the ability to detect, deter, prevent, and protect against threats to life and property. The tools to carry out these missions include (1) the collection of various forms of intelligence about the adversary's intent and capabilities; (2) building defense and response mechanisms that reduce the adversary's likelihood of success—or increase the adversary's cost—to a degree sufficient to deter him from attacking; (3) disrupting or incapacitating the adversary's ability to carry out plans if he is not deterred; and (4) hardening defenses so that an attack is mitigated or blunted. Depending on the scale of the threat, our security architecture should—again, within constitutional limits—maximize the flexibility to use all tools that serve the above goals on an international level. The decision as to which tools to use should then be guided by the sort of practical considerations and factors outlined earlier in this article.

Achieving this more seamless system may require eliminating organizational inhibitions that require certain agencies to cease their work at the water's edge; or it may mean filling gaps in our legal structure. For example, the current law on detention seems to force a choice between a military system devised in a day when war was conducted in uniform, and a civilian justice system with its non-criminal detention powers limited to sexual predators or the mentally unstable. Fashioning a process and rules for detention of terrorists would bridge the gap between these two drastically different regimes and allow the flexibility to incapacitate terrorists here and overseas with a suitably fair legal process.

Lastly, nowhere is the need for a nimble security architecture more urgent than in the area of cybersecurity. In a world in which cyberattacks can be launched remotely from any location, the concept of legal boundaries that differentiate between "domestic" and "overseas" is meaningless. When the likelihood of apprehending global cyberattackers is diminishing because of their ability to operate remotely and anonymously, prosecution cannot be the only tool for deterrence and prevention. When denial of service and destructive attacks may be motivated by criminal or ideological (and state-sponsored) impulses (or both), it will be fruitless to assign responsibility for defense exclusively to police or military authorities. The arena of cybersecurity will demand a holistic architecture of security that is not necessarily tethered to traditional considerations such as the origins of the attack or the citizenship of the attacker.

CONCLUSION

Much of the counterterrorism debate over the last ten years has revolved around efforts to characterize the threats as a military or law enforcement problem. This is a false choice, driven by an outmoded conception of security threats that is still embodied in our national security architecture and legal doctrine. But structure and law should be designed around current reality, rather than constrained by an intellectual straitjacket in which we struggle to confront terrorist threats. Recognizing that our international security is imperiled by a fluid set of dynamic threats is the first step to modernizing our response capabilities for the twenty-first century.

Congress has been largely absent in addressing the fundamental architecture of our new security challenges. Legislative enactments have typically focused on reacting to specific controversies or to the imminent expiration of statutory authorities. While both the Bush and Obama administrations have stepped in to fill the void with various executive orders, in the long run an enduring structure requires a congressional imprimatur. One useful approach now might be for the President and Congress to empanel a bipartisan group—similar to the National Commission on Fiscal Responsibility and Reform—to conduct a comprehensive review of our new security requirement and to formulate a set of recommendations to Congress for modernizing our legal architecture in the twenty-first century.

a unified defense against terrorists

EDWIN MEESE III
PAUL ROSENZWEIG

INTRODUCTION

Americans awoke on the morning of September 11, 2001 to a picture-perfect day across most of the nation. But the clear blue skies and moderate temperatures on the East Coast soon lost the promise of a pleasant day as two planes hijacked by terrorists slammed into the Twin Towers in New York City and a third exploded into the Pentagon, outside Washington, D.C. A fourth plane crashed in the fields of Pennsylvania, as brave passengers battled the terrorists to a standstill.

The events of September 11 were not the first battle in the war against terrorists, nor will they be the last. The challenge of responding to the terrorist threat continues today in America (witness the New York City Times Square attack last year) and elsewhere in the West, as vitally and immediately as it did that early morning. What made September 11 unique, however, was how it resonated in the conscience of the American public. For the first time since the surprise attack on Pearl Harbor, thousands of Americans died on American soil at the hands of our enemies. For a brief period, the result was a remarkable cohesion of the American body politic. Democrats and Republicans put aside their partisan differences in an effort to do what was needed in response to the attacks. In the first few months after 9/11, American leaders not only rejected a political response but went beyond politics altogether, putting aside parochial electoral concerns in an effort to enact a nonpartisan, non-political set of solutions, such as the Authorization for Use of Military Force and the USA Patriot Act.

Sadly, that moment was short-lived. Since 2001 our approach to the war on terror has rarely benefited from a sense of common purpose. Occasionally, Congress rises above politics to reach agreement. More frequently, our leaders descend into bickering, political battles. And, far more often than we would like, Congress is absent from the playing field; unable to reach consensus, the legislators simply take no action at all.

The tenth anniversary of September 11 is a good time to reflect on the successes and failures of our efforts to construct a cohesive national response to the terrorist challenge. Doing so also helps us assess how we can do better. From that perspective we see three areas that warrant discussion: issues related to the organization of the federal government; the authorization of military action; and legal reforms.

ORGANIZATIONAL CHANGES

Since September 11, we have seen two major changes in the structure of the U.S. government: the creation of the Department of Homeland Security (DHS) and the complete restructuring of the intelligence community (IC). Both of these reorganizations were, unfortunately, more the product of political struggle than of nonpartisan, rational assessment.[1]

Consider, first, the creation of the DHS. Initially, the Bush administration strongly resisted calls for government reorganization because of the delay and difficulties inherent in such an effort. Its reluctance was overridden by a congressional insistence characterized by a desire to appear politically "strong" on national security issues. The result was the amalgamation of twenty-two agencies into a single department.[2]

To be fair, some aspects of this consolidation have clearly been successful. For example, the consolidation of border inspection functions (customs, immigration, and agricultural inspection) into a single agency has generated real efficiencies and substantially increased security. Likewise, the decision to separate immigration enforcement from the citizenship and immigration adjudication process has proven to be wise. In the main, however, the massive undertaking to create a new department has been more of a burden than a benefit. Those who have worked in the department understand that the reorganization sapped at least two years of organizational energy from our counterterrorism activities, as managers and employees alike were forced to deal with the challenges and confusion of creating a new department from parts of other federal agencies. Anyone who doubts that should review the controversy over the new uniform for the merged Customs and Border Protection directorate.

Many outside observers recognize that some pieces of the department simply do not fit together. The Secret Service, for example, has almost no appreciable basis for inclusion in the department. Other agencies within the department, such as the Coast Guard, suffered from organizational confusion of roles as they attempt to fit their varied activities within DHS's primary counterterrorism mission.

Worst of all, however, is the way in which Congress has failed to honor the commitment it made in creating the DHS. To this day, oversight of the DHS is divided among more than one hundred congressional subcommittees. No effort has been made to adopt the 9/11 Commission's bipartisan recommendation that oversight be simplified by centralizing jurisdiction in a more limited number of committees and subcommittees.

The result of this failure is legislative chaos. Legacy agencies use congressional sponsors to protect their turf and avoid integration into a unified DHS. The efforts of the Federal Emergency Management Agency (FEMA) to leverage the jurisdiction of the House Transportation and Infrastructure Committee into administrative independence are particularly notorious. Private sector actors also continue to seek favored treatment through congressional influence. The most notable instance was the remarkable (and, fortunately, unsuccessful) proposal by the House Agriculture Committee to remove agricultural inspections from the DHS, in effect seeking to undo the unification of our border inspection function, a unification that many judge to be the single greatest success of reorganization.

In the end, the resulting confusion and organizational turmoil has been all too predictable. DHS is faced with a number of conflicting directions from congressional committees. Congressional turf fights frustrate any effort to ameliorate those conflicts through greater coordination. And when Congress and the administration are of different parties, the proliferation of congressional jurisdiction enables too much unnecessary oversight and micromanagement of particular programs.

The hope for greater coordination through centralized control is common on the American political scene. Precisely the same arguments in support of the creation of the DHS were made in support of the creation of an Office of the Director of National Intelligence (ODNI) and the restructuring of the IC. In these cases, too, a central focal point was thought necessary to achieve effective coordination of executive action.

The IC restructuring was on a scale equal to that of the DHS—it overturned a structure that had been in place since the dawn of the Cold War. The National Security Act of 1947 created the initial structure of the IC (and also reorganized our military so that each branch of service was subordinate to the Secretary of Defense), and authorized the creation of the CIA, whose director also managed the entire national intelligence effort in his role as the Director of Central Intelligence (DCI).[3] The DCI was charged with, among many tasks, coordinating intelligence collection requirements and priorities across the federal government and collecting intelligence through human sources. The 1947 Act has been modified on a number of occasions. Most recently, the Intelligence Reform and Terrorism Prevention Act of 2004 (IRTPA)[4] created the position of the Director of National Intelligence (DNI) and the ODNI, which took over most of the DCI's coordinating functions.

The ODNI was charged with overseeing the activities of the IC. The DNI was given a set of duties, including the coordination of the development of requirements for intelligence and the collection of information, its analysis, and dissemination. The

DNI was also explicitly obligated to "ensure compliance with the Constitution and laws of the United States by the Central Intelligence Agency" and to "ensure such compliance by other elements of the intelligence community through the host executive departments that manage the programs and activities that are part of the National Intelligence Program."[5] In other words, the new DNI was put in charge of intelligence.

But the DNI was not given the tools to do the job. The origins of the ODNI were swathed in "small 'p'" political considerations. Most notably, though the military intelligence functions represent well more than half of the nation's intelligence effort, the Department of Defense's activities were explicitly excluded from the DNI's direct control.[6] Understandably, cabinet secretaries and agency heads have consistently resisted organizational rules that constrain their ability to control the personnel and resources within their department. But what is understandable as a matter of bureaucratic politics is not ideal for American policy. The ideal concept for the ODNI is a lean headquarters charged with the following tasks: design of a blueprint for intelligence collection and analysis, allocation of resources, collection of intelligence products for use by decision makers (including conflicting views within the IC), and supervision of the sixteen separate agencies involved in intelligence activity. The ODNI has become a competing bureaucracy instead of an effective leadership model.

In the end, these intelligence coordination efforts may charitably be characterized as "works in progress" whose ultimate efficacy has yet to be conclusively determined. Less charitably, but more accurately, these efforts have turned out to be borderline failures. Perhaps the most recent example of this was the inability of the DNI and the Director of the CIA to agree on an assessment of the Muslim Brotherhood and its role in the Egyptian revolution: one thought it a benign secular influence, the other thought it a likely radical affiliate. If what we have tried to gain through these coordinating functions is a more rationalized, comprehensive and effective IC, we have not succeeded.

MILITARY USE OF FORCE

Our military response to September 11 began with a welcome degree of agreement across the political spectrum. The Authorization for Use of Military Force (AUMF) against terrorists and terrorist organizations passed with near-unanimity.[7]

Since that time we have been less successful in putting aside partisanship to foster the prosecution of our military efforts. To be fair, this is at least in part because of the difficulties of the legal and policy questions surrounding our war against non-state terrorist actors. The conflict with al-Qaeda and its affiliates poses a number of complex, novel questions. The war lies outside the traditional scope defined by the laws of armed conflict. Our enemies do not fight within the confines of the Geneva Conventions; they wage asymmetric warfare using the civilian population as a shield and they do not carry their arms openly. As a consequence, we have both practical and legal difficulties identifying who they are, which (for a country, like the United States, that *does* abide by the laws of war) makes targeting and disablement decisions highly problematic.[8]

Notwithstanding the difficulty of these issues, one would have hoped that by the tenth anniversary of the start of the war there would be a consensus emerging and a high degree of legal and practical clarity developing. Sadly, this has not been the case. We continue to be caught up in the symbolism of a few minor issues that prevent us from coherently addressing larger questions. We have even seen a muted argument by some that the successful operation to kill Osama bin Laden was unlawful—an argument that seems almost fanciful to most Americans. Consumed by the political salience of trial by military commissions and detention policy at Guantánamo Bay, Congress has had no political will to work with the executive branch and engage in the hard task of constructing the long-term legal and policy framework that will guide our war against terrorists and non-state enemies in the future.

The contrast between today's failure of political will and the more deliberative process of earlier eras is instructive, if a bit depressing. For example, in 1967 the Supreme Court held that the Fourth Amendment applied to electronic communications, and that a warrant was required for electronic surveillance conducted by law enforcement agencies in the United States.[9] To conform to this new ruling and yet empower investigators to combat organized crime and other major criminal activity, Congress codified requirements for such interceptions in Title III of the Omnibus Crime Control and Safe Streets Act of 1968.[10] Today, Title III continues to regulate the disclosure and use of authorized intercepted communications by investigative and law enforcement officers, though it has been modified over the years to take account of technological changes and now covers all forms of electronic communication (including, for example, emails). Legislative attention to the matter has been sustained and, for the most part, non-political. The war against terrorists demands the same type of practical solutions.

Perhaps the overly politicized atmosphere of Congress today will not permit that kind of careful and sustained attention to the legal and policy issues relating to our ongoing war against terrorists. But America needs this sort of effort now more than ever. A short list of topics for discussion would include: rules for preventive detention; definitions of armed conflict in cyberspace; rationalization of efforts to combat domestic radicalization; military preparedness for a biological attack; developing a legal and policy strategy for dealing with piracy;[11] and defining the boundaries of military/civilian intelligence domains. More could, of course, be added. That Congress has yet to find the political will to begin these efforts is deeply troubling.

LEGAL REFORM

Finally, there is the question of how to reform the legal system to allow us to prosecute the war against terrorists. Other contributors to this volume have written ably about the details of that effort. For our part, however, we see the efforts to frustrate necessary legal reforms as symbolic of a failure to come to grips with a changed reality. At bottom, the opposition reflects an unwillingness to realize that new legal regimes are necessary to deal with a new enemy.[12]

There is an overarching theme that animates criticism of the new legal authorities (such as the USA Patriot Act)[13] sought by the executive branch. Critics of the new laws frequently decry the expansion of executive authority in its own right. They generically equate the potential for abuse of executive branch authority with the existence of actual abuse. They argue—either implicitly or explicitly—that the growth in executive power is a threat, whether or not the power has been misused in the days since the anti-terrorism campaign began. In essence, these critics come from a long tradition of limited government (one that we generally favor ourselves) that fears any expansion of executive authority, notwithstanding the potential for benign and beneficial results, because they judge the potential for the abuse of power in the abstract to outweigh the benefits gained.

But the defense of the country against foreign enemies is a primary responsibility given to the federal government by the

Constitution. The Framers had a very different attitude about the powers that they granted the President for use in domestic as opposed to foreign or military affairs. The military and foreign affairs functions were ones in which the Founders determined the executive should be given considerable "energy" to protect national security.[14] Our republic's finest days have included times when the people and its institutions have been unified in response to major threats to the nation.

Political criticisms of legitimate investigative activity seem to misapprehend several important distinctions. First, they often blur potential and actuality. To be sure, many aspects of the Patriot Act (and other governmental responses) do expand the power of the government to act. And Americans should be cautious about any expansion of government power, for assuredly such expansion admits of the potential for abuse. But by and large, the potential for abuse of new executive powers has proven to be far less than critics have presumed. After ten years, a review of the operation of the Patriot Act, for example, shows little evidence of serious abuse.

Second, much of the belief in the potential for abuse stems from a misunderstanding of the true nature of the powers that the government has deployed. To a surprising degree, opposition to the executive response to terror is premised on a mistaken view of the powers actually involved in the counterterrorism laws. The investigative techniques authorized in the Patriot Act and related statutes have long been used against organized crime, drug trafficking, and other criminal activity.

More fundamentally, those who fear the expansion of executive power in the war against terrorists should not deny the officials charged with national security the tools to carry out their responsibilities. Instead, vigilance and oversight enforced through legal, organizational, and technical means are the answer to potential abuse. As a nation, we can have responsible counter-terrorism efforts without the erosion of civil liberties guaranteed by the Constitution.

Where there is genuine concern about potential abuse, there is ample opportunity for legal reform, as recent history illustrates. Through a series of amendments, aspects of the Patriot Act have been modified to provide for greater judicial review. This type of nonpartisan, constructive effort, combined with a practical understanding of the need for legitimate investigative activity, can pave the way for the successful achievement of both liberty and security.

CONCLUSION

Thomas Jefferson once said: "The natural progress of things is for liberty to yield and government to gain ground."[15] While accommodating the need for government to ensure domestic tranquility in these troubled times, a watchful America can guard against this natural tendency. Though Jefferson was right that we must be cautious, John Locke was equally accurate when he wrote: "In all states of created beings, capable of laws, where there is no law there is no freedom. For liberty is to be free from the restraint and violence from others; which cannot be where there is no law; and is not, as we are told, a liberty for every man to do what he likes."[16]

The obligation of the government is a dual one: to protect civil safety and security against violence and to preserve civil liberty. We can only do that through a unified and nonpartisan approach to the problem of terrorists. Efforts to resolve difficult questions of security and liberty raise a number of trenchant issues that can reasonably be debated, and deserve to be. But in doing so we must recognize a common obligation to restrain the politics of ambition in favor of the interests of the American public. Our initial post-9/11 efforts to do so—through reorganization, military action, and legal reform—were undertaken in the first flush of emergency. As we learn from the past ten years, we must be prepared to review and, if necessary, recalibrate our efforts. This decade of experience gives us the information we need to rationalize current laws and practices. It enables us to design policies and procedures that will enhance our defenses against terrorists in the future. We should get about doing so, in light of the experience of our forebears and the experience of our own time.

reforming the intelligence community[*]

THE HONORABLE
LAURENCE H. SILBERMAN

n 2004–2005, I enjoyed an extraordinary experience for a
sitting federal judge. I co-chaired, with ex-Senator Chuck
Robb, a Presidential Intelligence Commission. By executive
order, President George W. Bush charged the commission
to inquire into the intelligence community's conclusions regarding Saddam Hussein's possession of weapons of mass destruction
(WMD). It turned out, to my surprise, that the Canons of Judicial

---

[*] This essay is an edited version of a speech delivered to the Acadia Senior College, Bar Harbor, Maine, on July 15, 2010.

Ethics permitted a senior judge to take a temporary assignment in the executive branch, so long as I did not hear cases during my appointment. The bipartisan commission included the President of Yale, Rich Levin; the President of MIT, Chuck Vest; former White House Counsel in the Carter and Clinton administrations, Lloyd Cutler; former Undersecretary of Defense under Clinton, Walter Slocombe; my ex-colleague, Judge Patricia Wald, who had been appointed to the bench by President Jimmy Carter; and Senator John McCain. Two intelligence experts joined us: Henry Rowen, who had served in almost every administration since President John F. Kennedy; and retired Admiral Bill Studeman, who had headed NSA and been deputy Director of the CIA.

We were tasked with a careful examination of the intelligence community's conclusions regarding Iraqi WMD and any generic faults or political pressure that could have contributed to mistakes. We were also asked for reform suggestions. But we were not charged with considering the administration's (or Congress's) evaluation of that intelligence. That was a political issue in 2004 and the commission had no desire to enter into the political debate.

I feel less constrained now. Much time has passed, and the subject of the role of intelligence in the Bush administration's (and Congress's) decisions to invade Iraq can now be examined by scholars. So I will unburden myself of several conclusions that would have been inappropriate in 2005.

First, it is a grotesquely false charge that President Bush "lied us into war" by exaggerating our intelligence on Saddam Hussein's WMD. Karl Rove's recent book lays out the genesis of that accusation, first uttered by Senator Edward Kennedy and Senator John Kerry in 2004. And it is still peddled by tendentious commentators today. In fact, as our commission unanimously determined, the intelligence community had badly erred in its formal

National Intelligence Estimate (NIE) of 2002. It concluded, to a 90 percent certainty, that Saddam Hussein possessed WMD. That not only convinced the Bush administration, but also most members of Congress.

We also concluded unanimously that the administration never, in any way, pressured the intelligence community to reach that conclusion—the same conclusion the intelligence community had held during the Clinton administration. In light of these unanimous conclusions, there is not much room for the charge that the administration hyped or exaggerated the intelligence regarding Saddam Hussein's WMD. In fact, I have never found any comment by a Bush administration official that was inconsistent with the intelligence community's views, whether expressed in the 2002 NIE or in the President's Daily Briefs that we reviewed. Indeed, in the period leading up to the war, there is no difference between the Bush administration comments regarding Iraqi WMD and those by a host of Democratic congressmen who supported the war.

As it turned out, the intelligence community was, as we said, "dead wrong." More damning, its mistakes were quite incredible. Some were caused by a failure to share information; for instance, that Saddam Hussein had mobile labs to manufacture biological weapons. That conclusion appeared to be based on different sources, but it actually all came from one scoundrel, code named Curveball. He hornswoggled German intelligence and was never interviewed by American agencies. Another determination that Saddam had resumed his nuclear weapons program was based on a Defense Intelligence Agency (DIA) conclusion that he was importing tubes for centrifuges. It turned out that the tubes were for mortars. Amazingly, these tubes were exactly the same as the ones the U.S. Army used for mortars. The DIA analysts explained afterward that they were only familiar with foreign military weapons. Finally, the intelligence community's determination that Saddam had accelerated his chemical weapons production was based on satellite pictures, which showed that the large trucks—which we concluded were used to transport chemicals—were seen in increasing numbers. As it turned out, those trucks were not for that use, but that conclusion was defensible, even if incorrect. What was not defensible was the judgment that more and more trucks were observed. In fact, the intelligence community saw an increasing number of those trucks only because it had tasked satellites to pass over Iraq on a more frequent basis.

Still, it is important to recognize that it would have been virtually impossible for the intelligence community to have discovered that Saddam Hussein had destroyed his stockpile of chemical and biological weapons and stopped his effort to develop nuclear weapons. He had done so after United Nations weapons inspectors had detected his illicit programs in 1991. After all, his own top generals and his senior political officials were convinced he had them. Indeed, one of the most persuasive bits of intelligence, which came through a foreign intelligence agency, was from a very senior Iraqi official who was truthful, if mistaken. If the intelligence community had been doing a first-rate job, it would have reported to the President and Congress that it believes that Saddam has WMD. It should have reported that it knows he had them, it has no indication that he destroyed them, and he certainly behaves as if he has them, but it cannot be sure; it simply does not have sufficient hard intelligence. Had the intelligence community known that Iraqi WMD had been destroyed, I do not think that President Bush, nor Congress, would have wanted to go to war. Indeed, Saddam Hussein could have avoided war, even at the last moment, had he allowed the weapons inspectors free access.

Let us suppose, however, the 2002 NIE and the other report-ings of the intelligence community had followed this quite defen-sible probability line. Pondering this counterfactual scenario, I am inclined to believe that the United States would have gone to war anyway—which does not, of course, excuse the intelligence community, but does put mistakes in context. It is simply much too simplistic to say we went to war because of bad intelligence. I reach my counterfactual hypothesis based on the following considerations.

First, even had the intelligence community been more tenta-tive, virtually everyone in Washington would have believed that Saddam Hussein maintained his WMD capability for the same reasons that a more professional intelligence community would have reported that he "probably" had WMD. Second, Iraq was shooting at British and American planes patrolling the no-fly zone. It was only a matter of time before one or more were shot down. Third, Saddam Hussein was defying a series of UN resolu-tions since 1991, altogether ignoring UN inspection demands—perhaps most notably the UN Resolution 1441, which demanded "cooperation immediately, unconditionally, actively." Fourth, he had undisputedly sought to assassinate a former President, George H. W. Bush, in Kuwait. That incident was downplayed for obvious reasons by his son, but one might think that was a rather classic cause for war. Tony Blair—in my view one of the great statesmen of recent years—has made similar points. Finally, although there was no hard evidence that Saddam was cooperat-ing with al-Qaeda, given his hostility to the United States, he was certainly a threat post-9/11. Even the CIA, which strongly resisted the administration's suspicion of a direct connection between al-Qaeda and Saddam, recognized the possible threat.

Nevertheless, the United States would never have suffered the national embarrassment of General Colin Powell's presentation to the United Nations if the intelligence community had not convinced him with faulty intelligence. And Powell was determined to base his UN speech almost entirely on Iraqi WMD. According to newspaper accounts and post-war books, that was a rather disputed decision. A number of officials within the administration argued that the United States' reasons should have been set forth more broadly. Indeed, if American intelligence had been more tentative, the administration might not have gone to the United Nations at all as a precursor to war, any more than Clinton did a few years earlier vis-à-vis Serbia.

Admittedly, my hypothesis is speculative; but I would like to add a further consideration that leads me to believe that war with Saddam was coming, even if not in 2003. We know from the Duelfer Report commissioned by the CIA after the war and from other intelligence, including interviews with Saddam Hussein himself, that Saddam had every intention of resuming his WMD programs, including nuclear weapons, once the UN sanctions regime was disbanded. The sanctions regime was on its last legs because of increasing European disenchantment. It would have taken Saddam Hussein only a very short time—a matter of months—to re-establish both his biological and chemical weapons capabilities. Moreover, he retained a burning desire to punish Kuwait once again. In short, I think it is probable that it was only a matter of time before we would have been at war with Iraq, if not in 2003. I think that would have been so even had Senator Kerry become President in 2004.

This brings me to the fashionable theoretical dichotomy endorsed by political opponents of the war in Iraq. It has been argued by certain foreign policy specialists that the war in Iraq was only a war of choice, not a war of necessity and, since war should be thought of only as a last resort, it was improper—some would say immoral—to have attacked Saddam. That theory couples Iraq with Vietnam and distinguishes, for example, American entry into World War II, precipitated as it was by the Japanese attack on Pearl Harbor. I find this dichotomy rather simplistic and misleading. It ignores the uncomfortable fact that we were actually engaged in a de facto naval war with Germany in 1941, months before Pearl Harbor, and that the oil embargo against Japan in 1941 was a paradigmatic *casus belli*.

It is instructive in that regard to consider the situation Britain and France faced in the 1930s. We now know that if they had used military force to stop Hitler's march into the Rhineland in 1936, Hitler would likely have been overthrown by his own generals. The British and French political establishments surely saw such an action as a war of choice rather than necessity. And two years later, at Munich, again Prime Minister Neville Chamberlain chose peace rather than war. Churchill was, of course, prophetic when he said, "You were given a choice between war and dishonor. You chose dishonor and you will have war." When Hitler invaded Poland in 1939 the British and the French did declare war, but why was that a moment of necessity? After all, they were not attacked and Hitler actually expected that they would not declare war. Similarly, when the Japanese attacked Pearl Harbor, an undeniable ground for war, many of their leaders expected, after our fleet was destroyed, that the United States, like the Russians in 1905, would negotiate a peace rather than fight a long bloody war.

My point in this historical excursion is to establish that the fashionable dichotomy is false; there is no bright line that divides a war of necessity from a war of choice. Often, when we look in hindsight, a so-called war of choice was inevitable, and therefore can be described as necessary. Or, to put it another way, the choice is often not whether a country goes to war, but when. A nation's decision to go to war depends on a political cost-benefit calculation—a balancing test, if you will. When thinking defensively, a nation must weigh the imminence or likelihood of a threat against the importance of the interest to be protected and how vital it is. I do not mean to contend that the war in Iraq met that standard; we may not know that for some time. And certainly opposition to the war was and is quite respectable. I only mean to dispel some misconceptions about the role of intelligence, as well as some blatantly false charges and, as a thought experiment, to consider a counterfactual scenario.

Now I should like to turn to a different but related subject: the structure of the intelligence community. In the aftermath of the 9/11 Commission Report, Congress passed a wide-ranging new framework for the intelligence community. Most notably, a Director of National Intelligence (DNI), with cabinet rank, was created to oversee and coordinate the activities of the community. Our commission, faced with the legislation as a fait accompli, made a number of recommendations as to the implementation of that legislation.

We recognized at the outset that the Congress may well have placed great responsibility on the DNI that was not supported by his or her authority. Indeed, Congress, in effect, compromised between those who wanted merely a coordinating official— almost an extension of the National Security Council (NSC)— and those who wanted the DNI to have real supervisory authority over the main intelligence agencies—CIA, NSA, and FBI. It is still argued by some, including Judge Richard Posner, that the DNI should be akin to a White House aide, with authority only to call meetings at which disputes would be discussed. In that respect, Judge Posner expresses the view widely held in the CIA, which has always resented the DNI's emergence. Posner and like-minded critics look at the British system, but they overlook the fundamental difference in our government structures. A senior aide to the Prime Minister can play a more effective coordinating role than would be true in the United States because Britain fuses executive and legislative authority. Britain does not have a constant constitutional tension between the executive and legislative branches and correlative competition for control or influence over the bureaucracy. That is why we have so many more political appointees in the executive branch and larger legislative staffs than does Britain. Anyone charged with forcing coordination among the intelligence community agencies had to have some significant authority of his or her own. That is the reason why, in 1975, I turned down President Ford's request that I take on the job of Assistant to the President for Intelligence.

Without adequate authority, the DNI will never be as effective as Congress expected. I had hoped the DNI would have only a lean staff and much authority, which could be given by any President regardless of the legislative ambiguities. Instead, unfortunately, the reverse has been true under both President George W. Bush and President Barack Obama. The DNI, from the outset, has been a bureaucratic success story. A huge permanent staff was built and I am afraid it was not composed entirely of the very best the intelligence community had to offer. It would have been much preferable if a smaller number of top-notch professionals had been attracted to the DNI's office for career-enhancing temporary assignments, much like the joint staff in the Pentagon or under a combatant commander. And both Presidents could have given the DNI adequate authority truly to manage the community.

To be sure, the DNI has always faced a dilemma. The main purpose of the job is to manage the community—or at least see that it is managed—drawing on the President's authority if necessary. This was needed in order to adjudicate the enormous appropriations budget issues, encourage information sharing, and harmonize personnel practices. But DNIs have seen their prestige and clout dependent on the time spent with the President. There is, therefore, the temptation to present the President's daily briefing to him personally—which takes enormous time and energy. I understand that President Obama's first DNI, retired Admiral Dennis Blair, to his credit, tried to put his emphasis on management. Still, Presidents and their staffs are primarily concerned with the quality of the immediate intelligence provided—not longer-term improvements in intelligence gathering and analysis; so the incentives bearing upon the DNI, as well as the legislative structures, are problematic.

It seems to me it was foreordained in this administration that Admiral Blair had no chance to perform the DNI's job properly. As a career officer, he was supposed to oversee a major political figure, Leon Panetta, the director of the CIA. That could not possibly work, given the ambiguities of the legislation and Panetta's superior political clout. Then, to make matters even worse, President Obama put the man he originally wanted as head of the CIA, John Brennan, in a newly created White House position as Deputy National Security Advisor for Homeland Security and Counterterrorism, whose functions largely overlapped with those of the DNI. Brennan, not Blair, has become the administration's public spokesman on intelligence. Brennan has done so in a more openly political fashion than could a DNI. That has apparently increased his prestige within the White House, leading to an inevitable diminution of Blair's standing outside and inside the intelligence community. I was surprised Blair lasted as long as he did—he resigned in May 2010.

In conclusion, there is no question that the statutory structure in which the DNI operates is awkward. But if the DNI is actually to lead the intelligence community so as to reduce the glitches that have caused the community to be less than efficient in the past, the President has to place the proper personnel in the appropriate jobs and straighten out reporting authorities.

During my time on the commission, I developed a high regard for General James Clapper, then in charge of the National Geospatial Agency, one of the intelligence agencies within the Defense Department, and now President Obama's DNI. But General Clapper, like Admiral Blair, will hardly rival either Leon Panetta or John Brennan in political clout. Apparently, he was chosen, in part, because he saw the job of DNI a good deal more modestly than his predecessors. It remains to be seen whether a downgrading of the DNI position will adequately deal with the problems that prompted Congress to create the job in the first place.

the imperfect reconciliation of liberty and security

RICHARD A. EPSTEIN

NO SELF-INFLICTED PROBLEM

In the current state of American life, it is easy to identify the full range of economic issues brought on by the folly of a nation that thinks that it can tax, regulate, and subsidize its way to economic prosperity. For these issues, we have only ourselves to blame. In dealing with these problems, moreover, the correct solutions all move in one direction. Any set of viable reforms from the present status quo calls for less government—not more—which means that the basic problems of the nation are political, not substantive.

The question of national security, and the impact that national security has on individual civil liberties, is not cut from this cloth. As a general matter, many of the American left, which has long favored, or at least tolerated, extensive government regulation of economic markets, has taken quite the opposite view when it comes to civil liberties, where it often opposes government regulation on matters that could be justified even within the framework of a nation dedicated to the principles of individual liberty and limited government. One example is their opposition to punishing any news outlet that republishes, for a general readership, confidential information that it knows was stolen by other individuals. At the same time, many on the American right, who tend to be suspicious of government regulation on economic matters, take quite the opposite line on issues of national security: they favor fairly extensive levels of direct regulation, some of which, as I shall argue, are not consistent with these same principles of personal liberty and limited government.

On this, the tenth anniversary of 9/11, the key point about national security is all too obvious: these wounds are not, in any sense of the word, self-inflicted. They are often forced upon us by the worst actions of enemies sworn to our destruction. These groups would not be placated in the slightest by our return to small government policies on economic and social matters. Quite the opposite: on social issues, the authoritarian intolerance of al-Qaeda and its allies leads to their hatred of Western democracies. That hatred, in turn, fuels their willingness to engage in violence and terror against the United States and other nations that foster and protect an open society. There is little doubt that much of this antagonism toward the United States was cultivated by Osama bin Laden, who remained a symbol of the steadfast opposition to the United States for the nearly ten years in which he was in hiding. There is good reason to celebrate his demise at the hands of United States special forces, but no reason to think that his death means the end of the movement that he led for so long. On his death, a new generation of leaders will arise to continue the attack on American values and American institutions. It is unlikely that any of them can, at least in the short run, capture the bin Laden mystique. Yet by the same token they may bring a measure of youth and aggressiveness to their task that poses new threats to the United States and the West. No matter who is in charge, one truth remains: there is little that can be done to placate these diehard enemies. There is much that must be done to resist them.

THE NECESSITY OF BALANCING

The first consideration is methodological. The reason the issue is so difficult is that it is not possible to take a position that ignores the problem altogether. All groups in the United States, regardless of the differences in their substantive positions, do not look kindly on mass murder, the destruction of property, or the disruption of vital communications and transportation networks. What is the best way to deal with these issues?

At this point, we have to face the grim truth that the decision on when and how to intervene—nonintervention is the kiss of death—will be fraught with two types of errors. These errors have previously resisted any easy solution—even in separate contexts that carry none of national security's heavy freight. The key question deals with the mix between remedies that are imposed before any harm occurs and those that are applied only after it has taken place. In all cases, there are twin objectives: to punish the current offenders and to deter future offenses. There is simply no way in which to attack this task without making serious errors in execution that run in both directions. The more difficult the situation, the *higher* the error rate. This is true even for the *optimal* solution.

At this point, the potential sources of errors are legion. The first point is technical. Someone has to give weight to the various errors, and to the probabilities of their occurrence under different regimes. Next, there are unintended consequences. Getting tougher on terrorists does not necessarily reduce the levels of terrorism. It could easily lead to actions that offend large groups of individuals in ways that could radicalize them. Yet the effort to placate opposition can itself be the path to doom if it leads our enemies to think that they can outlast us.

It is a mistake to tarry too long at a high level of abstraction. Without getting down to cases it is possible that we will generate false disagreements that will disappear when the context becomes plainer. It is also likely at a high level of abstraction for people to take dogmatic positions they would not otherwise take if they proceeded either case by case or area by area. Therefore, I shall not dwell on the relative importance of either liberty or security or pretend that there is any global way in which to rank one ahead of the other. Security of the person necessarily requires that a society limit the way in which all people can use force and fraud against their fellow citizens. The ordinary laws of self-defense and defense of property are riddled with trade-offs that will not disappear as the contexts become more complicated. At root, the difficulties of international security reflect and magnify the difficulties in the common law of self-defense in all its rich variations.

In order to show how these trade-offs should be organized, I shall comment on two types of situations. The first deals with the efforts to ferret out terrorist activities before they can be undertaken. I limit myself to a discussion of the interception of communications and racial and ethnic profiling. The second deals with the apprehension and treatment of individuals who have engaged in terrorist activities, including conspiracies to commit offenses that involve harm to persons, the destruction of property, or the theft of government secrets. I address questions of detention and punishment, of both citizens and aliens.

THE PREVENTION OF TERRORIST ACTIVITIES

No responsible government could content itself with waiting until the moment a terrorist attack mobilized its resources. Death, bodily harm, property damage, and the like are too great a threat to liberty and security for government officials to simply stand aside. Of course, ordinary individuals and firms can, should, and do engage in their own protective activities. But neither private individuals nor groups have the resources or the power to deal with this task alone. The question, then, is what kinds of early devices are appropriate, and why?

1. Interception of Communications

One illustration of this issue concerned the revelations of late 2005 that the U.S. government had engaged in an extensive set of intercepts to ascertain the ways in which terrorist groups communicate. It should be evident that these efforts to expand the surveillance network must monitor the behavior of large numbers of individuals who are manifestly innocent. It should be equally clear that government efforts to track their connections and listen to their conversations will result in the kinds of personal intrusions that, if undertaken by one private individual against another, would be regarded as a serious invasion of personal privacy, punishable by the criminal law and actionable under private law.

Should government oversight escape the full range of criminal and civil sanctions? Under any rational system of balancing, surveillance has to be able to go forward. Looking for committed terrorists is trying to find the needle in the haystack. Rarely will investigations rest on anything more substantial than loose inferences and weak suspicions. To hold that government officials can go forward with their work only if they meet standards of probable cause gets the balance entirely wrong. A dragnet-like system that collects information about all sorts of individuals will not necessarily work a distinctive prejudice against any of them. As long as the information gathered is used solely to combat terrorism, it is best to take these invasions of privacy in stride. The success of these surveillance programs, moreover, cannot be judged solely by the number of suspects identified or the number of foiled plots. Their deterrent effect should never be ignored, even if there is no observable evidence of a terrorist cell or bomb plot.

The essential protection of civil liberties does not lie in curbing surveillance techniques; it lies in preventing the information that is collected from being misused: monitor use, not collection. This distinction has a lot of staying power in the eyes of ordinary individuals. President George W. Bush exceeded the scope of his "inherent" presidential authority when he authorized the monitoring of certain conversations involving foreign parties that did not meet the elaborate (and cumbersome) requirements of the Foreign Intelligence Surveillance Act of 1978 (FISA),[1] which was passed in response to the abuses of the Watergate affair. Congress had supplied a detailed statutory scheme for presidential searches that the President ignored. The President's power is at its low ebb when his actions fly in the face of a congressional mandate. The scuffles over presidential authority were, of course, eliminated once Congress amended FISA in 2008.[2] With the issue of authorization resolved, the only objection to the revised statutes stems from Fourth Amendment protections against unreasonable searches and seizures. On that issue, the Fourth Amendment offers only an uncertain guide:

> The right of the people to be secure in their persons, houses, papers, and effects, against unreasonable searches and seizures, shall not be violated, and no Warrants shall issue, but upon probable cause, supported by Oath or affirmation, and particularly describing the place to be searched, and the persons or things to be seized.[3]

The warrant provision is clearly inapplicable to this situation, for once a suspect has been identified by general surveillance, the government should be able to meet the warrant requirements of the Fourth Amendment, subject to the usual exceptions for emergency situations. But general surveillance, if it is covered by the amendment at all, is only reached by the first clause of the amendment, where the sensible argument in favor of an aggressive surveillance position takes two forms. First, some of the actions of the government, including tracking the connections between persons without examining the content of their communications, may not count as a search or a seizure. The second is that once a suspicious pattern emerges, these searches and seizures are not "unreasonable" in light of the seriousness of the underlying offenses and the modest nature of the intrusion.

Consider one concrete validation of this point of view. The reason George W. Bush's presidency survived the revelations of the unauthorized surveillance is that no one thought his conduct—however unwise or repugnant—was a rerun of Watergate, whereas the information collected by Nixon's operatives was used for personal reasons. Even a whiff of suspicion of improper use by the Bush administration would have completely changed the complexion of the political debate, for then impeachment would have been a real possibility, not just an idle suggestion.

2. Profiling

A second form of antecedent surveillance involves the use of various inspections of individuals, especially in airline transportation. It is easy to poke holes. Airline passengers are not the only parties vulnerable to attack: mass destruction can occur on trains, in public markets, or in stadiums. The current efforts at surveillance are thus both under- and over-inclusive. Yet no one wants to bring out the heavy constitutional artillery needed to deal with these serious problems of institutional and system design, given the strength of government interests and the sobering realization that no set of inspections for potential terrorists will be foolproof. This is not the area for strict judicial scrutiny.

If courts have displayed a genuine and sensible reluctance to deal with the overall design of surveillance activities, what about challenges based on the ground that individuals receive selective scrutiny—solely or primarily because of their race, nationality, or ethnic origins? Clearly, no one should lightly dismiss these serious concerns. But these concerns are not trumps for the interests on the other side, which strike me as far weightier. I have no firm conviction of how effective government surveillance should be best structured: is it best to focus on individuals born in some Muslim countries? Or on those that have displayed allegiance to certain Muslim causes? It is clear that any government program that adopted an uncompromising stance would be vulnerable to an effective counterstrategy: terrorist groups would look for individuals born in other places to carry out their programs. But this brute fact only proves that it would be foolish to target *all* resources against these selective groups, though it would not prove that it was equally unwise to devote a disproportionate set of resources.

I am therefore uneasy about the recent government decision to ramp up inspection on all individuals at airports. It could be that deploying those additional resources in other ways might prove far more effective. It ill behooves any law professor to claim that he has certain or even reliable information about the proper approach to profiling. It is sufficient to say that any attack appears to be indefensible in light of gains from rational search procedures relying on semi-solid information. There is little doubt that these programs will have disparate impact on virtuous individuals of certain religious and national groups. But there is no responsible way to deal with this problem and to maintain an effective system of surveillance at a sensible cost. Any effort to think in terms of compensation for selective ethnic or racial searches imposed would create such an administrative nightmare that it is not within the realm of plausible institutional arrangements. The national security angle swamps the claims for just compensation.

TREATMENT OF INDIVIDUAL SUSPECTS

1. Citizens and Aliens

The second major challenge involves the treatment of individuals who are suspected of engaging in terrorist activities. How should they be treated? The relative balance shifts as one considers the government interest in the prevention of terrorist activities and the high likelihood of certain individuals to engage in deadly activities. Yet the balance shifts in a more dramatic fashion on the other side. It is one thing to monitor telephone calls and email. It is quite another to lock up persons for an indefinite period of time without the benefit of a criminal trial or even some independent judicial review. The individual interest is large, and it should not matter that many of the individuals who are subject to the coercive power of the United States, either at home or abroad, are aliens. It is noteworthy that the two key constitutional texts make no distinction on the grounds of either citizenship or location. The Fifth Amendment's Due Process Clause states: "No person shall be . . . deprived of life, liberty, or property, without due process of law."[4] The protection of the writ of habeas corpus reads: "The privilege of the writ of habeas corpus shall not be suspended, unless when in cases of rebellion or invasion the public safety may require it."[5]

It is important to take these provisions to heart. Due Process contains what is best regarded as a form of constructive flexibility. The term "due" does not define itself. Rather, this constitutional riddle forces judges to figure out how much process is due in any situation. Nevertheless, by trial and error, it should be possible to make headway. It seems clear that the level of process needed for detention under battlefield conditions is quite low—indeed, virtually nonexistent. But that should apply whether we deal with American citizens or aliens. No process is due until people are taken to a position of relative safety behind the lines—far behind the lines. Similarly, with habeas corpus, the threat to public safety could come from any source at home or abroad. It is dangerous to draw invidious process distinctions based on citizenship status. By the same token, there is no reason to offer an extra measure of protection to citizen terrorists, either by birth or naturalization, who have become sworn enemies of the United States operating in foreign sanctuaries. They should be exposed to as much deadly force as aliens operating from the same locales. Anwar al-Aulaqi, an American citizen who operates out of Yemen, should not be entitled to any special immunity from air drones that target aliens in the same compound.

2. Detention and Trial

It is also critical to strike the right balance in those cases where an alien or citizen is taken into custody by the United States. What type of treatment the detained receives should not depend on the location of the prison. There are many abstruse debates over whether Guantánamo should be treated as American territory because it is held under a perpetual lease from Cuba, or whether it should be treated on a par with Bagram Airfield in Afghanistan. What is clear is that any person who is shipped to Bagram after being held securely elsewhere should not lose any rights otherwise possessed while near a combat zone. By clarifying that the place of detention does not influence the structure of rights, we can defuse the disputes over whether to close down Guantánamo and disperse its inmates elsewhere.

Once the case for uniform treatment is accepted, it remains to be decided what that treatment should be. The traditional view is that people held as enemy combatants could be detained without habeas corpus for an indefinite period of time until the conflict ran its course. This rule works well when it is clear who is picked up on the battlefield and equally clear when a war is over. It does not work when people are brought into custody under shady circumstances—as by bounty hunters—and when they could be held until the war on terror is over, an occasion that will not be marked by any armistice or treaty.

In the non-battlefield cases, the risk of error on both sides is high, and there is no clean solution. When the costs of error both ways are high, the government should invest a lot of resources to reduce them to the extent possible. The Suspension Clause does not offer much guidance because it only states when it is appropriate to suspend habeas corpus. It does not tell us when that "privilege" should be awarded in the first place. It is necessary to fashion an answer consistent with the basic desire to protect both liberty and security. In these cases, the government should not adopt a minimalist approach to legal rights, but should take the initiative to gather as much information as it can to determine who should stay or go. Nothing remotely close to certainty beyond a reasonable doubt, or even a preponderance of evidence, should be required to keep individuals in custody to prevent them from returning to the enemy. There is, moreover, no necessity to release those individuals who are subject to detention if they are not brought to trial, let alone before an Article III judge. It is enough that the evidence in question is sufficient to hold these detainees.

There is a serious quid pro quo for this exceptional power, which is the willingness to adopt extensive processes that give those in custody an opportunity to present their case to an independent judge, who need not be outside the military system. I have immense confidence in the willingness of military lawyers to defend their clients even at the cost of their own careers. But the Military Commissions Act of 2006,[6] drafted in response to the one-sided procedures struck down in *Hamdi v. Rumsfeld*,[7] while commendable in many of its specific provisions, seemed to go too far by denying any detainee the right to some independent determination of whether they should be classified as an enemy combatant. The government has no need to use one-sided procedures so long as it can control the forum. Indeed, it should go further and conduct internal reviews of each case to see whether the circumstances that justified the initial detention still hold, or whether new evidence is available. It should report to a judge within the military system about the status of the evidence, so that it does not look as though all detentions are ratified by kangaroo courts.

There may be ample evidence to hold most of those individuals who are in custody for the indefinite future. If so, no effort should be made to remove them from Guantánamo to a less controversial location. The detention facilities at Guantánamo are now among the best available; better to invite the hostile critics in for an inspection than to act as though the facilities were not worthy of American tradition. There are ample difficulties in dealing with detention without throwing on the government an added burden of fighting symbolic battles that can be won by better means.

CONCLUSION

One common theme links these disparate cases together. The pre-detention phase generally involves modest infringements on liberty that could generate substantial gains. Therefore, aggressive monitoring should be welcome, as long as the information collected is not used for improper ends. That distinction can be elusive on occasion, but for the most part it appears as though it has been scrupulously observed. At the other end of the spectrum, in the case of individuals potentially subject to detention, the stakes are higher. In those cases, unfortunately, neither form of error can be avoided; the best approach is one that uses additional resources to drive down both forms of error simultaneously.

The bad news in all these cases is that the imponderables on both sides of the scale are hard to weigh. The good news is that there is little doubt as to which side of the balance the individual weights belong. The relative consensus on both these issues should both shape legislative policy and limit judicial intervention to those extreme cases where due process becomes virtually no process at all. Those mistakes have been made, and they were checked. It is time now to move on with a greater awareness of the stakes on both sides.

torture and democratic accountability: an oxymoron?

ALAN DERSHOWITZ

One goal of terrorism directed against democracies is to provoke overreaction and repression. In the wake of the 9/11 attacks, many Americans did in fact overreact, and although the actions of the government did not approach "repression," there were some overreactions that seemed to play into the hands of the terrorists. Perhaps the most egregious were the acts of humiliation and torture that were captured by cell phone photographs at Abu Ghraib prison. These disturbing photographs went viral throughout the world and showed the ugly face of American torture. Surprisingly, the events of 9/11 also stimulated a debate within Western democracies: Is torture ever justified in the war against terrorism?

Rational discussion of this and other questions relating to torture proved difficult, because the issues are so emotional.[1] Indeed, to many absolutists, the very idea of a "rational" discussion of torture is an oxymoron. To them, the issue is simple and clear-cut: torture should *never* be employed or even considered, because it never works; it is incompatible with democratic values; it is barbaric; it will always lead to more barbaric practices; it is worse than any evils it may prevent; it will provoke even more terrorism; it strips any democracy employing it of the moral standing to object to human rights violations by other nations or groups; and it unleashes the "law of unintended consequences."

Most of these arguments are empirical in nature and may be true or false as matters of fact. But there is one fact that is indisputably true, has always been true, and, in my view, will always be true. That fact is that every democracy confronted with a genuine choice of evils between allowing many of its citizens to be killed by terrorists, or employing some forms of torture to prevent such multiple deaths, will opt for the use of torture. This, too, is an empirical claim, and I am entirely confident that it is true as a matter of fact.

That tragic truth is the underlying basis for my extensive writings about torture—both before and after 9/11—and especially for my controversial proposal for a "torture warrant." I have proposed as a prerequisite to the employment of torture—be it torture "light," waterboarding, psychological torture, or "extraordinary measures"—the attainment of judicial approval of a sworn affidavit detailing its need. The testing case, in the philosophical and legal literature, has always been the so-called "ticking bomb" terrorist in a situation endangering large numbers of innocent civilians.

Although the current administration, unlike its predecessor, has announced that it would never torture suspected terrorists, it has also resisted any judicial review of its counterterrorism measures. "Trust us," but don't ask us to justify that trust! Such an approach might be acceptable if men were angels, but no administration is run by angels. That is why visibility and accountability are essential to democratic governance. Neither is this an issue that divides along party lines. President Clinton implicitly acknowledged on National Public Radio that he would have used torture in an extreme case:

> We have a system of laws here where nobody should be above the law, and you don't need blanket advance approval for blanket torture. They can draw a statute much more narrowly, which would permit the President to make a finding in a [ticking bomb] case like I just outlined, and then that finding could be submitted even if after the fact to the Foreign Intelligence Surveillance Court.

Clinton was then asked whether he was saying there "would be more responsibility afterward for what was done." He replied: "Yeah, well, the President could take personal responsibility for it. But you do it on a case-by-case basis, and there'd be some review of it." He summarized his views in the following terms:

> If they really believe the time comes when the only way they can get a reliable piece of information is to beat it out of someone or put a drug in their body to talk it out of

'em, then they can present it to the Foreign Intelligence Court, or some other court, just under the same circumstances we do with wiretaps. Post facto . . . But I think if you go around passing laws that legitimize a violation of the Geneva Convention and institutionalize what happened at Abu Ghraib or Guantánamo, we're gonna be in real trouble.[2]

When I interviewed a former Australian Prime Minister following the terrorist attack in Bali that killed many Australians, he said essentially the same thing. Although I do not know what President Obama would say, I do know what his administration would *do* if faced with a real ticking bomb situation. No President would want to be responsible for the deaths of thousands of innocent citizens if he could have prevented these deaths by authorizing the use of nonlethal torture against a guilty terrorist.

If I am correct, then it is important to consider the following: if the use of torture is imminent, is it worse to close our eyes and tolerate it by low-level law enforcement officials without accountability, or instead bring it to the surface by requiring a warrant for it as a precondition to its infliction? The question is not whether some torture would or would not be used in the ticking bomb case—it surely would. The dilemma is whether it would be done openly, pursuant to a previously established legal procedure, or whether it would be done secretly, in violation of existing law. This is the important policy issue about which I have tried to begin a debate: how should a democracy make difficult choice-of-evil decisions in situations for which there is no good resolution?

Several important values are pitted against each other. The first is the safety and security of a nation's citizens. Under the ticking bomb scenario, this value may necessitate the use of torture, if torture is the only way to prevent the bomb from killing large numbers of civilians. The second value is the preservation of civil liberties and human rights. This value requires that we reject torture as an illegitimate part of our legal system. In my debates with two prominent civil libertarians, Floyd Abrams and Harvey Silverglate, both have acknowledged that they would want nonlethal torture to be used if it could prevent thousands of deaths, but they did not want torture to be officially recognized by our legal system. As Abrams put it: "In a democracy sometimes it is necessary to do things off the books and below the radar screen."

Abrams' approach illustrates a conflict with the third important democratic value: open accountability and visibility. "Off-the-books actions below the radar screen" are antithetical to the theory and practice of democracy. Citizens cannot approve or disapprove of governmental actions of which they are unaware. Experience has shown that off-the-books actions can produce terrible consequences. Richard Nixon's creation of a group of "plumbers" led to Watergate, and Ronald Reagan's authorization of off-the-books foreign policy in Central America led to the Iran-Contra scandal.

Only in a democracy committed to civil liberties would a triangular conflict of this kind exist. Totalitarian and authoritarian regimes experience no such conflict, because they subscribe to neither the civil libertarian nor the democratic values that come in conflict with the value of security. The hard question is: which value is to be preferred when an inevitable clash occurs? If we do not torture, we compromise the security and safety of our citizens. If we tolerate torture, but keep it off the books and below the radar screen, we compromise principles of democratic accountability. If we create a legal structure for limiting and controlling torture, we compromise our principled opposition to torture in all circumstances and create a potentially dangerous and expandable situation.

In 1678, François de La Rochefoucauld wrote, "hypocrisy is the homage that vice renders to virtue." In this case we have two vices: terrorism and torture. We also have two virtues: civil liberties and democratic accountability. Most civil libertarians I know prefer hypocrisy, precisely because it appears to avoid the conflict between security and civil liberties. But by choosing the way of the hypocrite, these civil libertarians compromise the value of democratic accountability. Such is the nature of tragic choices in a complex world. As Bentham put it more than two centuries ago: "Government throughout is but a choice of evils."[3] In a democracy, such choices must be made, whenever possible, with openness and democratic accountability, and subject to the rule of law.

The moral dilemma posed by torture can be ignored only if we assume, as some do, that torture never works. I have been criticized for raising a red herring since it is "well known" that torture does not work. The tragic reality is that torture sometimes works, though many people wish it did not. There are numerous instances in which torture has produced self-proving, truthful information that was necessary to prevent harm to civilians. The *Washington Post* has recounted a case from 1995 in which Philippine authorities tortured a terrorist into disclosing information that may have foiled plots to assassinate the Pope, crash eleven commercial airliners into the Pacific Ocean, and fly a private Cessna filled with explosives into CIA headquarters. For sixty-seven days, intelligence agents beat the suspect "with a chair and a long piece of wood [breaking most of his ribs], forced water into his mouth, and crushed lighted cigarettes into his private parts." After successfully employing this procedure, they turned him over to American authorities, along with the lifesaving information they had beaten out of him.[4] And following the killing of Osama bin Laden, CIA officials claimed that valuable information elicited by waterboarding helped in locating the world's most wanted terrorist. It is impossible to avoid the difficult moral dilemma of choosing among evils by denying the empirical reality that torture *sometimes* works, even if it does not always work. No technique of crime prevention always works.[5]

The goal of the torture warrant proposal is to reduce the use of torture to the smallest amount and degree possible, while creating public accountability for its rare use. I see it not as a compromise with civil liberties but rather as an effort to maximize civil liberties in the face of the realistic likelihood that torture does and will, in fact, take place below the radar screen of accountability. It seems to me logical that a formal, visible, accountable, and centralized system is somewhat easier to control than an ad hoc, off-the-books, and under-the-radar-screen non-system. I believe, though I certainly cannot prove, that a formal requirement of a judicial warrant as a prerequisite to nonlethal torture would decrease the amount of physical violence directed against suspects. At the most obvious level, a double check is always more protective than a single check. In every instance in which a warrant is requested, a field officer has already decided that torture is justified; in the absence of a warrant requirement, the officer would simply have proceeded to implement torture. Requiring that decision to be approved by a judicial officer will result in fewer instances of torture even if the judges rarely turn down a request. Moreover, I believe that most judges would require compelling evidence before they would authorize so extraordinary a departure from our constitutional norms. A record would be kept of every warrant granted, and although it is certainly possible that some individual agents might torture without a warrant, they would have no excuse, since a warrant procedure would be available. They could not claim "necessity," because the decision as to whether the torture is indeed necessary has been taken out of their hands and placed in the hands of a judge. In addition, even if torture were deemed totally illegal without any exception, it would still occur, though the public would be less aware of its existence.

I also believe that the rights of the suspect would be better protected with a warrant requirement. He would be granted immunity, told that he was now compelled to testify, threatened with imprisonment, and given the option of providing the requested information. Only if he refused to do what he was legally compelled to do—provide necessary information, which could not incriminate him because of the immunity—would he be threatened with torture. Knowing that such a threat was authorized by the law, he might well provide the information. If he still refused, he would be subjected to judicially monitored physical measures designed to cause excruciating pain without leaving any lasting damage.

It should be noted that, in the context of searches, our Supreme Court opted for a judicial check on the discretion of the police by requiring a search warrant in most cases. The Court has explained the reason for the warrant requirement as follows: "The informed and deliberate determinations of magistrates . . . are to be preferred over the hurried actions of officers."[6] Of course, there is something different about torture that makes us loath to bring torture within the oversight of our judicial officers. In addition to the horrible history associated with torture, there is also the aesthetic of torture: the very idea of deliberately subjecting a captive human being to excruciating pain violates our sense of acceptable conduct. Yet what moral principle could justify the death penalty for past individual murders, while condemning nonlethal torture to prevent future mass murders? Bentham posed this rhetorical question as support for his argument regarding torture. In the United States we execute convicted murderers, despite compelling evidence of the unfairness and ineffectiveness of capital punishment. Yet many who support capital punishment recoil at the prospect of shoving a sterilized needle under the finger of a suspect who is refusing to divulge information that might prevent multiple deaths.[7] In our modern age, the death penalty is underrated, while pain is overrated. That we put the prisoner "to sleep" by injecting a lethal substance into his body covers up that death is forever while nonlethal pain is temporary. Despite the irrationality of these distinctions, they are understandable. But in the end, the absolute opposition to torture may rest more on historical and aesthetic considerations than on moral or logical considerations.

Then there is the slippery slope argument. If nonlethal torture of one person is justified to prevent the killing of many important people, what if it were necessary to use lethal torture? What if it were necessary to torture the suspect's mother or children to get him to divulge? What if it took threatening to kill his entire village? Under simple, quantitative utilitarianism, anything goes as long as the number of people tortured or killed does not exceed the number that would be saved. This is morality by numbers, unless there are other constraints on what we can do. These other constraints can come from rule utilitarianism or other principles of morality, such as the prohibition on deliberately punishing the innocent. Unless we are prepared to impose limits on the use of torture or other barbaric tactics that might be of use in preventing terrorism, we risk hurtling down a slippery slope into the abyss of amorality—and, ultimately, tyranny.

The slippery slope is an argument of caution, not a debate stopper, since virtually every compromise with an absolutist approach to rights carries the risk of slipping further. For example, if nonlethal torture were legally limited to convicted terrorists who had knowledge of future massive terrorist acts, were given immunity, and still refused to provide the information, there might still be objections to the use of torture, but they would have to go beyond the slippery slope argument. Moreover, the process of obtaining a warrant, which would include judicial review, would cabin the use of torture and slow the slide down any slippery slope.

There are other, somewhat more subtle considerations that should be factored into any decision regarding torture. There are some who see silence as a virtue when it comes to the choice among such horrible evils as torture and terrorism. Commentators argue that the decision to torture should be left to the low-visibility discretion of low-level functionaries rather than be legitimated by high-level, accountable decision makers. Justice Jackson's dissenting opinion in the *Korematsu* case observed the dangers of judicial sanctions of certain conduct:

> Much is said of the danger to liberty from the Army program for deporting and detaining these citizens of Japanese extraction. But a judicial construction of the due process clause that will sustain this order is a far more subtle blow to liberty than the promulgation of the order itself. A military order, however unconstitutional, is not apt to last longer than the military emergency. . . . But once a judicial opinion rationalizes such an order to show that it conforms to the Constitution, or rather rationalizes the Constitution to show that the Constitution sanctions such an order, the Court for all time has validated the principle of racial discrimination in criminal procedure and of transplanting American citizens. The principle then lies about like a loaded weapon ready for the

hand of any authority that can bring forward a plausible claim of an urgent need.[8]

A similar argument can be made regarding torture: if an agent tortures, that is an incident; if the courts authorize torture, it becomes a precedent. There is, however, an important difference between the detention of Japanese-American citizens and torture. The detentions were conducted openly and with presidential accountability; torture would be done secretly, with official deniability. Besides, history has proved Jackson wrong about the *Korematsu* decision. Had the Supreme Court merely allowed the executive decision to stand without judicial review, a far more dangerous precedent might have been established: namely, that executive decisions during times of emergency will escape review by the Supreme Court. That far broader and more dangerous precedent would then lie "like a loaded weapon," ready to be used not only by dictators but by decent government officials without fear of judicial review.

We cannot have a "don't ask, don't tell" policy on torture that enables our President and attorney general to close their eyes to uses of torture while simultaneously denying torture categorically—the kind of willful blindness condemned by the courts in other contexts. With no limitations, standards, principles, or accountability, the use of torture techniques will expand.

My arguments have apparently been credited in unexpected corners. Recently the ACLU brought suit on behalf of the father of an American citizen and terrorist, Anwar al-Aulaqi, whom the Obama administration has chosen to target as a combatant. The ACLU's suit demands that the government "disclose the criteria that are used in determining whether the government will carry out the targeted killing of a U.S. citizen." It also demanded that the government present evidence of "concrete, specific, and imminent threats to life or physical safety, and [that] there are no means other than lethal force that could reasonably be employed to neutralize the threats."[9] What the ACLU is now seeking is, in effect, a "killing warrant." They are demanding, as a precondition to targeted killing, essentially the same mechanism that I have proposed as a precondition to the imposition of nonlethal torture. The virtue of a "torture warrant," like that of a "killing warrant," is that it requires articulation of standards, visibility of actions, and ultimate approval by democratic institutions. The ACLU seems to understand this when it comes to "killing warrants." It should understand that, when it comes to the inevitable use of torture in ticking bomb situations, there is also a virtue in visibility and accountability.

Torture, like any other topic, deserves a vigorous debate in a democracy such as ours. Even if government officials decline to discuss such issues, academics and advocacy groups have a duty to raise them and submit them to the marketplace of ideas. There may be danger in open discussion, but there is far greater danger in actions based on secret discussion. What is a quintessentially democratic problem requires a quintessentially democratic response. In short, it is not inconsistent to be opposed to torture and yet in favor of a torture warrant. Democratic accountability for torture is not an oxymoron.

nuremburg revisited and revised: the legitimation of torture in the united states

JONATHAN TURLEY

The greatest triumph for terrorists is not the destruction of a people but to get a people to destroy their own values. When it comes to torture, our enemies can claim such a victory after the Bush administration responded to the September 11, 2011 attacks by ordering the waterboarding of detainees, as well as an array of other abusive measures. This chapter focuses on the advent of an American torture program and how lawyers rationalized the commission of alleged war crimes in the name of fighting terror. It was no small feat, however. In order to legitimize torture, Bush administration officials had to revisit and revise one of the touchstones of international law: the Nuremburg Principles.

This dubious accomplishment was only achieved by using carefully selected government attorneys to validate a facially unlawful program. The damage done to the rule of law is difficult to capture in a brief essay, but it should be featured prominently in any list of the lasting impact of the September 11 attacks. As on so many occasions of our history, our greatest wounds from this tragedy proved to be self-inflicted. It will take decades for the United States to recover from these legal losses and regain our position as the world's defender of the rule of law. However, the damage is not (as is often claimed) the redefinition of torture. We never changed international law; we simply violated it. Rather, the lasting effect of the Bush program will be in the use of defenses against alleged war crimes and specifically the use of lawyers to avoid accountability of officials who order the torture of detainees.

The prohibition of torture under international law is considered *jus cogens* and the UN Convention Against Torture defines torture as:

> any act by which severe pain or suffering, whether physical or mental, is intentionally inflicted on a person for such purposes as obtaining from him or a third person information or a confession, punishing him for an act he or a third person has committed or is suspected of having committed, or intimidating or coercing him or a third person, or for any reason based on discrimination of any kind, when such pain or suffering is inflicted by or at the

instigation of or with the consent or acquiescence of a public official or other person acting in an official capacity. It does not include pain or suffering arising only from, inherent in or incidental to lawful sanctions.[1]

Common Article 3 of the Geneva Conventions[2] and other international agreements prohibit torture. Various federal laws, not the least of which is the Torture Act, 18 U.S.C. § 2340, address torture. Government records show that Abu Zubaydah was waterboarded at least 83 times and Khalid Sheikh Mohammed at least 183 times.[3]

I will not spend time or effort arguing the obvious: torture is prohibited under both domestic and international law. In overturning the dismissal of a complaint based on torture in Paraguay in *Filartiga v. Pena-Irala*,[4] the U.S. Court of Appeals for the Second Circuit stated:

> Indeed, for purposes of civil liability, the torturer has become like the pirate and slave trader before him *hostis humani generis*, an enemy of all mankind. Our holding today, giving effect to a jurisdictional provision enacted by our First Congress, is a small but important step in the fulfillment of the ageless dream to free all people from brutal violence.

By extension of the Second Circuit analysis, President Bush and his aides put this country in a position of being viewed as "an enemy of all mankind" by ordering torture. In what appeared to be a case of blind rage meeting blind ambition, Bush administration lawyers set out to justify the unjustifiable and create America's first officially sanctioned torture program.

THE "WATER CURE" AND THE ADVENT OF THE BUSH
TORTURE PROGRAM

Outside of the core Bush administration officials and advocates, there has never been serious dispute that waterboarding constitutes torture. This long-established fact has been recognized by officials ranging from President Barack Obama to Attorney General Eric Holder to Senator John McCain to Colin Powell. A wide array of Republican and Democratic experts have also stepped forward to denounce this torture, including Susan J. Crawford, a former judge and convening authority for the Bush military tribunals, and former State Department official Richard Armitage.

For centuries, waterboarding has been recognized as a form of torture.[5] Indeed, it is one of the oldest and most practiced forms of torture. In the fifteenth century, waterboarding was embraced by the Spanish Inquisition and called *la tortura del agua*—often involving the placement of a cloth into the mouth of the victim and then pouring water on the victim to simulate drowning. The following century, Anabaptists were tortured during the Flemish Inquisition with a similar technique. Later, waterboarding was used by the Dutch East India Company against natives.

Previously, American soldiers were accused of using waterboarding during the occupation of the Philippines (a practice picked up from the Spanish). American prison officials were also accused of this form of torture at Sing Sing prison and other prisons in the nineteenth century. Conversely, U.S. soldiers faced waterboarding at the hands of the Japanese and Germans in World War II. The United States prosecuted Japanese officers for waterboarding American and Allied soldiers. One Japanese officer, Yukio Asano, was sentenced to fifteen years of hard labor for waterboarding. In Vietnam, American servicemen, like John

McCain, were tortured with waterboarding. It was also a preferred form of torture used by the Khmer Rouge in Cambodia.

Thus, waterboarding was not some new or novel form of "interrogation" when Bush officials began to contemplate its use after the 9/11 attacks. Indeed, in 1983, Texas sheriff James Parker and three deputies were found guilty of torturing six prisoners between 1976 and 1980 to force confessions through the use of waterboarding.[6] This case and other past cases were left out of the so-called "Torture Memos" that were used to justify waterboarding under the euphemism of "enhanced interrogation" techniques. United States officials had for decades denounced waterboarding and other forms of torture around the world. There was no serious ambiguity or uncertainty as to its status as torture—until the Bush administration.

Of course, the United States' decision to join such countries as North Korea, Egypt, Saudi Arabia, Iran, and Burma as practitioners of "*la tormenta de toca*" still faced such considerable obstacles as the Geneva Conventions[7] and the Convention Against Torture and Other Cruel, Inhuman or Degrading Treatment or Punishment.[8] Not only did the Bush administration approve of the use of waterboarding, it also allowed for a variety of other acts identified by the Red Cross[9] as prohibited practices. These included, but were not limited to, forcing detainees into prolonged stress positions, beating detainees, sleep deprivation, exposure to extreme temperatures, and other forms of ill-treatment.

Despite the best (or worst) efforts of Bush administration lawyers, waterboarding remains torture and torture remains a war crime. The authors of the "Torture Memos" struggled mightily to avoid decades of precedent to the contrary and, in the end, convinced few. Indeed, the memos were valued less for offering persuasive analysis than a basis for plausible deniability for Bush officials. Ultimately, the Bush administration itself rejected the memos as flawed and those memos are no longer cited by any reputable commentator as offering credible legal analysis. Rather, they have been cited primarily as a defense by officials, including President Bush and Vice President Cheney, when challenged over the alleged torture program. Various officials have admitted that they were concerned about being prosecuted for torture. Indeed, the CIA was later found to have knowingly destroyed tapes of these sessions, anticipating that they could be demanded as evidence. These memos functioned as a ready-made defense for those who ordered the torture of detainees.

The Justice Department ultimately declared that John Yoo had "violated his duty to exercise independent legal judgment and render thorough, objective and candid legal advice."[10] Associate Deputy Attorney General David Margolis went further to state, "I fear that John Yoo's loyalty to his own ideology and convictions clouded his view of his obligation to his client [President Bush]." Jay Bybee was found to have "acted in reckless disregard" of his ethical obligations in authoring the Torture Memos.[11]

While some top Bush officials admitted that the memos offered obviously poor and incomplete analysis, they insisted that they were still right in relying upon the memos in ordering the waterboarding and abuse of prisoners.[12] It was an ironic argument for the Justice Department (which ultimately accepted this view) given its general opposition to the "advice of counsel defense" in criminal cases. While steadfastly opposed to such claims by average citizens,[13] the Justice Department readily embraced the defense when administration officials were facing international calls for prosecution.

Thus, the lasting impact of the Bush administration on torture is not the redefinition of torture, but the reduction of accountability for advocating or committing torture. It is on this question that the Bush administration succeeded in revising the Nuremburg Principles in a new and troubling image. The Bush administration revived the use of lawyers in shielding officials from accountability and—most troubling—resuscitated the "superior orders" defense.

THE BUSH PRINCIPLES AND THE REVIVAL OF THE SUPERIOR ORDERS DEFENSE

The establishment of a torture program by the Bush administration produced shock and outrage around the world. As the existence of the program was gradually confirmed, calls increased for the United States to fulfill its international obligations to prosecute those responsible for ordering and carrying out the torture of detainees. The United States has a clear and mandatory obligation to investigate and prosecute such crimes. The Convention Against Torture provides for states either to prosecute those responsible for torture or to extradite those individuals.[14] Despite these obligations, the Bush administration refused to investigate and prosecute those responsible for criminal conduct, including refusal to appoint a special counsel—given the involvement of both President Bush and prior Attorneys General. Later, both Bush and Cheney admitted that they were personally involved in the ordering of the systemic torture of detainees.[15]

The Convention Against Torture (signed by President Ronald Reagan) expressly states that "just following orders" is no defense and "no exceptional circumstances whatsoever" will be considered. Yet President Obama pledged soon after he was elected that he would not allow any CIA employee to be prosecuted for torture and would block international efforts to investigate these alleged crimes. Despite the fact that he was dealing with alleged war crimes, President Obama insisted that it was necessary "to provide [CIA officers] with the confidence that they can do their jobs." In this case, that confidence included being shielded from war crimes investigations. Various high-ranking officials also stated that Obama promised them before his inauguration that he would prevent anyone from being charged for the torture program.

If there was one defense that stood out from the Nuremburg Trials, it was *"Befehl ist Befehl,"* or "orders are orders." Since 1474 and the trial of Peter von Hagenbach for atrocities committed during the occupation of Breisach (Germany), this defense has been rejected. When von Hagenbach insisted that he was merely following the orders of Charles the Bold, the Duke of Burgundy, the Holy Roman Empire tribunal rejected the defense.

Various Nuremburg defendants tried to argue that they were only following orders and were therefore not responsible for war crimes. The United States and its allies not only rejected the defense, but executed many of those who used it. It became the foundation for human rights law for decades—informing government officials and police around the world that they are independently responsible for criminal acts. Nuremberg Principle IV stated "[t]he fact that a person acted pursuant to order of his Government or of a superior does not relieve him from responsibility under international law, provided a moral choice was in fact possible to him."

At Nuremburg, defendants such as German Armed Forces Command Chief Wilhelm Keitel insisted that he was not only carrying out superior orders but orders that derived from the legal system. This included the *Nacht und Nebel* ("Night and Fog") directive allowing for the capture and execution of those who threatened the "security or state of readiness" of German forces. Not only was Keitel convicted, so were lawyers and Justice Ministry officials like Franz Schlegelberger for their role in supporting war crimes through the legal system. The court found that "by his exhortations and directives, Schlegelberger contributed to the destruction of judicial independence." The court acknowledged that "his ideas were less brutal than those of his associates, but they can scarcely be called humane."

No one would suggest that the alleged war crimes of the Bush administration reached the horror of the Holocaust. However, it is also important to recognize that torture is a war crime and that the United States is obligated to prosecute those responsible for acts of torture. Under the Bush principles, any war crime could be excused by a President relying on hand-picked lawyers who predictably ratified and legitimized his intended actions.

Ironically, Bush was adamant about the prosecution of war crimes *in other countries*. In 2003, he insisted, "War crimes will be prosecuted, war criminals will be punished and it will be no defense to say, 'I was just following orders.'" On June 26, 2003, conservatives applauded as Bush told the United Nations, "[the United States] is committed to the worldwide elimination of torture and we are leading this fight by example." He then proceeded to order the commission of torture and insist that such orders are by definition legal because they were reviewed on some level by lawyers.

President Obama revived the *"Befehl ist Befehl"* defense when he announced a blanket immunity for CIA officials and his intention to protect CIA officials "as vigilantly as they protect our security." Attorney General Holder insisted that the officials were simply following orders that were sanctioned by the Justice Department. CIA Director Leon Panetta went further and said that the "CIA responded, as duty requires"—ignoring the commission of an alleged war crime in the commission of torture. The result is devastating for Nuremburg Principle IV. Government officials now understand that they cannot be held personally liable if they follow orders from their superiors, even in the commission of torture. Moreover, future Presidents understand that they need only select a group of willing lawyers to issue self-serving analysis to shield themselves and their subordinates from prosecution.

Once again, no one is suggesting that the Bush administration committed atrocities analogous to the Nazis. However, the Bush principles are ready-made for a host of crimes committed more commonly on a smaller scale. This defense can be asserted again in a variety of more insular cases of officials "following orders."

The logic of the Bush and Obama administrations became circular when they excused torture by CIA officials as based on legal advice and then refused to discipline those lawyers responsible for the advice. The Justice Department would block any prosecution or disciplining of the attorneys who facilitated the torture program, in particular former Justice officials John Yoo, Jay Bybee, and Steven Bradbury. The Bush administration insisted that, no matter how transparent or poor the analysis of the Torture Memos, reliance on those memos excused officials ranging from President Bush to the CIA agents in torturing detainees. Attorney General Michael Mukasey insisted that "[w]hatever was done as part of a CIA program at the time that it was done was the subject of a Department of Justice opinion through the Office of Legal Counsel and was found to be permissible under the law as it existed then." Mukasey then proceeded to excuse the lawyers for those unsupported memos. Thus, the officials were excused because of the lawyers and the lawyers were then excused because they were performing a legal advisory function.

The use of lawyers as shields is nothing new. The United States helped create the precedent holding lawyers responsible for their roles in war crimes and rejecting the "legal counsel" defense of war criminals. The third of the twelve Nuremburg Trials for war crimes involved sixteen German jurists and lawyers. Nine had been officials of the Reich Ministry of Justice; the others were prosecutors and judges of the Special Courts and People's Courts of Nazi Germany.[16]

The result was a new, immaculate commission of a war crime where no one could be punished. Indeed, Bybee was given the one job that would largely insulate him from the backlash against his unethical conduct: a lifetime appointment as a federal judge on the U.S. Court of Appeals for the Ninth Circuit. For those faced with any questionable order or program in the future, Bybee will stand as a troubling case study of how one can be rewarded despite of (or perhaps because of) one's involvement in alleged crimes.

CONCLUSION

At a critical meeting in which top-ranking Bush officials deliberated the use of torture, then Attorney General John Ashcroft reportedly asked, "Why are we talking about this in the White House? History will not judge this kindly."[17] Of course, Ashcroft was right. History will not judge Bush officials or this country kindly for the use of torture. Accounts of the atrocities committed by these terrorists will be followed by accounts of alleged war crimes committed by the United States in response. The effort by the Bush administration to blame attorneys like John Yoo and Jay Bybee for flawed and unsupportable analysis will not alter that historical judgment. The embrace of their analysis was at best a case of willful blindness by Bush and his administration—a transparent effort to justify torture. Indeed, the effort to put all of the blame on these lawyers combined a lack of morality with a lack of integrity on the part of Bush officials.

One of the lessons of history is that no country is invulnerable to the relapse to extralegal abuses that come during moments of national fear or rage. In every country, there remain men and women who harbor a preference for authoritarian measures. In this sense, the desire for torture and other abuses rests like a dormant virus within a country—a virus that is allowed to take over a body politic in feverish periods of war or internal strife. What was astonishing was the willingness of academics and lawyers to facilitate the use of these measures to lead it to the destruction of core international and domestic principles.

Magnifying this moral and legal relativism is the effort of some to claim that, putting aside the use of a possible war crime, it worked. Literally within hours of the announcement of the killing of Osama bin Laden, many of those accused of ordering or facilitating torture from Dick Cheney to John Yoo were claiming that the killing was made possible by waterboarding.[*] They insisted that Khalid Sheikh Mohammed supplied the name of an associate of bin Laden after being tortured in 183 waterboarding sessions. Those initial claims were later refuted by the Director of Central Intelligence Leon Panetta as well as others familiar with both the prior intelligence and the operation.[†] However, putting aside the support for this claim, the more relevant question is, even if it were true, why would it matter? The clear import of this claim is that, even if it is a war crime, it was somehow justified by killing a hated enemy. Of course, history has shown that all war criminals believe that their use of torture is justified by their cause or their enemy. The entire premise of the Nuremburg Principles (as well as the Convention Against Torture[‡]) is that the

---

[*] Lawrence Rafferty, "Torture is still Torture, and it is Still Illegal," *Jonathan Turley* blog, May 7, 2011, http://jonathanturley.org.

[†] Luiza Savage, "Did torture help the U.S. find bin Laden?" *Maclean's*, May 30, 2011.

[‡] The Convention Against Torture provides that "no exceptional circumstances whatsoever, whether a state of war or a threat of war, internal political instability or any other public emergency, may be invoked as a justification of torture."

ends do not justify the means. Killing a war criminal with a war crime would not be a sign of distinction but of defeat—embracing the same consequentialist morality of our enemy.

There are credible allegations of war crimes in the torture of detainees against those who ordered it, justified it, and carried it out. Each of these accused individuals also has credible defenses to make, but they should have been required to make those arguments to a special counsel or a grand jury. If these officials had persuasive arguments, they would have withstood an independent criminal investigation. Instead, like so many countries we have accused of human rights violations in the past, we barred a full and independent investigation under sweeping claims of privilege and immunity.

Ultimately, no one who ordered or committed torture under the Bush program was prosecuted—a lesson that will not be lost on future government officials in this country and abroad. We will pay that price when Americans are waterboarded in other countries or when we try to condemn others for blocking war crimes investigations. Indeed, many fear that it will be our service members who will pay the price of our hypocrisy at the hands of our enemies.[18] What neither the Bush administration nor the Obama administration understood is that the investigation and prosecution of alleged war crimes do not weaken a nation. They reaffirm the difference between ourselves and those we are fighting. To abandon our principles for politics is to hand al-Qaeda its greatest victory—not the destruction of lives or buildings, but our self-inflicted wound of hypocrisy and immorality. True victory against our enemies is only to be found on the other side of prosecuting those who, like our enemies, claim the right to wage war by any means.

stopping the terrorists

MARC THIESSEN

Where were you on September 11, 2001?

Think back to that time—to the smoldering rubble at Ground Zero, the Pentagon with a hole in its side, the shock we all felt at the ability of terrorists to penetrate our defenses and wreak such destruction in our midst. All of us wondered: Who had attacked us? What did they want? And what else were they planning?

If someone had predicted back then that we would reach the year 2011 without another successful catastrophic terrorist attack on the American homeland, no one would have believed it. We all thought, inside and outside government, that the attacks of 9/11 were the first of many.

I was in the Pentagon on September 11, 2001, working on a speech for Secretary of Defense Donald Rumsfeld. I was blessed not to be at the point of impact. But I remember feeling the walls of my office shudder, and the smell of the smoke that filled the hallways. One memory stands out: to my surprise, no evacuation alarm ever sounded. All of us simply filed out onto the lawn outside, where we looked back at the broken and burning building. In the months that followed, the evacuation alarms in the Pentagon went off on numerous occasions, as false reports came in that other planes were headed our way. Each time, we exited and stood on the lawn looking up at the sky waiting for the next attack. That attack never came. There are only two possible explanations: the terrorists lost interest in attacking America, or we uncovered their plans and stopped them. The answer is self-evident.

In those early days after 9/11, we knew very little about the enemy that hit us. We knew that al-Qaeda was behind the attacks. But we did not know that Khalid Sheikh Mohammed (KSM) was the operational commander of al-Qaeda or the mastermind of 9/11. We did not know who his key accomplices were. And we did not know what follow-on attacks al-Qaeda had planned.

Unbeknownst to us, there were two terror networks at large planning a "second wave" of attacks. The first was the KSM network that had carried out 9/11. The second was the Hambali network—Southeast Asian terrorists recruited by KSM because he believed that the United States would be on the lookout for Arab men. Both of these networks had set terrorist plots in motion. These included: a plot to blow up high-rise apartment buildings in the United States using natural gas; a plot to replicate 9/11 in Europe by flying hijacked airplanes into Heathrow Airport and buildings in downtown London; a plot to replicate the East Africa embassy bombings in Pakistan by blowing up the U.S. consulate and Western residences in Karachi; a plot to blow up the U.S. Marine camp in Djibouti; an al-Qaeda cell that was developing anthrax for attacks inside the United States; and a plot to carry out a second wave of attacks in America by flying a plane into the Library Tower in Los Angeles. The United States government did not know any of this; it was completely blind to the coming danger.

Then, beginning in 2002, we began to capture and interrogate senior terrorist leaders. The first to be captured was Abu Zubaydah, a top aide to Osama bin Laden who served as al-Qaeda's terrorist travel facilitator. Zubaydah helped lead the CIA to Ramzi bin al-Shibh—KSM's right-hand man in the 9/11 attacks—just as he was finalizing plans for the Heathrow Airport attack. Together, Zubaydah and bin al-Shibh led us to KSM. And these captured terrorists gave the CIA information that allowed the agency to round up virtually all the key members of the KSM and Hambali networks, dismantling them and disrupting all of the planned attacks in the process.

They also provided the key intelligence that allowed the United States to kill Osama bin Laden. U.S officials have acknowledged that the key piece of intelligence that led the CIA to bin Laden's lair—information on the al-Qaeda leader's principal courier—came from detainees in CIA custody. In response to a direct question about the role of enhanced interrogation in the bin Laden operation, CIA Director Leon Panetta confirmed that, "Obviously there was, there was some valuable intelligence that was derived through those kind of interrogations." His immediate predecessor, former CIA Director Mike Hayden, went further, declaring: "let the record show that when I was first briefed in 2007 about the brightening prospect of pursuing bin Laden through his courier network, the briefing was anchored on information provided by three CIA detainees, all of whom had been subjected to some form of enhanced interrogation." Hayden compares those who deny the critical role CIA interrogations played in the bin Laden operation to "9/11 'truthers' who, despite all evidence to the contrary (or more precisely, lacking any evidence to the positive) persist in claiming that 9/11 was a Bush administration plot."

Hayden says the program played a critical role in virtually every counterterrorism success since the war on terror began. As Hayden explains, "it is nearly impossible for me to imagine any operation like the one that was so successful on May 2nd that would not have made substantial use of the trove of information derived from CIA detainees, including those on whom enhanced techniques had been used."

When KSM was captured, he was asked about his plans for new attacks. He told his interrogators: "I'll tell you everything when I get to New York and see my lawyer." If we had given KSM the lawyer he had requested—had we told him, "you have the right to remain silent"—there would likely be craters in the ground in Los Angeles, London, Karachi, Djibouti, or other cities to match the one at Ground Zero in New York City.

Fast forward to January 2009. President Barack Obama takes office and eliminates the CIA interrogation program that had allowed us to discover, dismantle, and disrupt the two terrorist networks that were planning the second wave of al-Qaeda attacks. Obama even goes to CIA headquarters in spring of 2009 and tells the assembled officers that he understands his decision will force the government to protect the American people "with one hand tied behind our back. . . . And that's OK."

As Obama was busy tying one hand behind the CIA's back, new dangers were rapidly emerging. A mysterious new terror network—al-Qaeda in the Arabian Peninsula (AQAP)—began plotting to attack the American homeland. And in December 2009, this network managed to penetrate America's defenses, get an operative onto civilian planes headed for the United States, and nearly succeed in blowing up Northwest Airlines Flight 253 as it prepared to land in the city of Detroit. By the Obama administration's own admission, it was under the impression that AQAP was focused on regional attacks, and was completely unaware that this terrorist network had developed the capability or intent to attack us here in America. Yet they very nearly blew up a plane over Detroit on Christmas Day.

Why was America caught blind? Because—unlike the period immediately after 9/11—the United States is no long capturing and interrogating high-value terrorists who could tell us al-Qaeda's plans to attack the homeland. In fact, even when a high-value terrorist fell into our hands—as in the case of the Christmas Day bomber—instead of aggressively interrogating him the Obama administration gave him a lawyer and told him he had the right to remain silent.

On Christmas Day we avoided disaster by pure luck. The Detroit airline bombing was not a *foiled* terrorist attack; it was a *failed* terrorist attack. The bomb malfunctioned. But that has not deterred AQAP from trying again. Less than one year later, AQAP penetrated our defenses a second time—this time getting two package bombs aboard planes headed for the United States. The sophisticated bombs were designed to go off just as the planes reached the eastern seaboard of the United States. As with the Christmas Day attack, we did not foil this plot either.

This time disaster was averted only because we got a last minute tip from Saudi intelligence that allowed us to track down the explosives before they went off.

Twice in less than a year AQAP nearly succeeded in killing hundreds of innocent people. What has the Obama administration done about it? To this day, the United States has not captured or killed any of the top AQAP leaders behind these two attempted attacks on the American homeland—including AQAP's spiritual leader, the radical cleric Anwar al-Aulaqi. In November 2010, the *Washington Post* reported that President Obama had deployed unmanned Predator drones to Yemen to go after the leaders of AQAP. Obama has also reportedly given the order to kill Anwar al-Aulaqi. But the drones have not been used. Why? According to the *Post*,

> The United States has . . . not fired missiles from the unmanned aircraft because it lacks solid intelligence on the insurgents' whereabouts, senior U.S. officials said. . . . Current and former U.S. intelligence officials said the drones' surveillance prowess is often overstated and will be of limited use in identifying al-Qaeda operatives in Yemen without the aid of signal intercepts or human sources on the ground. "All Land Rovers look pretty much alike," said a former high-ranking U.S. intelligence official familiar with operations in Yemen. "You have to have something that tells you this is the one to follow."[1]

Despite AQAP having nearly succeeded in blowing up a passenger plane over Detroit and two cargo planes over the eastern seaboard, we still have no idea where Aulaqi or the other key leaders of this terrorist organization are hiding, where its operatives are training, or what they are planning—so we can't hit them.

AQAP is just one al-Qaeda terror network that threatens us. We face another emerging terrorist network that wants to attack us—this one based in East Africa. The Somali terrorist group al-Shabab recently merged with al-Qaeda, pledged loyalty to Osama bin Laden, and promised to carry out attacks across the world on al-Qaeda's behalf. Where have they set their sights? One clue: al-Shabab is actively recruiting Americans. In October 2010, a twenty-year-old Northern Virginia man, Zachary Adam Chesser, pled guilty to charges of attempting to travel to Somalia to join al-Shabab as a foreign fighter.[2] Before his planned departure, Chesser had been in direct communication with Anwar al-Aulaqi, the AQAP cleric behind the attempted Christmas Day bombing over Detroit.

Al-Shabab's top military commander, Omar Hammami, is also an American citizen. Hammami grew up in Alabama, has justified the September 11 attacks, and affirmed his group's allegiance to bin Laden. Al-Shabab has also recruited more than twenty American citizens of Somali descent to be suicide bombers. al-Qaeda does not need suicide bombers with American passports to conduct terrorist attacks in Africa—it only needs operatives with American passports for an attack against the American homeland.

The Obama administration should be desperate to capture senior terrorist leaders in East Africa so it can learn more about al-Shabab and its plans for new attacks, and avoid a repeat of the Christmas Day debacle—or worse. President Obama had a golden opportunity to do just that—and he passed it up.

In February 2010, the *Washington Post* reported in a front-page story that the United States had tracked down a senior terrorist leader named Saleh Ali Nabhan. Nabhan was al-Qaeda's leader in East Africa and also a senior leader in al-Shabab. Indeed, he was the man responsible for the merger of the two groups. He was clearly someone with whom U.S. officials ought to be interested in speaking. When it located Nabhan, the U.S. military gave President Obama three options. First, U.S. Special Operations Forces could kill Nabhan with an airstrike while he was driving through southern Somalia. Second, they could kill him by firing from helicopters, and then land to collect DNA to confirm the kill. Third, they could try to capture him alive and bring him in for interrogation. The military wanted Nabhan alive. "We wanted to take a prisoner,"[3] a senior military officer told the *Post*. But Obama chose to have him killed. He chose the second option—sending a helicopter crew to take Nabhan out, after which Special Operations commandos rappelled down to recover his remains. Obama could have taken Nabhan alive, but consciously chose not to do so.

Think of the intelligence that was lost with that decision—the information Nabhan could have shared about al Qeada's networks in East Africa, its relations with bin Laden, its recruitment of American citizens, and its plans to attack the homeland. All of it was vaporized—on President Obama's order. As a result, the *Post* reported, "the opportunity to interrogate one of the most wanted U.S. terrorism targets was gone forever."[4] If al-Shabab succeeds in carrying out an attack on America, we can trace it back to that fateful choice made in the Oval Office.

In addition to these new terror networks that are emerging to threaten us, we still face a threat from al-Qaeda central. The Obama administration believes that al-Qaeda has been set back by the Predator campaign in Pakistan's tribal regions—and that may well be the case. But al-Qaeda now also has in place its most dangerous and capable external operations commander since KSM held the post—a terrorist named Adnan El Shukrijumah. In 2002, the CIA began asking al-Qaeda detainees, "Who will be picked to lead the next big attack on America?" Abu Zubaydah, KSM, and other detainees all pointed to Shukrijumah. A global manhunt ensued, but Shukrijumah went to ground and evaded capture. He has since risen through the al-Qaeda ranks to assume one of the top positions in the global terrorist hierarchy.

Shukrijumah is more than a highly trained operative; he is an American who lived among us for fifteen years and who is intimately familiar with our country. Think about this: the man who now occupies the position once held by KSM when he planned 9/11 is an American citizen. What does this American al-Qaeda terrorist have planned for his country? We don't know. We are no longer capturing and aggressively interrogating senior leaders who could tell us.

The fact is that the government cannot protect the homeland unless it is able to interrogate captured terrorists. Why is terrorist interrogation so essential? Without it, we cannot obtain an accurate picture of the capability and intent of our enemies. Former CIA Director Michael Hayden explained it to me this way: intelligence is like putting together a large puzzle. You have all the pieces laid out on the table in front of you—and you must put them all together. But you must do so without being allowed to see the picture on the cover of the box.

That is the challenge facing our intelligence officers. They have lots of puzzle pieces from different sources: tips, signals intercepts, and sources that they have recruited inside al-Qaeda. But they don't know how the pieces all fit together, or what the final picture looks like. There is only one way to obtain that final picture: by capturing the terrorist leaders who know what the picture on the cover of the box looks like. When we interrogate a terrorist mastermind like KSM, he is not simply giving us more puzzle pieces that we could find another way; he is providing information that is available in no other place—*how* the various pieces that we already have fit together. He is giving us the picture on the cover of the box.

That is what we have lost by eliminating the CIA's capability to detain and interrogate terrorist leaders. According to senior intelligence officials, well over half of the information our government learned about al-Qaeda after 9/11—how it operates, moves money, communicates, recruits operatives, picks targets, plans and carries out attacks—came from the interrogation of terrorists in CIA custody. Consider for a moment that without this capability, more than *half* of what we knew about the enemy would have disappeared.

To this day, we are still using the information that the CIA obtained from KSM and other high-value terrorists to help disrupt terrorist plots and keep our country safe from new attacks. But with each passing year, that information becomes increasingly dated. New leaders rise through the ranks; new terrorists operatives are recruited; and new methods are used to communicate, move money, recruit operatives, and plan new attacks. We are no longer replenishing information about al-Qaeda's inner workings because we are no longer capturing and detaining the terrorist leaders who could refresh our knowledge about al-Qaeda's operations.

What can be done now to remedy this situation? First, we must resume capturing high-value terrorists alive, instead of killing them. There are times when it is necessary to kill a terrorist with an unmanned drone—he may be in a remote region where we cannot send a Special Operations team, or the intelligence that we have may be perishable and our only choice is to kill him or lose him. But the default option should be to capture terrorists alive whenever possible and bring them in for interrogation.

Second, we need somewhere to detain and interrogate them. In June, the top military official involved in the bin Laden raid,

Vice Admiral William McRaven, testified before Congress that the Obama administration has no clear plan for handling suspected terrorist leaders if they are caught alive outside a war zone. In response to senators' questions, McRaven said that "in many cases" captured terrorists are taken to a U.S. Navy ship until they can be tried in a U.S. court or transferred to the custody of an allied country. But if neither option turns out to be feasible, "then we will release that individual," Think about that: The United States' top Special Operations commander told Congress that because the United States has no place to hold captured terrorists, we simply let them go.

President Obama has closed the CIA's black sites for good. But current CIA Director Leon Panetta recently suggested another viable option. Testifying before the Senate Intelligence Committee, Panetta was asked what the United States would do if we captured senior al-Qaeda leaders. He replied that the Obama administration would probably transfer them to military custody and send them to Guantánamo Bay. Panetta is right: Guantánamo is the logical place to conduct terrorist interrogations. The facility is not closing anytime soon—the outgoing Democratic Congress saw to that by cutting off funds for any transfer of Guantánamo detainees to the United States. And according to press accounts, the base has a state-of-the-art CIA detention facility, which already houses KSM and other high-value detainees. This facility could easily accommodate fresh captures.

Third, we need to place the CIA back in charge of terrorist interrogations. The Obama administration's High-Value Interrogation Group—which was supposed to replace the CIA interrogation program that Obama eliminated—has been a colossal failure. The CIA has a cadre of trained interrogators with a proven record of success. They should be put back in charge of capturing, detaining, and questioning senior terrorist leaders.

Fourth, we must give interrogators the tools they need to question terrorists effectively—tools beyond those currently in the Army Field Manual on interrogation. When President Obama eliminated the CIA program and released thousands of pages of documents detailing how our interrogators operated, he removed the veil of mystery that surrounded our interrogation techniques. This was a grave mistake. During the Bush administration, the CIA interrogation program usually worked without the application of *any* interrogation techniques—because the terrorists did not know the limits. For example, in 2007, a senior al-Qaeda terrorist named Abd al-Hadi al-Iraqi was captured and taken into CIA custody. When his interrogators told him he was in the hands of the CIA, he replied: "I've heard of you guys. I'll tell you anything you need to know." The mere existence of the CIA program, and the uncertainty of what it included, was enough to get this al-Qaeda terrorist talking. That would not happen today. Obama has revealed the secrets behind how we question terrorists. And with the Army Field Manual on interrogation available on the Internet, terrorists can study our techniques and train to resist them.

Obama can correct this situation without bringing back the most controversial techniques that he opposes. On the morning Obama issued his executive order, CIA Director Mike Hayden called White House Counsel Greg Craig and made a simple suggestion: Just add the words "unless otherwise authorized by the President." Adding these words today would allow the administration to provide U.S. interrogators with additional lawful techniques. The President could also simply announce that he is adding a classified annex to the Army Field Manual with additional interrogation techniques. The classified annex could be a blank page—so long as our enemies did not know it. Taking these steps would restore a level of uncertainty for our enemies about what they would face in the interrogation room—which would increase the odds that other terrorists would respond the way that Abd al-Hadi al-Iraqi did.

Such steps are desperately needed because the danger to our country is growing. In the past three years, America has suffered three near misses: the plot to blow up a plane over Detroit; an attempted bomb attack in Times Square; and the plot to blow up two package bombs on planes over the East Coast of the United States. We must be crystal clear: As Americans commemorate the tenth anniversary of the 9/11 attacks, the terrorists are meeting in caves in Waziristan, Yemen, and East Africa planning the next 9/11. We all hope and pray they fail—but hope and a prayer do not make a national security policy.

confronting the animating ideology of the enemy

ANDREW C. MCCARTHY

I n the aftermath of 9/11, consensus formed around two conclusions. The first, an instinctive reaction to a new threat environment in which American lives were in immediate jeopardy, was based in brute fact. The government had failed in its primal responsibility to secure the governed. It had no alternative but to rethink its approach and execute it ASAP.

The second conclusion involved a matter every bit as significant: the matter of *why*. Why had Muslim terrorists crash-hijacked jumbo jets into iconic symbols of American financial and military might, mass-murdering our citizens? What was it that had fueled 9/11, the capstone of atrocities tracing back to 1993, or perhaps even 1979? In the near term, it was obviously a higher priority to take action against the threat than to draw final conclusions about its animating cause. Still, the fact that there had been no careful, dispassionate probing of our enemies' motives, despite the many attacks that predated 9/11, displayed a mulish resistance.

For all its horror, the carnage of 9/11 did not overcome this resistance. In the end, there was no consensus—at least among opinion elites and policy makers—about what impelled our enemies. Consensus was instead limited to what *would not* be mentioned: Islam. But, of course, the only common denominators connecting all the attacks are Islam and our enemies' "civilizational jihad"—a campaign whose arsenal includes far more than violence, aimed at "eliminating and destroying Western civilization from within," as a 1991 Muslim Brotherhood strategic memorandum put it. Determined to absolve Islam—and "Islamist" ideology, a term fastidiously employed to stress a divide between the belief system of 1.4 billion and the Muslim supremacists who would impose it on the rest of the world—the resulting consensus was rooted not in fact but in misplaced hope.

Where we drew fact-based conclusions, our national security has dramatically improved. After a decade of ideological controversy, those who decried the law enforcement paradigm— Clinton-era counterterrorism—have been vindicated. It was by treating a national security threat as a mere crime problem that the government failed to protect its citizenry.

Initially, vindication came in the palpable success of the Bush administration's war paradigm. In unleashing the U.S. armed forces to root out terror cells and topple abettors, in giving intelligence gathering and prevention pride of place over evidence collection and prosecution, the nation avoided another 9/11. The Bush administration had markedly degraded the capacity of al-Qaeda and its affiliates to project power.

In more recent years, vindication has come in the grudging acceptance by the Obama administration of an array of Bush policies once vilified by the then-presidential candidate. In the run-up to the 2008 election, Bush counterterrorism was portrayed as a Constitution-shredding program that crossed the line from heedless provocation into actionable war crimes. Once elected President and actually accountable for public safety, however, Barack Obama continued military interventions in Iraq; escalated military presence in Afghanistan; authorized Predator drone strikes more widely and frequently than Bush (even in friendly countries, against at least one American citizen); detained enemy combatants indefinitely (a fact that changing their label to "unprivileged belligerents" cannot camouflage); continued to operate the prison camp at Guantánamo Bay (after promising in the first hours of his presidency to close it within a year); convened military commissions (after attempting to shut them down) and endorsed legislation that made only cosmetic tweaks to their Bush-era procedures; defended the state secrets doctrine; reserved the right to practice extraordinary rendition (a procedure made a counterterrorism staple not by Bush but by Clinton); and continued stepped-up surveillance of foreign agents in the United States (formerly condemned as "domestic spying") under the cloak of sweeping court authorizations (once panned as a judicial "rubber stamp" of executive excess).

Alas, there was also the second, divergent path—consciously avoiding the gleaming nexus between Islamic doctrine and Islamist supremacism. This has been a catastrophe. Willful blindness to the ideology that inspires our enemies has rendered Americans more vulnerable, particularly by eroding our liberty culture—the conceit that society flourishes when individuals are free to pursue their highest interests, not when a central authority imposes what it claims is best for them.

The *ne plus ultra* of security is to know thy enemy—a maxim attributed to the ancient Chinese strategist Sun Tzu, but also rooted in common sense. The study of what animates one's adversaries, in order to anticipate and thwart their operations, is the irreducible core of military threat doctrine, and basic even to competent law enforcement. Without knowing the enemy, our nation will never arrive at the most effective counterterrorism policy, much less defend our society from the civilizational jihad's stealthier encroachments.

A law enforcement paradigm is incompatible with gathering the intelligence needed to know your enemy. Yet the Obama administration came to power determined to reinstate the Clintonian view of terrorism as a criminal justice nuisance to be contained rather than a national security challenge to be quelled. In the wake of 9/11, one might have thought this astonishing. The law enforcement approach had proven an abject failure. Between the bombing of the World Trade Center on February 26, 1993, and the destruction of the complex on 9/11, the United States was repeatedly targeted by jihadists tied to al-Qaeda and to Iran: the foiled 1994 "Bojinka" plot to blow up U.S. airliners over the Pacific (in which one Japanese air passenger was killed and a plane nearly taken down during a preparatory strike); the 1996 Khobar Towers attack in Saudi Arabia (in which nineteen members of the U.S. Air Force were murdered by Iran's forward militia, Hezbollah, almost certainly with assistance from al-Qaeda operatives); the 1998 bombings of U.S. embassies in Nairobi and Dar es Salaam (in which al-Qaeda's East African cells murdered 224 innocents); the unsuccessful 1999 "Millennium" plot to bomb Los Angeles International Airport; and the attack on the USS *Cole* on the eve of the 2000 election (in which al-Qaeda's cells in Yemen—to this day, among its most deadly—killed seventeen American sailors and nearly sank the destroyer). As if this rampage had not made clear that something several dimensions more serious than a crime wave was afoot, bin Laden and his votaries publicly declared war against the United States several times—including their 1998 announcement of an intention to kill all Americans, including civilians, wherever on earth they could be found.

Through the eight-year terror campaign, when prosecution in the criminal justice system was the principal counterterrorism strategy, the United States managed to neutralize only twenty-nine terrorists with prosecutions. A mere handful of these were major players. In a ringing testament to the limits of the justice system, bin Laden himself was under U.S. indictment since June 1998. His deputy, Ayman al-Zawahiri, has been under indictment for a dozen years.

In contrast, the Bush war paradigm—which proceeded under a bipartisan congressional Authorization for Use of Military Force (AUMF)—was a swift and decisive success. It did not relegate law enforcement to the sidelines, for it required aggressive investigation and prosecution of nascent conspiracies in the homeland and of those who provide terrorists with material support. Rather than spearheading the government's response, though, the Justice Department and criminal investigators moved to a position more appropriate for a nation on a war footing. The heavy lifting would now be done by the armed forces and the intelligence community. Meanwhile, not only the Justice Department but all relevant federal agencies would pitch in, including the State Department (which would turn up diplomatic heat in countries where terror cells flourished) and the Treasury Department, whose tracking of financing was essential to drying up terrorist resources while serving as an underappreciated intelligence tool where U.S. assets (particularly, human intelligence sources) were scarce.

Within weeks of 9/11, al-Qaeda's top hierarchy was in disarray and on the run. Its Afghan patrons, the Taliban, were quickly toppled and, like bin Laden's network, put to flight. In the ensuing years, thousands of operatives were killed or captured. Over time, it has become commonplace to ask why al-Qaeda and its affiliates have failed to replicate their 9/11 success, especially when there are so many inviting targets. The best answer—though not one that devotees of law enforcement and "outreach" responses like to hear—is brute force. Killing and capturing terrorists before they can strike saves lives. It does far more than outreach efforts to discourage would-be recruits. New jihadists cannot replace the lost competence of senior terrorists who had trained (and, indeed, become trainers) for years before their demise. Coupled with the push to stanch the money flow through Islamic charitable fronts, Bush counterterrorism made life inordinately difficult for bin Laden and thus made the nation incalculably safer.

One wonders how a candidate such as Senator Obama could remain viable upon urging a return to September 10 America. The answer begins with President Bush's announcement of what became known as the "Bush Doctrine." In its original articulation, it was—and remains—the only blueprint to victory in a very different kind of war against transnational terror networks. A week after 9/11, Bush pledged that the United States would (a) hunt down and destroy the cells of al-Qaeda and its affiliates wherever they operated, and (b) treat all nations that abetted the terrorists as enemies. The latter did not necessarily mean America would militarily attack every terror-sponsoring regime; but it left the option of attack, and every other arrow in our government's quiver, on the table.

Unfortunately, the Bush Doctrine was ultimately not sustained. In its initial implementation, the doctrine was a resounding success because it was backed by the AUMF. The AUMF meant that American forces could attack jihadist havens in places like Afghanistan, where American law and law enforcement had not proven to be a meaningful deterrent. More important, it also meant that those captured by U.S. forces would be deemed enemy combatants under the supervision of the executive branch, not criminal defendants under the supervision of the courts. Matters related to the detention of alien enemy combatants, including whether to try them by military commission for war crimes, are committed to the discretion of the commander-in-chief.

In the present conflict, moreover, the enemy targeted civilians and mocked the threshold requirements for treatment as honorable combatants under the laws of war. This meant the jihadists could be interrogated. U.S. law forbade the use of torture, but that was the sole restriction. While human rights activists would later argue that detainees were protected against treatment that was cruel, inhuman, or degrading (CID) by the UN Convention Against Torture, the United States' ratification of that treaty interpreted CID provisions as limited to conduct already prohibited by the Fifth, Eighth, and Fourteenth Amendments. Those constitutional protections—against "cruel and unusual punishment" and treatment that "shocks the conscience"—were essentially confined to detainees in the criminal justice system and did not, in any event, apply outside U.S. sovereign territory.

The Bush Doctrine and the AUMF ensured that the nation could strike effectively at its enemies. Taking the military initiative moved the battlefield away from places like Manhattan and Washington and to the enemy's overseas strongholds. Special focus was placed on gathering intelligence from high-level captives—the only truly effective way to prevent secretive terror networks from striking. State sponsorship was severely discouraged, and in its absence no mere terror network, however extensive its tentacles, could project power on the scale of a nation-state.

Alas, there developed a hypersensitivity for Muslim sensibilities. It dismissed the very possibility, to say nothing of the patent reality, that Islamic doctrine—or, at the very least, a mainstream interpretation of Islam followed by millions of Muslims worldwide—is the principal reason Muslim extremists resort to terrorism.

Many analysts denied the centrality of doctrine to terrorism out of a well-meaning but utterly naïve hope. They believed that it was somehow within their power to repeal or change the troubling aspects of Islam by ignoring or reinventing them—as if fundamentalist Muslims would care what they thought. Others worried that conceding the nexus between doctrine and terror would be tantamount to declaring "war on Islam"—as if neither Americans nor the millions of authentic moderate Muslims were capable of sorting out and explaining whom we were fighting and whom we were not. Finally, there were commentators on the hard left whose rationale for bleaching the Islam from Islamic terror was calculated. If Islamic doctrine is not the cause of terrorism, something else must be. Conveniently, that something else is always some issue (using the military against terrorists, detaining jihadists at Guantánamo Bay, military commission trials, Israel, etc.) over which the left is agitating. Claiming that the policies one opposes trigger mass-murder attacks has great demagogic value, especially when matter-of-factly repeated by the media.

Ironically, Bush counterterrorism policies were also undermined by their own success. The combat operations, the aggressive surveillance, the intelligence haul, the money tracking, and the stepped-up prosecutions *worked*. The dreaded second wave of attacks never came, enabling critics to portray the threat as exaggerated.

But the watershed event—turning public and judicial opinion against overseas aspects of the Bush counterterrorism program—was the 2004 Abu Ghraib scandal. Assiduous investigations showed that the abuse undertaken by U.S. military guards at the infamous Iraqi prison was the deplorable work of a rogue unit with no connection to any authorized interrogation program. The abuse, moreover, was humiliation and degradation, not torture. None of this mattered. The shocking images of Abu Ghraib were broadcast nonstop in the United States and abroad, and left-wing commentators repeated the libel that they were emblematic of prisoner treatment at Guantánamo Bay (decried as a "legal black hole") and of the CIA's enhanced interrogation program for high-value detainees. The smear discredited the war effort—especially when the insurgency in Iraq turned bloody and difficult. It also put pressure on the courts, which imposed an unprecedented level of judicial scrutiny on the President's power to detain enemy combatants and subject them to military commission trials.

A second misstep, a question of priorities, further undermined the Bush Doctrine. When the Taliban rapidly fell and the remnants of al-Qaeda's leadership were driven into hiding, it seemed the United States meant business. One sensed that terror cells would not be safe in northwest Pakistan, Yemen, Somalia; that the days for terror sponsors in Iran and Iraq were numbered; and that faux allies like Saudi Arabia would need to mend their ways or face a hostile America. But the campaign stalled. The Bush administration elected to confront Saddam Hussein's regime next, essentially ignoring the worse offender in Tehran while beseeching the unreliable regime in Pakistan to continue the fight in its own territory. It became clear that the Bush Doctrine would not be enforced with the ardor of its proclamation.

The final, fatal blow to the doctrine actually came well before these events. Starting in 2002, the Bush administration opted to emphasize as the *casus belli* what intelligence services the world over believed were Saddam's thriving weapons of mass destruction (WMD) programs. This gave short shrift to the only rationale that connected Iraq to the war on terror: the regime's extensive record of ties to al-Qaeda and its affiliates—connections once thought so strong that the Clinton administration had cited them as the basis for a cruise missile strike in Sudan.

The rest is history: WMD were not found in Iraq in the copious quantities anticipated. In the public mind the case for connections between Iraq and al-Qaeda was never made. Shamefully, the anti-war left, Muslim activist organizations, and leading Democrats accused the Bush administration of intentionally "lying" the nation into war. Though Saddam's regime had been driven from power with unanticipated ease, Sunni terrorists, Shiite militias, and Baathist loyalists hunkered down for a brutal insurgency. Under blistering criticism over the once popular decision to overthrow Saddam, and with Iraq seeming to disintegrate into chaos, the Bush administration shifted the emphasis of the Bush Doctrine from defeating terrorists to building stable democracies.

There were several problems with this approach. Most immediately, it did not gain popular support. Americans were unified behind the use of our military to defeat enemies who had attacked our homeland and murdered more Americans than had been killed at Pearl Harbor. There was no such consensus on democracy promotion.

Furthermore, there was no logic to democracy promotion as a national security strategy. Even if democratic nations tend not to go to war with each other, that is irrelevant in a threat environment where the challenge is sub-national terror networks. Indeed, 9/11 was largely planned and executed in places like Hamburg, Madrid, Connecticut, San Diego, Florida, Arizona, Washington, Boston, and New York. Although anti-terrorist operations are still being carried out—reducing what would otherwise be strident criticism against the democracy project from the political right—deploying the armed forces for the primary purpose of building stable democracies is not popular, and the war thus became ever more unpopular.

To add context: there is no tradition of democracy in the Islamic world. This political landscape is not without religious and cultural rationales. First, sharia (Islam's legal and political framework) rejects core tenets of Western democracy, including the principle that the governed may make law for themselves irrespective of religious code. Mainstream Islamic ideology holds that sharia is Allah's perfect plan for human existence, and departures from its strictures are deemed blasphemous. Sharia rejects freedom of conscience (apostasy is a capital crime); it establishes a state religion; it rejects Western notions of privacy (adultery and homosexuality are death penalty offenses); it stifles economic liberty (the charging of interest is forbidden); it rejects equal protection under the law (women and non-Muslims are discriminated against); it endorses cruel and unusual punishments; and it promotes the settlement of political disputes by violent jihad.

Second, there is a virulent hostility in Islamic law and culture to the planting of Western ideas and institutions in Islamic countries—and particularly to the presence of Western armed forces in those countries. Even if one believed promoting democracy by military means was a worthy idea, it would make little sense to try it in the Islamic world, where the costs in blood and treasure will be immense and the chance of creating a Western-style democracy is minimal. Americans do not like putting their young men and women in harm's way over a Hail Mary pass.

The Bush administration reacted to these uncongenial realities by elevating the procedural aspects of democracy: popular elections and constitution writing. These measures, however, do not inculcate democratic culture—they are the tail wagging the dog. What's more, the emphasis on popular elections favors the most organized and disciplined factions. In places like Afghanistan, Iraq, the Palestinian Territories, Lebanon, and Egypt, these factions tend to be Islamists and Muslim terrorists. Thus another sad irony: the democracy project undertaken to defeat terrorists has tended instead to empower them—the Taliban, Muqtada al-Sadr, Hamas, Hezbollah, the Muslim Brotherhood, and the rogue regimes that abet them are prospering.

Also undermined is the stated goal of creating democracies that will ally with the United States. If, for example, hostilities eventually erupt with Iran—which, despite the Bush Doctrine, has been permitted to facilitate the killing of U.S. troops and edge closer to developing nuclear weapons—it is not certain that Iraq would side with us. Despite all our sacrifices, Iran has close ties with the new "democratic" regime and operates extensively throughout Iraq.

All of these factors contributed to what became deep public dissatisfaction with the war in Iraq and with President Bush, whose approval ratings were extraordinarily low by the end of his term. The sad fact is that this was avoidable. By suppressing any consideration of the role of Islamic doctrine in Islamist ideology and jihadist terror—even to the point of attempting to purge such terms as "jihad" from our discourse—our government missed the patent flaws in its strategy that makes democracy promotion in the Muslim world a key plank.

At home, Islamist leaders were invited to consult with policy makers. Since their ideology was not deemed problematic as long as they purported—however unconvincingly—to condemn terrorism, they became liaisons between the U.S. government and the Islamic community. Rather than increasing national security, "outreach" to these Muslims has advanced their goal of insinuating sharia principles into our law enforcement and intelligence protocols, our law, and our society.

It was the discontent with President Bush and the war in Iraq that emboldened then-candidate Obama to urge a return to Clintonian counterterrorism. The Obama presidency, however, demonstrates that the left overplayed its hand: conflating the unpopularity of the war with what it hoped was disaffection in general with Bush counterterrorism.

In point of fact, Americans are passionately supportive of counterterrorism policies that they are convinced make the country safer. Even if they were skeptical about Iraq (and are ever more skeptical about nation-building in Afghanistan), they want terrorists neutralized—killed, captured, and detained. They do not want trained terrorists brought to the United States, where they justifiably fear that courts may order release, and they do not want enemy combatants given full-blown civilian trials, which stand to endanger the surrounding communities while serving as a discovery bounty for our enemies. That is why President Obama has been forced to adopt most of the Bush counterterrorism program. To return heedlessly to the September 10 paradigm would fatally damage his 2012 reelection hopes. Thankfully, Obama's political survival instinct has left us more secure from terrorist attacks.

It has also served Obama extraordinarily well. On May 1, 2011, U.S. Special Forces raided Osama bin Laden's compound near Islamabad, Pakistan, killing the terror network's emir and, according to administration leaks, seizing a trove of intelligence about al-Qaeda's global operations. Bin Laden had been under Justice Department indictment for thirteen years, but it was the nation's war footing—and intelligence derived in large part from the Bush-era interrogation program for high-level al-Qaeda detainees—that finally "brought him to justice." Bush counterterrorism, the target of candidate Obama's disdain, brought about the signal achievement of President Obama's term.

Still, it is critical to remember that bin Laden was a practitioner of terror, not its cause. Islamic doctrine must be studied so we can understand not only why terrorists strike but what Islamists in the United States hope to accomplish. As the Justice Department proved in the successful terrorism financing prosecution against the Holy Land Foundation, a charitable front for Hamas, Islamist organizations led by the Muslim Brotherhood presently consider themselves engaged in what they call a "grand jihad" aimed at destroying Western civilization from within, by "sabotage." Yet our government continues to engage these groups, turn to them for advice on counterterrorism policy, impose them on our law enforcement and intelligence agencies for Islamic "sensitivity training," indulge their efforts to write sharia principles into our law, and permit them to intimidate industrious investigators and journalists with smears of "profiling" and "Islamophobia."

A comprehensive and effective national security program will have to address both the savage jihadist threat to our lives and the stealth jihadist threat to our liberties. Back on September 11, 2001, it was understandable to focus myopically on the danger of more massacres. But on this tenth anniversary, an effort to understand what inspires those massacres—what causes Islamic supremacism—is long overdue.

Interrogation

JOHN YOO

INTRODUCTION

In the space of forty minutes on May 1, 2011, two Navy SEAL teams descended on a compound in Abbottabad, Pakistan, and killed Osama bin Laden. They brought a rough measure of justice to the man responsible for the killing of 3,000 Americans on September 11, 2001, and thousands of others in countries from Spain to Iraq. President Obama's greatest victory to date in the war on terror vindicated the intelligence architecture—put into place by his predecessor—that marked the path to bin Laden's door. According to current and former administration officials, CIA interrogators gathered the initial information that ultimately led to bin Laden's death. The United States located al-Qaeda's leader by learning the identity of a trusted courier from the tough interrogations of Khalid Sheikh Mohammed, the architect of the 9/11 attacks, and his successor, Abu Faraj al-Libi. Armed with the courier's nom de guerre, American intelligence agencies later found him thanks to his phone call to a contact already under electronic surveillance. Last August, the courier traveled to bin Laden's compound, but it took another eight months before the CIA became certain that the al-Qaeda leader was hiding inside.

The successful operation to kill bin Laden followed in the steps of earlier victories in the war on terror made possible by the enhanced interrogation program. Interrogation of Abu Zubaydah, thought at the time to be al-Qaeda's operations planner, in the spring of 2002 led to the capture of much of al-Qaeda's top leadership at the time.

On September 11, 2002, Pakistan captured Ramzi bin al-Shibh, the right-hand man to Khalid Sheikh Mohammed (KSM) and the primary conduit between al-Qaeda leaders and 9/11 commander Mohammed Atta.[1] Six months later, American and Pakistani agents landed KSM, the "principal architect" of the 9/11 attacks and a "terrorist entrepreneur."[2]

Not only did the captures of these three commanders take significant parts of the al-Qaeda leadership out of action, they also yielded intelligence that prevented future terrorist attacks. The 9/11 Commission Report is a testament to the large amount of information that they provided.[3] Both Porter Goss, then-Director of the CIA, and Pat Roberts, then-chairman of the Senate Intelligence Committee, said publicly that they provided "actionable intelligence."[4] General Michael Hayden, CIA Director at the end of the Bush administration, reported that most of the United States' information on al-Qaeda during the first years of the war came from the interrogation of these al-Qaeda leaders.

If civil libertarians had their way, however, this information would not have come into the hands of the United States. They argue that any effort to coerce a detainee constitutes "torture"—conflating any interrogation method that goes beyond standard police-house questioning with a war crime.

Furthermore, human rights lawyers and some in the media have spun a broader "torture narrative."[5] The Bush administration allegedly deprived al-Qaeda of Geneva Convention protections as part of a conscious conspiracy to torture al-Qaeda leaders. These interrogation methods "migrated" to Iraq, where they produced the horrible abuses at Abu Ghraib.

This conspiracy theory is nothing but an exercise in hyperbole and partisan smear. The Bush administration went through its internal struggles over the Geneva issue only three months after the 9/11 attacks. American forces were still in Afghanistan and President Bush would not launch his political offensive on Iraq until the fall of 2002. Iraq presented a different situation entirely—a war between nation-states that was clearly covered under the Geneva Conventions.

Instead of conspiracy theories, the war on terror presents us with hard questions on coercive interrogation. Federal law prohibits torture. But limiting a captured terrorist to six hours' sleep, isolating him, interrogating him for several hours, or requiring him to exercise does not constitute "severe physical or mental pain or suffering" within the meaning of that law. Surely the United States is not required to treat captured terrorists engaged in war against the United States as if they were suspects held at an American police station. Limiting our officials to polite questioning, and demanding that terrorists receive lawyers, Miranda warnings, and eventually a court trial, are more than likely to be ineffective in stopping future attacks.

Our government has a responsibility to take reasonable measures in self-defense. In 2004, Senator Charles Schumer (D-NY) acknowledged during a Senate Judiciary Committee hearing that "very few people in this room or in America . . . would say that torture should never, ever be used, particularly if thousands of lives are at stake."[6] Even John McCain (R-AZ)—who helped craft a 2005 law that prohibited the American military not just from using torture (which was already prohibited), but also from employing a much broader category of cruel, inhuman, and degrading treatment—conceded that the President ought to violate his own law if al-Qaeda has hidden a nuclear bomb in New York. "You do what you have to do," McCain said in the fall of 2005. "But you take responsibility for it."[7]

Unfortunately, these are no longer hypothetical questions. We face an enemy that is intent on carrying out surprise attacks on innocent civilians, with weapons of mass destruction (WMD) if possible, by using covert cells of operatives within the United States. The enemy refuses to obey any of the basic principles of civilized warfare, and its lack of territory, population, or regular armed forces means that gaining intelligence is the only way to prevent attacks successfully.

CLARITY IN INTERROGATION STANDARDS

Federal statute, international agreement, and presidential policy all ban torture. But the law draws a distinction between torture and coercive interrogation. Torture is not all forms of interrogation that go beyond questioning, just as first-degree murder does not include all deaths. Physical or mental coercion, for example, could include threats of poor treatment or promises of better treatment. It could include non-harmful physical contact. Inter-rogators, for example, could use standard methods for Marine basic training without committing torture.

In 1994, the United States ratified the Convention Against Torture (CAT). The CAT makes a clear distinction between tor-ture, which states must criminalize, and less harmful "cruel, inhu-man, or degrading treatment." President Reagan understood the treaty this way when he first sent it to the Senate: "[I]n order to constitute torture, an act must be a deliberate and calculated act of an extremely cruel and inhuman nature, specifically intended to inflict excruciating and agonizing physical or mental pain or suffering."[8] The Reagan administration reported to the Senate: "rough treatment as generally falls into the category of 'police brutality,' while deplorable, does not amount to 'torture.'"[9]

Congress maintained this distinction when it criminalized torture outside the United States in 1994 as "an act committed by a person acting under the color of law specifically intended to inflict severe physical or mental pain or suffering (other than pain or suffering incidental to lawful sanctions) upon another person within his custody or physical control."[10] Congress intended its prohibition on torture to be narrow. The alleged torturer must have acted with "specific intent," the highest level of criminal intent known to the law.[11]

Notice that Congress only prohibits "*severe* physical or men-tal pain or suffering," not *any* pain or suffering, whether physi-cal or mental. It prohibits only severe acts, though it does not define "severe." Standard dictionaries define "severe" in the con-text of pain as something that is "grievous," "extreme," "sharp," and "hard to endure."[12] The only other place where Congress has used similar words is in statutes defining health benefits for emergency medical conditions; in these statutes, "severe pain" occurs when an individual's health is placed "in serious jeopardy," "serious impairment to bodily functions," or "serious dysfunction of any bodily organ or part.[13] Obviously, Congress's terminology here is not exactly on point, but it is the closest Congress has come.

Civil libertarian critics imply that the Bush administration interpreted torture to include only physical abuse. They have claimed, for example, that under Bush, the Justice Department would allow the denial of medical care, or the use of psychotropic drugs, or Russian roulette, or the threat of imminent death to a detainee or his family members. These claims ignore the words of the 2002 legal opinion issued by the Justice Department's Office of Legal Counsel (OLC) and the 1994 law. Congress clearly prohibited the infliction of severe mental pain or suffering, which it more precisely defined as "the prolonged mental harm" caused by four specific acts: (1) the threat of or actual physical pain and suffering, (2) the threat or administration of "mind-altering substances or other procedures calculated to disrupt profoundly the senses or the personality," (3) the "threat of imminent death," or (4) the threat of inflicting these harms on a third person.[14] Congress's definition prohibited certain actions, but allowed others—that is the nature of drawing a line.

Congress declined to prohibit the broader category of "cruel, inhuman, or degrading treatment or punishment" on the grounds that these words were too vague.[15] A European court, for example, suggested that German officials had violated this standard by refusing to recognize a prisoner's sex change.[16] Executive branch officials wanted to make sure that the United States did not adopt any international legal obligations that exceeded American law. They suggested, and the Senate adopted, a definition by which "cruel, inhuman, or degrading" meant acts that were already prohibited by the Constitution's Fifth, Eighth, or Fourteenth

Amendments.[17] This followed the American practice of ratifying human rights treaties so as to require no change in domestic law. It would have been remarkable for the United States to accept an enormous extension of constitutional rights to all foreign citizens whenever they were detained by the U.S. government.

Critics charge that the Bush administration sought to redefine torture so as to allow mistreatment. The critics rarely provide any definition, nor do they explain how such a definition might apply to the capture of al-Qaeda leaders. Critics further claim that the United States acted contrary to world opinion, but neglect to consider the experience of democracies that have confronted severe terrorism threats. Counterterrorism agents in the United Kingdom and Israel had developed similar interrogation methods without inflicting severe physical harm. Although the European Court of Human Rights found the British methods to be inhumane and degrading treatment, it also found that they "did not occasion suffering of the particular intensity and cruelty implied by the word torture."[18] Israeli experience teaches the same lesson. In response to the Palestinian intifada and a campaign of suicide bombings, Israel's General Security Service employed a combination of stress positions to interrogate terrorist suspects. Israel's Supreme Court found that legislative authorization was needed for the methods because they were inhumane and degrading—but not torture.[19] Other democratic nations, with legal traditions not unlike our own, addressed their terrorist challenges with policies similar to our own.

Some critics believe it is wrong for our elected leaders even to ask about the legal limits of their powers. President Bush and his advisors should not have inquired about the meaning of the anti-torture law, according to Professor Jeremy Waldron, because merely asking about it would encourage policy makers to go to far.[20] Apparently, government lawyers in the OLC should have refused to answer the White House's question out of moral outrage. This is absurd. A President would be derelict in his duty if he did not review the full legal extent of his options when confronted by the challenges of a new kind of war.

The critics' desire to impose their policies by misreading the law comes through loud and clear on the question of defenses. American law presumes self-defense and necessity defenses to exist for violations of any criminal law unless explicitly precluded by Congress. Before 9/11, legal scholars had debated whether necessity or self-defense could justify or excuse torture.[21] Necessity, or as it is known, the "choice of evils," is the most discussed justification for violations of criminal law.[22] The defense depends on weighing probabilities of outcomes and costs and benefits. Discussion of the necessity defense employs the well-known "ticking bomb" scenario. Congress also did not explicitly rule out self-defense when it passed the anti-torture law. Like necessity, whether a claim of self-defense is upheld will depend on the facts.[23] It is also possible a nation's right to self-defense from attacks supports an individual agent's claim to the use of force in self-defense.[24] If self-defense is a standard defense to homicide, it is difficult to see why it would not be a defense to torture. Congress specifically considered but decided against the elimination of defenses for government officials engaged in harsh interrogation. It intentionally omitted the CAT provision that eliminated defenses based on war or public emergency.[25]

We cannot ask our intelligence and military officers to put their lives on the line in a state of dangerous ignorance and uncertainty. We do not send our police officers onto the streets without fully understanding the rules on the use of force, including self-defense. Our intelligence officers deserve the same clarity. Critics want to keep intelligence officers in the dark with vague standards, behind which lurks massive liability. Our agents in the field deserve better.

EXECUTIVE POWERS IN TIMES OF WAR

A broader constitutional issue is whether Congress can interfere with the President's authority to wage war. The Bush Justice Department concluded that the torture statute could not limit the President's constitutional exercise of his commander-in-chief power to dictate the interrogation of enemy prisoners during wartime. I believe that in times of crisis, the Constitution grants the President broad powers to respond to unforeseen circumstances and dangerous threats to protect the nation. This was the very essence of the executive power at the time of the framing of the Constitution and the reason it is concentrated in one person: so that the nation can respond with speed, decision, and force, particularly in times of war. Presidents such as George Washington, Andrew Jackson, Abraham Lincoln, Franklin Roosevelt, and Ronald Reagan all shared this understanding of presidential power.[26]

Nevertheless, a collection of law professors and human rights and liberal activists attacked this as "an unprecedented and under-analyzed claim that the Executive Branch is a law unto itself" which is "incompatible with the rule of law and the principle that no one is above the law."[27] They argued that the OLC opinion's conclusion that the commander-in-chief power could override the anti-torture statute violated professional ethics standards because it did not discuss certain dicta in *Youngstown Sheet & Tube Co. v. Sawyer*,[28] a famous separation of powers case.

The OLC had not cited *Youngstown* in 2002 because earlier OLC opinions, reaching across several administrations, had concluded that the case did not apply to the President's conduct of foreign affairs and national security. *Youngstown* reached the separation of powers outcome because the Constitution clearly gives Congress the exclusive power to regulate the economy.[29] But *Youngstown* does not address the scope of the commander-in-chief power where strategy or tactics in war are involved, and even supports the proposition that one branch may not intrude on the clear constitutional turf of another. Justice Jackson recognized that, even at its lowest ebb, the inherent powers of the President would prevail if "he can rely only upon his own constitutional powers minus any constitutional powers of Congress over the matter."[30] Detention and interrogation policy in war are not a matter of Congress's domestic powers but of the President's commander-in-chief power to wage war. All administrations similarly have refused to acknowledge the legality of the War Powers Resolution, and have started military conflicts without congressional approval.

In 1994, Janet Reno's OLC (then headed by Duke law professor Walter Dellinger) opined that the President could "decline to enforce a statute that he views as unconstitutional."[31] This is especially true, Dellinger observed, "of provisions limiting the President's authority as commander-in-chief." The Reno OLC later found unconstitutional a congressional effort to prohibit American troops from serving under foreign or international commands as an infringement of the President's power over war and the military.[32] Dellinger's opinion cited *Youngstown* only once—in support of the proposition that the President has the right to *refuse* to execute a law. Far from inventing some novel interpretation of the Constitution, the claim that Congress cannot interfere with legitimate exercises of the commander-in-chief power was long the position of Presidents and Justice Departments in the past.

COERCIVE INTERROGATION IN LAW AND POLICY

Some believe that coercive interrogation is never justified in a moral society, even if the consequences are another 9/11 or worse. When confronted with the hypothetical of using "excruciating pain" to learn the location of a nuclear bomb in an American city, Waldron has said, "my own answer to this question is a simple No."[33] For Waldron and other absolutists, the ban on coercive interrogation overrides any other consideration. The number of lives that could be saved is irrelevant.

Most Americans, and certainly anyone of either political party who must actually run a government, would adopt a more reasonable position. We are repelled by the idea of using physical or mental pressure to elicit information, but we cannot rule it out in all cases. It would be morally wrong for a leader to allow the deaths of thousands of citizens rather than consider coercive interrogation of a single terrorist leader. Civil libertarian absolutists often dismiss the nuclear bomb scenario as an artificial hypothetical. That is simply mistaken. We continue to face an enemy that killed 3,000 citizens on September 11, 2001; that enemy has attempted to acquire biological and nuclear weapons, and will use them against us if possible. Coercive interrogation of al-Qaeda leaders made possible the capture or killing of the top ranks of al-Qaeda's leadership, including Osama bin Laden himself.

Most of the arguments against coercive interrogation are not about absolutes, but about whether the costs outweigh the benefits. Critics usually understate the benefits and overstate the costs. One common claim is that coercive interrogation does not work and produces unreliable information.[34] But, as

Marc Thiessen has shown, there is substantial evidence that coercive interrogation can produce valuable information and even actionable intelligence.[35]

Critics commonly make claims about the costs of coercive interrogation based on highly speculative assumptions. They assert that relaxing the prohibition on physical pressure will make torture the norm.[36] Or that it will encourage the enemy to fight harder.[37] Or that it will undermine the advancement of international human rights.[38] Or that it will reduce cooperation from allies or cause us to lose the moral high ground. Coercive interrogation in an individual case might make sense, a critic might even concede, but because we cannot rationally balance costs and benefits under the pressure of war, we should follow a prohibition in all cases.

These pragmatic objections fall apart under closer examination. Take, for example, the commonly heard claim that if we allow the use of coercive interrogation with regard to terrorists, it will undermine the ban on physical pressure in other situations.[39] This is the familiar "slippery slope" argument.[40] Other democracies such as Israel and Great Britain have not allowed coercive interrogation to spread to their broader military or law enforcement activities. There is no claim that France's use of torture against Algerian terrorists infected its investigation of garden-variety crimes in metropolitan France. We have laws that permit the police to use force—even deadly force—against suspects to protect themselves or the lives of others. Under the slippery slope argument, this ought to lead to a weakening of the respect for the rights of suspects. That, however, is not the case.

Critics point to the mistreatment of Iraqi prisoners at Abu Ghraib as an illustration of their argument. Journalists charge that the use of coercive interrogation methods against al-Qaeda leaders led to their use at Guantánamo Bay. This culture then migrated to Iraq, where it inspired the abuses of detainees by military police and intelligence units at Abu Ghraib. But individual instances of rule violation differ from slippery slopes produced by policy choices. At Abu Ghraib, individuals committed awful abuses of detainees under their control that were not authorized as a matter of policy or law or "atmosphere." Breaches of regulations are not reason enough for changing the policy. To make a domestic comparison: we have many cases of police brutality or prison abuse in the United States every year, but violations do not prove that the rules promote or facilitate police or prison brutality.

Multiple investigations have shown that the Abu Ghraib abuses arose because of a lack of sufficient resources and personnel at the prison. Defense Department officials had not devoted sufficient troops to detention operations. These failures of leadership and judgment do not represent a conspiracy to abuse Iraqi detainees. In fact, military investigators had discovered—and initiated disciplinary proceedings against the perpetrators of—the abuses at Abu Ghraib long before media revelations.

Nor should unpopularity abroad, taken alone, veto American policy. Our elected leaders have to estimate the benefits of pressuring al-Qaeda members to reveal actionable intelligence. The Bush administration decided that the intelligence gained through coercive interrogation could prevent another attack on the United States, and that this outweighed the cost in public opinion and international support. To look at the problem from a different perspective, consider the costs of inaction. Suppose a second attack in the United States, on a par with or greater than 9/11, had occurred. al-Qaeda has a record of follow-on attacks, it has sent more operatives to the United States since 9/11, and it has actively sought WMD technology. Would an American leader have found the death and destruction caused by a second attack an acceptable price to pay for an absolute ban against coercive interrogation?

Flat prohibitions leave no room for discretion, which may be needful in unforeseen or catastrophic circumstances. The Israeli Supreme Court recognizes a general ban against torture, but also allows a necessity defense. In this book, Alan Dershowitz proposes that the government go to court for warrants that would allow torture, permitting methods far beyond coercive interrogation. Eric Posner and Adrian Vermeule argue that our legal system should handle coercive interrogation as it does the use of deadly force by the police: with training, special rules, and immunity for those who follow the rules.[41]

Each proposal has its advantages and disadvantages. Absolute prohibitions may be clear, but they are clumsy in situations such as national security and war, where uncertainty and circumstances demand flexibility. Dershowitz's proposal suffers from the same problem because it requires judges to approve events before the fact. Judicial competence is at its nadir in national security. The probability of an attack and the magnitude of the destruction depend on events in the future rather than crimes in the past. This is classically a job for the political branches.

The 2005 McCain amendment is not unlike the Miranda rule. Both tie the government's hands with a blanket prohibition, which prevents decision based on all of the circumstances at the time. Miranda is less costly because the harm an individual criminal can inflict on society is limited, while WMD technology, rogue nations, and terrorist groups make terrorists far more dangerous.

The legal system could adopt effective approaches toward coercive interrogation. A President could decline to prosecute an officer whom he believed to have acted properly in self-defense or out of necessity (particularly if the President ordered the interrogation). A President could pardon those involved. The necessity defense can maintain society's declaration that such interrogation is wrong, while also recognizing an exception for emergencies. It allows future decision makers with better information to decide on coercive interrogation rather than blindly follow an *ex ante* one-size-fits-all rule.

If prosecution is the primary tool to enforce these standards, we would still have all the problems of courts: lack of secrecy, exposure of sources and methods of intelligence gathering, unpredictable juries, and the basic, structural lack of executive, managerial, and policy planning expertise.

The executive branch should continue to bear primary responsibility for any decision to use coercive interrogation, but it must brief the House and Senate Intelligence Committees generally. The intelligence agencies have understood for many years that congressional support is essential for the long-term success of their missions. They have been and will increasingly be reluctant to carry out any dubious action without both the approval of the President and the political support of Congress.

Covert actions developed by the President and his staff and briefed to the intelligence committees have included targeted killings and paramilitary operations against foreign nations. Courts have not intervened, nor have they been necessary. These institutional arrangements should be equally suitable to the realm of interrogations.

CONCLUSION

September 11 requires us to make choices about whether coercive interrogation is worth the cost. The law we passed did not give us the answers, but instead required our elected leaders to make a policy judgment. That is how it should be. Coercive interrogation can produce information from al-Qaeda leaders and operatives that helps our military, intelligence, and law enforcement personnel prevent future attacks. It has produced the information that led to the capture or killing of high-ranking al-Qaeda leaders, ultimately including Osama bin Laden himself. The practice may have costs in foreign policy, organizational discipline, and enemy morale. But we should also not lose sight of the benefits—for it was much more than luck that allowed our government to frustrate and disrupt terrorist efforts to carry out another 9/11.

fear: the tail wagging the post-9/11 policy dog

BOB BARR

The cowardly attacks on the World Trade Center towers, the Pentagon, and the U.S. Capitol on September 11, 2001 did not succeed in achieving their primary goal of bringing America's political and economic systems to their knees. In the years since the attacks, the non-governmental actor—al-Qaeda—under whose auspices the 9/11 attackers operated has been weakened considerably as a result of military and other actions taken by the United States and its allies.

In one important and perverse way, however, these terrorists did succeed in at least one of their aims. Their actions indirectly but significantly changed the relationship between the American citizenry and the government. The terrorists diminished the freedoms—freedoms the 9/11 perpetrators so disdained—that citizens of this great country enjoy. Fear has become the tail wagging the public-policy dog in the early twenty-first century.

Throughout our nation's history, America has always met and overcome major challenges. We have met and repelled every military attack on our sovereignty, and have emerged stronger for our efforts. This is the bright side of America's use of military power. Unfortunately, as with most governmental actions, there is another side. As James Madison noted in *Federalist No. 51*, men are not angels.[1] This recognition led Madison and his *Federalist Papers* co-authors, Alexander Hamilton and John Jay, to argue masterfully that a constitution was essential in order to keep government itself within limits.

The remarkably concise system of checks and balances, incorporated in the three-branch government provided for in the U.S. Constitution, emphatically envisioned an executive branch with clear powers. Some powers are shared with the legislative and judicial branches, and others are unique entities, but none was intended to be exercised absolutely or unchecked. As Chief Justice Marshall noted in the seminal case of *Marbury v. Madison*, even though certain political acts of a President are not reviewable by the courts, official acts of the President and those working under him must be reviewable to ensure that the President and all executive branch officials operate within the law and the Constitution.[2] Were it otherwise, the fundamental principle underpinning the Constitution itself—that ours is a government of limited and enumerated powers—would be rendered null. Yet this is precisely what occurred as a result of the 9/11 attacks.

The federal government has often used crises and "emergencies" as justification to expand its powers, as it did in the days, weeks, and months following the 9/11 attacks. For example, even before the United States entered the nineteenth century, the government's commitment to freedom of speech and assembly was tested when, in 1798, the infamous Alien and Sedition Acts were passed.[3] Citing crisis, President Andrew Jackson on more than one occasion exceeded the limits on his Article II powers, daring the judiciary to stop him.

This trend toward aggressive expansion of executive power continued during America's first century. During the Civil War, Abraham Lincoln—exalted by many historians and academicians above all other Presidents—usurped powers explicitly not granted to the President in the Constitution, offering as rationale what he believed to be the implied, absolute power to preserve the Union. In the early twentieth century, Woodrow Wilson and his Attorney General, Alexander Mitchell Palmer, pointed to the threats allegedly posed by anarchist and communist ideologies to justify the infamous "Palmer Raids." Moreover, in what is assuredly one of the darkest stains on American history, one of the country's most liberal chief executives, Franklin Roosevelt, ordered the summary internment of Japanese-Americans shortly after the Pearl Harbor attack.

President Richard Nixon gave the grandest rendition of the doctrine that when a President exercises what he believes to be a power granted him in Article II of the Constitution, such acts not only are permissible, but are not reviewable by either of the other two branches of government. In an interview following his resignation, Nixon stated candidly that whatever a President does is by definition lawful, simply because the President does it.[4]

This is the darker side of many U.S. Presidents exercising otherwise commendable leadership in overcoming serious threats to our nation. Thankfully—if belatedly in some instances—in virtually every instance in which a President has expanded the powers of his office, the courts, very occasionally the Congress, and sometimes the President's successors in office, have taken actions to restore at least partial constitutional balance.

However, unlike earlier conflicts or "emergencies" that precipitated unconstitutional actions, which receded when the conflict or emergency passed, the current "global war on terror" has no discernible or definable end point. Any person, at any time, and in any location is capable of committing an act of terrorism. Every person is a potential terrorist combatant and every city, neighborhood, or block a potential target. The terrorism "battlefield" is everywhere.

In this terrorism battlefield, whenever the President dons his hat as "commander-in-chief," he claims power over virtually anywhere on the face of the earth. This makes the current environment dramatically different from—and significantly more threatening to liberty than—any previous exercise of extra-constitutional powers by a President. The "temporary" has morphed into the "permanent."

The abject fear of terrorism that has gripped our country since 9/11 has led to a seismic shift in the relationship between the government and the citizenry. This shift, measured in terms of liberties lost and power gained, has been a one-way street from the people to the government. And it has occurred with astonishing speed and lack of widespread concern.

As a member of Congress from 1995 to 2003, I witnessed firsthand various executive branch agencies petitioning Congress for additional powers on behalf of the President, citing various "crises": the drug crisis, the Wall Street crisis, the Enron scandal, and the terrorism crisis. The attack on the Alfred P. Murrah Federal Building in Oklahoma City in April 1995 precipitated just such an episode. Hardly had the dust settled from this domestic terrorist attack when the Clinton administration made the rounds on Capitol Hill, soliciting support for broad new investigative and prosecutorial powers for the FBI and the Department of Justice. While some proposals reflected legitimate and reasonable measures to update federal laws relating to electronic surveillance and data collection, others went far beyond what was reasonably necessary.

In a preview to the behind-the-scenes battle over the USA Patriot Act[5] six years later, some House members were willing to grant the government limited and reasonable new powers to meet threats presented by modern-era, ideology-driven criminals, but opposed sweeping powers undermining Fourth Amendment guarantees. We fashioned a floor amendment that scaled back the legislation sought by President Clinton and supported by the Republican House leadership. The Antiterrorism and Effective Death Penalty Act of 1996[6] thus struck a proper balance between legitimate law enforcement needs and the time-honored liberties guaranteed in the Bill of Rights (particularly the Fourth Amendment).

The compromise, which was eventually incorporated in the legislation signed into law, resulted from many weeks of hard work by a group of people who put aside serious differences in order to protect essential civil liberties against unnecessary erosion by the government in the name of "fighting terrorism." Members of this informal group included myself, the ACLU, the NRA, Americans for Tax Reform, Eagle Forum, and others. This coalition would replicate itself in the fall of 2001 to fight similar efforts by President George W. Bush, though with far less success.

It is axiomatic that the 9/11 attacks were a game-changer. Despite repeated assurances by President Bush and other top administration officials that their responses to the attacks would not change our way of life, they have done just that. People who cling to the Pollyannaish notion that they have as much freedom from government intrusion now as they did on September 10, 2001 have been living in a time warp.

The post-9/11 power grabs by the federal government were aided by a number of factors that have converged to create a "perfect storm" for erosion of privacy and other constitutional liberties. These phenomena include the full blooming of the Internet, the arrival of mass corporate data-mining, and the explosion of social networking. The list is endless:

- Consumers clamor for discounts, oblivious to the fact that in return for a miniscule price cut, their buying patterns are recorded.
- Drivers concerned with saving time as they traverse toll booths purchase automatic toll passes, enabling the government to register the points at which their vehicles enter and exit the toll road, how fast the vehicles travel between toll booths, and the date and time of their travel.
- "Behavior Detection Officers" now roam America's airports looking for persons whose behavior may be "suspicious," even if unrelated to air travel.
- The Global Positioning System (GPS) of satellites now monitors and retains data on cell phones and other individual electronic devices.
- Passports now issued by the State Department are equipped with tiny RFID (Radio Frequency Identification) chips that allow quicker scanning by government agents at points of entry; the holder does not have access

to the kind of information stored on the chip. RFIDs can be monitored by persons or entities other than official government stations.

- In order to make the delivery of consumer products and services available more "efficient," companies increasingly turn to RFID chips for inventory control and retail tracking.

- RFID chips are used to track pets, the elderly, and even schoolchildren.

- RFID chips are finding their way into trash bins in some cities, as a way to determine whether citizens are properly separating their trash according to local recycling mandates.

- Financial transactions of virtually any amount, handled by a wide array of institutions, are subject to increased monitoring by an ever-growing cadre of private and government officials.

- Foreign investors are increasingly subject to extensive privacy-invasive reporting requirements for transactions having no link to suspicious activities or persons.

- As a result of the "threat" of illegal immigration, federal, state, and local governments are increasingly turning to employment-verification and housing-approval databases.

- The legal and practical barriers that the government must meet before its agents are able to gather personal information in the control of a third party (e.g., retail establishments, medical offices, libraries, or credit agencies), have been dramatically lowered as a result of provisions in the USA Patriot Act and other post-9/11 legislation.[7]

- As local and state governments face budget shortfalls, pressure has mounted to install speed-detection and red-light cameras, which have significantly enhanced government revenues and created electronic databases of drivers' behavior and locations. This practice is denigrating the sound, individual judgment of the law enforcement officer, which previously provided the basis for police action. Technology has become the Holy Grail of federal, state, and local law enforcement.

- Biometric identification and measuring devices are being used at venues as diverse as sporting events, government installations, and airports.

- USA Patriot Act warrants, which are non-judicial, allow government access to hotel registries and rental car records, even in the absence of any suspicion of unlawful or improper activity.

- Under the 2008 amendments to the Foreign Intelligence Surveillance Act (FISA) of 1978,[8] any international communications (including phone calls, emails, and other Internet-based communications) are subject to warrantless electronic surveillance by the government, based on nothing more than the fact that the communications are "international" in nature.

- In order to "coordinate" state and local "anti-terrorism" efforts with federal efforts, "Fusion Centers" are being developed across the country. They enlist local citizens and law enforcement to develop information on, and awareness of, the need for expanded reporting of a ridiculously broad array of "suspicious activity."[9]

- Certain emergency reporting devices in consumer vehicles (e.g., "OnStar") can be programmed to monitor what is taking place inside the vehicles, and made available to law enforcement.

- "Watch lists" containing hundreds of thousands of names, based on information unavailable to citizens, are maintained by private industry and government agencies. These lists can provide the basis for denial of the basic right to travel or access services, such as consumer credit.
- "Scent tracking" has now been employed by the government to help identify potentially threatening individuals (reportedly used, for example, at the 2007 G-8 summit in Germany).[10]
- Local governments across the country, especially in large cities, are installing surveillance cameras, or forcing businesses to do so, in order to reduce crime and terrorism.
- Neighborhood surveillance cameras are now being supplemented in some locations by sound detection devices to alert police to suspicious sounds.
- Fear of drunk driving now provides an excuse for police in some jurisdictions (such as Fairfax County, Virginia) to begin testing people for alcohol inside bars or restaurants, regardless of whether they would have driven after leaving.
- And, of course, we now have employees of the federal Transportation Security Administration (TSA) routinely demanding that law-abiding and suspicion-free air travelers submit to invasive, manual pat-downs like those that police perform on common street criminals, or forcing men, women, children, and the elderly alike to stand in glass cages while TSA employees view naked x-ray scans of their bodies.

This is by no means an exhaustive list of government actions taken in the post-9/11 world, or of powers that represent a clear and significant break from the relationship between the citizenry and the government. Certainly not all of these privacy-invasive actions can be tied directly to the attacks of 9/11. All of them, however, reflect the pervasive fear that has become the currency of public policy in the wake of those terrorist attacks. Fear is their common element. Fear of terrorism. Fear of crime. Fear of environmental damage. Fear of being lost. Fear of being hurt. Fear of kidnapping. Fear of losing a pet. Fear of anything that might pose or reflect a risk. Fear that only government can address.

In the days and weeks leading to the floor vote on the Patriot Act, Justice Department lawyers met with hesitant members of Congress to "alert" them to the possibility of further terrorist attacks, including possible use of crop-duster planes to spread poisonous gasses. No evidence that such activities were reasonably expected was provided, but the message was clear: vote for the legislation or risk being blamed for another attack. This is a tactic employed often by government personnel urging passage of everything from the 2008 FISA amendments to all manner of authorization and appropriation bills.

Modern American Presidents—especially the one Republican and one Democrat who have governed since September 11, 2001—understand Edmund Burke's prescient observation in 1757 that "no passion so effectually robs the mind of all its powers of acting and reasoning as fear." One of our own Founding Fathers, John Adams, observed that "fear is the foundation of most governments."

These maxims are even more relevant today. Our Founders established a constitution-based government structure—described in eloquent detail in the eighty-five essays that compose *The Federalist Papers*—to serve us in peacetime as well as in war, protect liberty, and keep government within proper bounds. Sadly, this has not lasted, and the trend away from individual liberty toward government power has accelerated greatly in the years since September 2001.

This massive shift toward government power and the inevitable reduction in individual liberty and freedom have led to some unusual views toward our government at home and abroad. For example, due to the degree of surveillance within its borders, the United States now receives some of the lowest "privacy rankings" among the several dozen countries ranked annually by UK-based Privacy International.[11]

Domestically, trust in government has eroded even as Americans appear willing to cede more and more power to government to make them "safer." In the most recent survey conducted by the nonpartisan Ponemon Institute, the Department of Justice, which should be among the most trusted of agencies, enjoyed a "trust" ranking of only 21 percent.[12]

Some observers justify or excuse the intrusions by the current President and his immediate predecessor—and a number of their predecessors, such as Lincoln—based on "changed circumstances." In their analyses, the constitutional framework bequeathed to us contemplated a world in which terrorist cells or other non-state actors did not figure, a world in which threats were more easily definable and considerably less menacing than those faced by modern Presidents.[13] In this brave, new post-9/11 world, filled with potential terrorist threats of all manner and design, the outdated, narrow and limited interpretation of Article II must yield to extreme flexibility and the broadest possible delineation of commander-in-chief powers.

This is the world of the so-called "neocons" and those who support a "unitary executive" theory of constitutional interpretation. In this world, a President exercising powers as the "commander-in-chief" alone determines what actions are needed and when they must be taken. Insofar as neither the Article I branch

(Congress) nor the Article III branch (the judiciary) is explicitly charged with this responsibility, neither of those two branches may interfere with or limit a President's "unitary" power.

In a world such as this, it is facile to justify a President's usurpation of the power to suspend the "Great Writ" of habeas corpus as Lincoln did, and as former Attorney General Alberto Gonzalez implied in remarks before the Senate Judiciary Committee.[14] It is easy for these neocons to justify a President ignoring a law such as FISA, which (prior to its amendment and expansion in 2008) prohibited a President from engaging in warrantless electronic surveillance of an American citizen's international phone calls absent reasonable suspicion that he or she is communicating with a known or suspected terrorist or an associate of a known or suspected terrorist. After all, the theory goes, an Army field commander is clearly empowered to learn surreptitiously what his enemy is up to without resort to judicial process, and the President is the commander-in-chief.

Even America's long-held aversion to and condemnation of torture has yielded to the exigencies of this post-9/11 view of the world. Yet, if the law of the land—including provisions of a treaty ratified by the Senate—prohibits government officers operating under presidential "directive" from engaging in torture, then under what reasonable interpretation of that law and of the Constitution should executive branch officials be allowed to order that torture be employed?

Individuals favoring the use of torture and other controversial actions often rely for their justification on the success of a particular course of action; a form of *ex post facto* justification for otherwise clearly or arguably unlawful actions by a President or an administration. The argument essentially is set forth thus: "America has not suffered a serious attack by terrorists since 9/11; therefore whatever we have been and are doing is working, and is therefore proper since such actions have enabled the President successfully to fulfill his primary responsibility of protecting the nation." This in fact was a refrain heard repeatedly in the aftermath of the military operation that resulted in the killing of Osama bin Laden on May 2, 2011, since according to some reports, the intelligence information that led eventually to bin Laden's death was derived from "enhanced interrogation" of suspects. This form of rationalization is the slipperiest of slopes—justifying otherwise prohibited government action based on results. Preventing such actions constituted a principle underpinning of the Constitution, and for the limitations on government actions incorporated in the Bill of Rights. That the doctrine of *ex post facto* justification has now become a cornerstone of federal policy is clear evidence of the degree to which 9/11 has changed our constitutional landscape.

Scenarios such as this, with statutory prohibitions already in place, are distinct from situations in which the law is silent and a President makes a case that national security requires that he engage in acts not otherwise prohibited to him. This distinction reflects the fundamental difference between a government of men and a government of laws. John Adams correctly identified America as falling in the latter category. Sadly, the post-9/11 world—in which virtually every controversial public policy is tied in some manner to protecting the nation against terrorism—has transformed America to a nation of men: the President and those operating at his direction.

This is not to argue against robust executive power to protect the nation and its vital interests. I agree—and have done so publicly in numerous debates—that a President has and must be permitted a great deal of flexibility to protect our sovereignty and national interests. However, when there is a law of the land—duly passed by Congress and signed by the President—that expressly prohibits a President from acting, or which clearly defines the manner in which he must act, if we are to remain a "nation of laws and not of men," the President must be bound to abide by the law, even if he does not wish to.

There are remedies for a President who honestly believes the law unduly limits his ability to carry out his duty to protect the nation. He can seek to have the law amended. If he is persuasive— and most Presidents are—Congress will agree and change the law. The President can challenge the law in the courts. Because most federal judges are overly deferential on matters of national security, the President is more likely than not to prevail.

But to sanction a President's defiance of law, a treaty ratified by the Senate, or a clear provision in the Constitution, would openly invite despotism, albeit benign. It undermines the foundations of our heritage and history and weakens the very fabric of freedom that is our Constitution. No fear, no risk, and no enemy, no matter how powerful or insidious, is worth that. And no President, no matter how well-intentioned, should be permitted to place himself above the law or the Constitution. Unfortunately, we have traveled far down this road since September 11, 2001; but, I hope and pray, not so far that we cannot begin to reverse course and reconnect with that "constitutional road" identified for us by James Madison in 1788.[15]

liberty, security, and the USA patriot act

JOHN D. ASHCROFT
VIET D. DINH

INTRODUCTION

At the time of this writing, nearly a decade has passed since the 9/11 attacks, and fortunately our terrorist enemies have not successfully engaged in any large-scale attacks on American soil since. This is a testament to the remarkable efforts of an alert citizenry and of law enforcement, intelligence, and homeland security personnel. The hard work, dedication, and increased coordination have been greatly aided by the tools, resources, and guidance provided by the Uniting and Strengthening America by Providing Appropriate Tools Required to Intercept and Obstruct Terrorism Act (USA Patriot Act).

Proposed less than a week after the terrorist attacks of 9/11 and enacted a month later, the Patriot Act is among the more important national defense legislative measures in American history. The act enables government to combat a protracted and difficult war against those who wish to rob us of our way of life—a way of life defined by freedom. At the same time, the Patriot Act constrains attempts by governmental actors to extend the government's reach inappropriately.

SECURING LIBERTY

Since the 9/11 attacks, Americans have been told that a choice must be made between security and liberty. Frequently, it is suggested that there is a necessary balancing act between individual liberty and security, where enhancement of one is only possible at significant cost to the other. In the search for this elusive balance, commentators often cite Benjamin Franklin's dictum that those who "give up essential liberty to obtain a little temporary safety deserve neither liberty nor safety." Liberty (let alone "essential liberty") is not to be traded for safety (let alone "a little temporary safety"). At its core, Franklin's maxim is correct. Security is not an end in itself, but rather a means to the greater end of liberty.

Freedom is a value that is without parallel. Freedom never requires balancing. What it requires is enhancement. Freedom must be supported and safeguarded. Freedom must be secured. Security, then, is not a counterweight to freedom, but rather a means to ensure that freedom remains intact and contributes positively to the character of humanity. Simply put, appropriate security enables freedom, rather than competes against it. Thus, searching for a "balance" between liberty and security is counter-productive because such an approach is based on a false dichotomy. It is the function of security to safeguard liberty. Unless it does, it should not be undertaken.

The essential issue Americans face today is not a trade-off between security and liberty, but rather an inquiry into what liberty entails, and how security is best utilized to protect that liberty. Perhaps Edmund Burke said it best: "The only liberty I mean is a liberty connected with order; that not only exists along with order and virtue, but which cannot exist at all without them."[1] In other words, true liberty is by necessity an ordered liberty. The stability and legitimacy essential for a government under law can only be obtained through the maintenance of this symbiotic relationship.

Consider liberty without order. Absent order, liberty is an unbridled license allowing men to do as they choose. Liberty without order is unstable, and arguably illegitimate. In such a world, the weak must submit to the will of the strong. One man's expression of his desires deprives another of his freedom. True, legitimate liberty is achievable only in an ordered society, in which rules and laws govern and limit the behavior of men.

Just as liberty without order is illegitimate and unstable, so too is order without liberty. A society of order without liberty is plausible only by exerting force to compel obedience, thereby creating the mirage of stability. In any ostensible order maintained by brute force, the ruler has no greater claim to the use of force than the ruled. The two are in constant conflict—one seeking to maintain the mirage of stability created by the use of force, the other striving to achieve his freedom by the use of force. Order and liberty are, therefore, not competing concepts that need to be offset to maintain some sort of democratic equilibrium. Rather, they are complementary values symbiotically contributing to the stability and legitimacy of a constitutional democracy.

THE AGE OF TERROR

On September 11, 2001, Osama bin Laden attacked those values, and thousands died tragically. al-Qaeda aimed not only at our physical structures, but at the very foundation of our ordered liberty.

On that one day, a handful of individuals, having spent only several hundred thousand dollars, inflicted greater damage on America and its citizens than most modern armies would be capable of doing by striking directly at our nation's order and freedom. On that day it became clear that warfare is no longer the exclusive domain of nation-states.

That some wish to inflict such damage on the United States and its people is neither new nor surprising. What is surprising is that they identified the means of doing so—that they were able to do that which no enemy nation had ever been able to do in the history of the United States.

There were signposts leading to the 9/11 attacks. For many years, individual terrorists and terrorist organizations sought to execute state-like force. It was not a watershed moment on 9/11 when a breach of the monopoly on force of nation-states occurred. Rather, it merely marked a shift—though in a most dramatic way. On that day, twentieth-century warfare was amplified by a modality of destruction that shocked mankind. Old-style battles, characterized by conflict among nation-states, yielded to the chaotic modernity of the twenty-first century. The 9/11 barbarism dramatically marked the beginning of an era that threatens to replace governed order with pervasive disorder.

Because terrorists owe no allegiance to any particular place or polity, and willingly sacrifice human life, including their own, in an effort to impose their rigid theocratic agenda, the threat to national and global security is posed to freedom—the freedom respecting all nation-states collectively. In this new era, the threat to security no longer emanates only from hostile nation-states, but is one rooted in ideology and independent of geography. This global terrorist movement, and its ability to inflict mass destruction, poses a pervasive and asymmetric threat to order on an international level. The threat is pervasive because the movement is a loose network united by shared objectives and ideals; it is asymmetric because the new breed of warriors exploit the vulnerabilities of open, freedom-focused liberal democracies, inflicting terror on easily accessible targets—the masses of humanity.

Modern terrorists engender fear by undermining the stability of consequence. Acting without the bonds of a geographic base or the restraint of a national polity, the enemy is faceless and, in this way, impregnable. That nation-states no longer have a monopoly on the motives and means of war, the lesson at the core of 9/11, has ominous implications for law, policy, and international relations.

Terrorism, whoever its perpetrator and whatever the goal, poses a fundamental threat to the ordered liberty that our constitutional democracy is designed to protect. The terrorist seeks not only to kill, but also to terrorize. Increasing the body count is designed to instill fear in those who survive. The terrorist is unlimited in the choice of victims and indifferent as to the traditional "combat" value of the targets. Part of an international conspiracy of evil, terrorists operate across boundaries. They capitalize on borders as barriers to enforcement and prevention. They use violence to disrupt order, kill to foment fear, and terrorize to paralyze normal human activity. By definition the methods and objectives of terror attack the foundations of ordered liberty.

In this sense, the terrorist is fundamentally different from the criminal offender normally encountered by our criminal justice system. By attacking the foundation of societal order, the terrorist seeks to demolish the structure of liberty that governs our lives. By fomenting mass terror, the terrorist seeks to incapacitate the citizenry from exercising the liberty to pursue our individual and collective ends. This is not mere criminality. It is an act of war against our polity.

In waging that war, the terrorist employs means that fundamentally differ from those used by traditional enemies encountered on battlefields governed by the established rules of war among nations. Those rules clearly distinguish uniformed combatants on the battlefield from innocent civilians who are off-target. This distinction is advantageously exploited by the terrorist. In this war, the international terrorist against whom we fight differs even from guerilla warriors of the past who mingled among civilians and on occasion targeted innocent civilians.

Countering the threat to liberty, our traditional and essential responses have been through the valiant efforts of our men and women on foreign battlefields and the constant vigilance of our men and women of law enforcement on the streets of America. Both professional soldiers and law enforcers have been aided and supported most valuably by alert citizens. However, given the unorthodox nature of the new threat, the traditional approach of the past—to allow situations to develop until the last possible moment so that traditional criminal charges could be brought—became untenable. The dire consequences of fully executed terrorist plots became too catastrophic to adopt any policy other than aggressive prevention.

After 9/11 and faced with a new kind of threat, the Department of Justice refocused its investigative and prosecutorial resources toward one overriding and overarching objective: to prevent terrorist attacks before they happen. This massive effort was undertaken to defend the foundations of our ordered liberty—to deliver freedom from fear by protecting freedom through law.

Proper adaptation to this reprioritization required that law enforcement be furnished with new tools. Before 9/11, the terrorists had a technological advantage: our own law enforcement personnel did not have the tools and technology to compete with terrorist intelligence. Immediately following the terrorist attacks, the Justice Department worked tirelessly to prepare a legislative proposal containing the tools investigators and prosecutors needed in the war against terror.

Following a month of deliberation and consideration, the USA Patriot Act passed with overwhelming bipartisan support.[2] The House of Representatives voted 357 to 66, and the near-unanimous vote of the Senate was 98 to 1. Signed into law by former President George W. Bush on October 26, 2001, the Patriot Act contained more than one thousand anti-terrorism measures that have helped law enforcement investigate, prosecute, and most importantly, prevent acts of terror.

In the years leading up to 9/11, a system designed to separate law enforcement functions from intelligence and national security functions hampered America's law enforcement efforts. The premise that law enforcement powers should be separated from intelligence gathering formed the basis for this system. Fear that evidence gathered during intelligence operations could taint evidence gathered for the purposes of criminal prosecution led to the serious restriction of communication between law enforcement and intelligence gatherers. Constitutional safeguards for criminal prosecutions—often irrelevant to the process of gathering national security intelligence—were interpreted as a deterrent to the detection and diffusion of terrorist plots. In 1995, the Justice Department issued a memorandum titled "Instructions on

Separation of Certain Foreign Counterintelligence and Criminal Investigations," which both reinforced and enhanced this practical and philosophical wall, chilling communications between prosecutors and intelligence officials. As a result, different agencies such as the CIA and the FBI could not communicate freely, and the FBI's intelligence division was prohibited from sharing certain kinds of information with its own criminal division.

Although well intentioned, the "wall" was a cause for concern, even before 9/11.[3] The Patriot Act dramatically reduced the devastating effects of seriously curtailed communications between intelligence and law enforcement officials. The act sought to ensure that information could be shared and the dots connected. At the same time, the Patriot Act maintained the appropriate respect for constitutional requirements in criminal prosecutions.

The information sharing authorized by the Patriot Act put the good guys on an equal footing with the bad guys, who for too long had been able to evade law enforcement. While it now seems incomprehensible that we ever countenanced a communication prohibition between law enforcement and intelligence operatives—a prohibition that endangered the lives and liberties of our citizens—it existed across administrations through much of the last quarter of the twentieth century. It frustrated those to whom we entrust our safety and our freedom.

Section 218 of the Patriot Act amended the Foreign Intelligence Surveillance Act (FISA) to facilitate increased cooperation between agents gathering intelligence about foreign threats and investigators prosecuting foreign terrorists. The provision reconfigured the requirement that intelligence be the "primary purpose" of an investigation with a "significant purpose" test.[4] Because of this change, intelligence and law enforcement authorities can now share information without fear that such coordination will jeopardize the legal validity of the investigation and attendant orders.

The Patriot Act actually created a protection that the FISA statute in its original form did not afford. Passed in 1978, section 1804(a)(7)(B) of the FISA statute required "that the purpose of the surveillance" be "to obtain foreign intelligence information." However, at some point both the Justice Department and the courts read into this provision the "primary purpose" test, despite no evidence, and indeed despite substantial legislative history to the contrary, that Congress had intended such a test. The result was to limit surveillance under the FISA to only those situations where foreign intelligence surveillance was the government's primary purpose. This "primary purpose" test became the norm in interpreting the statute, and even prevailed in FISA decisions after the passage of the Patriot Act's amendment providing for the "significant purpose" test.

In 2002, the U.S. Foreign Intelligence Surveillance Court ("FISA Court") authorized certain surveillance requested by the Justice Department but imposed severe restrictions on the surveillance, intended to comply with the previously prevailing "primary purpose" test. The restrictions included prohibiting law enforcement officials from making certain recommendations to intelligence officials or from directing or controlling the use of FISA procedures.

This perpetuation of the "wall" by the FISA Court, despite Congress's clear action less than a year before in the Patriot Act, forced the Justice Department to bring the first ever appeal of a FISA Court decision. In that appeal the FISA Court of Review reversed the lower FISA Court's orders to the extent they imposed restrictions on the conduct of the surveillance, and ordered the FISA Court to grant the applications as submitted.[5] In so doing, the Court of Review found that the "primary purpose" test had been a "false dichotomy," never actually required by the congressional mandate in the original 1978 FISA statute.[6] As a result, the Patriot Act's language requiring "a significant purpose" in fact established a higher standard that afforded greater protection from potential improper government utilization of FISA orders. Ironically, a complete repeal of the Patriot Act would likely result in a reduction of the safeguards against overreaching use of the FISA authority.

The Patriot Act's clarification of the FISA's capacity to thwart terrorist activity equipped prosecutors with the tools necessary to take convicted terrorists off the streets. Due to the harsher penalties for terrorism provided in the Patriot Act, terrorists can now be detained for significantly longer periods.

Terrorists require funding to complete their attacks. Title III of the Patriot Act helped stem this flow of money. Title VIII of the act improved cyberterrorism laws, and filled gaps in criminal law by creating a new crime of attacking a mass transportation system.

Terrorist activities often span several federal districts, and so too must the investigations of these activities. In these investigations the ability to act swiftly is imperative, because the opportunity to prevent an attack can be fleeting. With the mandate for prevention (rather than reliance on post-disaster prosecution), it was no longer feasible to lose time petitioning several judges in multiple districts for search warrants related to a single investigation. To address this problem, section 220 of the Patriot Act authorized out-of-district warrants in certain terrorism cases.[7] This tool ensured the Justice Department's success in disrupting and prosecuting the Northern Virginia Jihad operation.

The Patriot Act also allowed law enforcement to conduct investigations without tipping off terrorists. Informing a terrorist of an investigation prematurely allows the terrorist the opportunity to flee, destroy evidence, intimidate or kill witnesses, cease contact with associates, or take other evasive measures. For decades, federal courts in other law enforcement settings have allowed law enforcement to delay notifying the subject of an investigation that a search has been executed. This same authority to delay notification in terrorist cases, supervised by federal judges, gives law enforcement the ability to identify the conspiring terrorists' associates, coordinate the arrest of multiple subjects without tipping them off, and diffuse threats to our communities.

Finally, the Patriot Act harmonized law with current technology. For decades, law enforcement officials had used multi-point wiretaps to track drug traffickers and mobsters. The Patriot Act allowed federal agents to use this same technology to track terrorists. Instead of requiring law enforcement officers to apply for separate warrants for every phone, fax, and communication device used by a single terrorist, warrants can now authorize the terrorist himself as the subject of the surveillance. As a result the surveillance order can apply to all communication devices he uses. This capacity makes it much harder for terrorists to evade detection by switching from device to device.

REAUTHORIZATION

During the debate over various provisions of the Patriot Act, the drafters struggled with important constitutional questions. For example, in forming the "significant purpose" test of section 218, the drafters considered whether the change comported with the Fourth Amendment's protection against unreasonable search and seizure (it does), and whether there is adequate process for criminal defendants to seek to exclude intelligence evidence from non-terrorism trials (there is). Ultimately, the drafters were confident of the answers and of the constitutionality of the resultant legislation.

Nonetheless, the safeguards of the Patriot Act are vulnerable to abuse by zealous enforcers, just as the provisions of the act can be violated by those whose aim is the destruction of American freedom. Each type of violation requires redress. It must be recognized, however, that there is a distinct difference between a violation of a law and a law that itself offends liberty. For example, an individual might offend or violate the Constitution, but that violation would not render the Constitution infirm. Consequently, the potential that a law may be violated should not render the authority expressed in the law infirm or invalid. In the course of domestic law enforcement duties, a police officer may misuse a commonly accepted power, such as his power to arrest and detain; but this does not mean that the power of a police officer to arrest and detain is either unconstitutional or unwise. It merely means that the individual police officer has abused that power and that the abuse of the power should be remedied. Similarly, if an individual improperly or illegally misuses the Patriot Act provisions, it does not follow that the provision itself is improper.

A Justice Department audit in March 2007 found that the FBI had "improperly and, in some cases, illegally used the Patriot Act to secretly obtain personal information"[8] about United States citizens. This does not mean the Patriot Act itself is improper. This understanding is imperative to provide for a constructive discussion of the issues surrounding various provisions of the act, their ongoing necessity, and the need to monitor how the provisions are applied in specific cases.

One of the many safeguards of the Patriot Act was the inclusion of a "sunset" clause for certain provisions—meaning the provisions would expire on a date certain unless Congress acted affirmatively to reauthorize them. In 2005, Congress had the opportunity to discuss the effectiveness and appropriateness of many of the act's provisions in determining whether to reauthorize the sunsetting provisions. Congress found the tools provided by the Patriot Act to be invaluable and enacted two bills to continue their effect.

The USA Patriot and Terrorism Prevention Reauthorization Act of 2005 reauthorized all but two of the provisions of Title II that would have expired. Many provisions, including section 218, were made permanent. Although the reauthorization was largely without amendment, Congress did take the opportunity to include a small number of amendments before voting to reauthorize. Although section 215—the National Security Letter provision, which allowed national security investigators access to business records in certain circumstances—already contained significant checks to prevent abuse, Congress added to it a judicial review process for recipients to appeal the request for information.[9] Additionally, Congress adopted a sunset date of December 31, 2009 for three particular provisions, including the National Security Letter provision. In 2010, President Obama signed a one-year extension of these three sections.[10] As a consequence of these sunsetting provisions, the Patriot Act has been continuously refined. Congress's reauthorization stated clearly that the purpose and implication of each provision is in furtherance of, and in keeping with, our ultimate goal of securing liberty.

CONCLUSION

Securing liberty is a constantly evolving battle of the utmost importance to the United States. The Patriot Act has provided essential, valuable tools that have enabled law enforcement, intelligence, and Homeland Security personnel to cooperate in the prevention of terrorist attacks since 9/11. Its transformation of the traditional agencies from segmented, independent actors into a dynamic, cohesive network has provided a means of protection against the threats of today while anticipating threats in the future. The reauthorization and support of the Patriot Act is a firm testament to the effectiveness and continued need for these tools as we continue our battle in the ongoing war on terror.

protection of our national security—revisited

MICHAEL B. MUKASEY

INTRODUCTION

When I spoke at the Federalist Society convention in Washington, D.C., on November 13, 2009, I intended simply to review where we stood in the war on terror, but events overtook me. The speech coincided with the announcement by Attorney General Eric Holder that instead of being tried before a military commission at Guantánamo Bay, Khalid Sheikh Mohammed (KSM) and others said to have been responsible for planning and executing the September 11, 2001 attacks would be brought to the United States and tried before a civilian court—in the Southern District of New York. That took some of the focus off the larger picture, although I did touch on it. Events since have provided no reason to disturb the observations I made that day, about both the KSM trial and other matters, and supplied several reasons to confirm them. An edited version of the speech is included in this chapter, after this introduction.

Tactically, news from the war is certainly not all bad. Increased drone attacks in and around Pakistan continue to take a toll on al-Qaeda and Taliban organizers and fighters, and keep them on the defensive. Strategically, however, the Obama administration has intentionally failed to consider the nature of the adversary that we confront. Our enemy is motivated by a religious ideology that offers to infidels three choices: conversion, dhimmitude, or death. Americans live in a culture in which we hesitate to ask questions about a person's religion, and we consider religion to be only one among many aspects of life. For those who embrace Islamist ideology, there is no other aspect.

We are facing a militant ideology that is not based in any particular country or location, but motivates a network of individuals around the world to translate their religious beliefs into concrete, violent action. The only way we can prevail is to stay one jump ahead, and the only way to do this is through intelligence gathering, both electronic and (when we can get it) human. I would not downplay the importance of human intelligence, as some have done. Even the drone strikes depend on human intelligence to provide at least the general location of the target, and often to verify that the proper target in fact was hit. General Michael Hayden, former director of the CIA, has compared failure to use intelligence to trying to solve a giant jigsaw puzzle without being able to look at the picture on the box.[1] Occasionally, we get hold of a person who can describe the picture on the box, and that sort of intelligence is highly valuable. Unfortunately, we now have a program for questioning potentially valuable detainees that is limited to the Army Field Manual on interrogation, which is available on the Web and already used as a training manual by terrorists. We use tactics that increasingly rely on killing rather than capture, and on dealing with those we do capture as criminal defendants rather than as intelligence sources. Consequently, we will find our ability to gather human intelligence limited unless we resort to what is called extraordinary rendition, which involves turning people over to foreign governments that are less restrained in their interrogation techniques. That, potentially, involves inhumane treatment and takes us out of control.

The week before my 2009 address, Captain Nidal Malik Hasan, who had been in touch with Anwar al-Aulaqi (spiritual advisor to at least two of the 9/11 plotters) shouted "*allahu akhbar*" before shooting to death thirteen fellow soldiers and wounding about thirty others at Fort Hood, Texas. The response was indicative of the official view of Islamist terrorism then and now. President Obama told the nation not to jump to conclusions as to what may have motivated the attack, and the official Pentagon review of the tragedy nowhere referred to Islam or its teachings.

On Christmas Day of 2009, Umar Farouk Abdulmutallab was arrested after trying to detonate a bomb in an airplane over Detroit. Rather than being considered an intelligence asset, he was treated as a criminal defendant. Similar treatment was accorded Faisal Shahzad, who was charged with planting a bomb in a vehicle in New York's Times Square. Had it gone off, it would have killed and maimed hundreds, if not thousands, of people.

The government conceded that Abdulmutallab should have been questioned by the high-value interrogation team that was supposed to replace the CIA interrogation program; President

Obama abolished the latter upon taking office because he thought it coercive. But it turned out that that team had not yet been constituted. However lax the administration was about replacing the CIA interrogation program it had abolished, it acted with alacrity in carrying out the Attorney General's decision to investigate a half dozen CIA agents who had conducted questioning under that program. Those agents had previously been cleared and detailed written memoranda describing why no prosecution was warranted, but the Attorney General reopened the investigations without reading the memoranda. Those investigations, unlike the high-value interrogation unit, were already up and running by Christmas 2009, a fact which speaks loudly as to the Justice Department's priorities.

Lost in the Abdulmutallab episode was the opportunity to investigate in a timely fashion the source of the bomb he carried. The cost of that lapse became apparent months later, when bombs of the same type began to show up in packages that originated in Yemen.

The administration's plan to try KSM and others for the 9/11 attacks in civilian court was supposed to receive a boost from first trying Ahmed Ghailani for the 1998 East Africa U.S. embassy bombings in the same forum. Initially, Ghailani was to be tried before a military commission in Guantánamo, but that proceeding was aborted and he was brought to the United States to stand trial on an indictment that had been filed years before—and on which two other defendants had already been convicted. Notwithstanding the important differences between Ghailani's case and KSM's (the evidence against Ghailani had been gathered specifically for presentation in a court, with all governing protocols observed, while at least some of the evidence against KSM was not admissible in a civilian court), the Ghailani trial was supposed to show the feasibility of trying a Guantánamo detainee in a civilian court, and thereby dissipate the pressure and criticism behind the planned KSM prosecution into a ditch. The Ghailani trial failed to do that. The trial judge excluded a significant government witness, and Ghailani was acquitted of all of the hundreds of murder counts against him. He was convicted only of conspiring to damage government buildings.[2]

Notwithstanding the dozens of Islamist plots uncovered in the United States since 9/11, the criminal law paradigm is again limiting the U.S. response. Abd al-Rahim al-Nashiri, the alleged mastermind of the USS *Cole* bombing, was supposed to be tried before a military commission at Guantánamo last summer. Instead, on a summer Friday afternoon, the Justice Department filed a brief in another case disclosing that there are no charges pending against al-Nashiri, which is to say the military commission proceedings against him have been halted.

Although the White House promised to disclose the forum in which KSM and other 9/11 plotters would be tried, after their initial choice of New York was hooted down, subsequent announcements remained inconsistent for a time. Faced with legislation that barred the use of federal funds to try Guantánamo detainees in the United States, Attorney General Holder announced reluctantly on April 4, 2011 that KSM and others would be tried by military commission after all. However, in July 2011, he disclosed that a Somali suspect, Ahmed Abdulkadir Warsame, who had been captured abroad and held on naval vessels rather than at Guantánamo, would be brought to the United States and tried in a civilian court. Notably, Warsame, unlike Shahzad and Abdulmutallab, was reportedly debriefed extensively following his capture by the high-value interrogation team promised at the time the CIA interrogation program was abandoned in 2008. The interrogation techniques, however, are still limited by the Army Field Manual. Moreover, military officials have conceded candidly that we have no detention program; we simply improvise from one capture to the next.

It is true that Guantánamo remains open, but it is also true that President Obama remains as committed as ever to closing it. He seems determined to figure out a way to release those detained there despite a growing body of evidence that alumni of Guantánamo have returned to terrorism. A recent example is an interview with Sheikh Abu Sufyan al-Azdi, deputy commander of al-Qaeda in the Arabian Peninsula, a group based in Yemen, published in the October 2010 issue of that organization's English language magazine. Abu Sufyan was released from Guantánamo and turned over to the Saudis for participation in their vaunted re-education program, but made his way to Yemen to resume his jihadi activities. In the interview, he urges Muslims to emulate Nidal Hasan, the Fort Hood shooter, and Abdulmutallab, the airplane bomber.

Abu Sufyan is by no means the first alumnus of Guantánamo to return to the battlefield. In March 2010, the supreme leader of the Afghan Taliban announced that he was promoting mullah Abdul Qayyum Zakir to replace a top deputy captured by U.S. forces; Zakir had also been in detention at Guantánamo, and was released to the Afghanis.[3] In fact, more than 20 percent of those released from Guantánamo have returned to the battlefield, and of course those are only the ones we know about because they have been recaptured or killed. How many others remain in the fight is anyone's guess.

It has become increasingly obvious since 2009 that the administration is resolutely opposed to looking at militant Islamism squarely, whether in its terrorist manifestation or otherwise. For example, in 2010 at the Center for Strategic and International Studies, deputy national security advisor John Brennan said that this talk of a war on terrorism or on terror is highly misleading because terrorism is simply a tactic and terror is a state of mind. Brennan cautioned against describing our enemies as jihadists because jihad, as he put it, "is a holy struggle, a legitimate tenet of Islam."[4] And then, just so no one missed the point, he said that jihad actually means something innocuous. It means simply, as he put it, "to purify oneself or one's community."[5] Brennan, by the way, believes that the 20 percent-plus recidivism rate for those released from Guantánamo is not bad because it compares favorably with the rate of U.S. prisons,[6] where we have considerably less trouble determining who has returned to a life of crime than we do with Guantánamo alumni.

Our current Deputy Attorney General, appointed while Congress was in recess so as to avoid the need for Senate confirmation, is James Cole. Cole criticized Attorney General Ashcroft in 2002 for, among other things, helping to create military tribunals and using the classification "enemy combatant." Of course, the laws of war have recognized the enemy combatant status for many years. It was used to classify the German saboteurs who landed in 1942 off Long Island and Florida and were tried before military tribunals.[7] In 2002, Cole wrote:

> Attorney General [Ashcroft] is not a member of the military fighting a war—he is a prosecutor fighting crime. For all the rhetoric about war, the September 11 attacks were criminal acts of terrorism against a civilian population, much like the terrorist acts of Timothy McVeigh in blowing up the federal building in Oklahoma City, or of Omar Abdel Rahman in the first effort to blow up the World Trade Center. The criminals responsible for these horrible acts were successfully tried and convicted under our criminal justice system, without the need for special procedures that altered traditional due process rights.[8]

Warming to his subject, he added: "Our country has faced many forms of devastating crime, including the scourge of the drug trade, the reign of organized crime, and countless acts of rape, child abuse, and murder. The acts of September 11 were horrible, but so are these other things." This is the new chief operating officer of the U.S. Department of Justice.

Meanwhile, in New York, there is a project afoot led by a Muslim cleric of questionable background to build a mosque close to where the World Trade Center stood. Both President Obama and Mayor Bloomberg appear to have endorsed the project, to the consternation of approximately 70 percent of the country and the overwhelming majority of those who lost loved ones in New York on September 11, 2001.

Small miracles saved us from disaster in Detroit and again in New York in the last two years. In view of our leadership, it appears that we will have to rely on more such miracles, which is a poor substitute for a strategy.

SPEECH DELIVERED AT THE FEDERALIST SOCIETY LAWYERS CONVENTION IN WASHINGTON, D.C., ON NOVEMBER 13, 2009

When I addressed this group last year, I had concluded my speech by expressing the hope that what was then the administration in formation would take a good look at what the outgoing administration had done in good faith to keep this country safe, would conclude that those measures were both lawful and effective, and would, by and large, keep in place the programs and the policies that had succeeded in protecting the security of this country for the eight years since 9/11. What I wish to do this afternoon is briefly to examine a few programs, policies, and issues that have been in place since the Obama administration took office to see to what extent that last hope that I expressed was realized and to what extent it was not. I will start with the positive—the instances in which my wishes were fulfilled—and then proceed to the instances in which they were not. I had prepared my speech before the announcement this morning—that the Obama administration intends to bring to this country several detainees, including Khalid Sheikh Mohammed and Ramzi bin al-Shibh, the architect and principal operative, respectively, in carrying out the September 11, 2001 attacks on this country, and to try them in a civilian court—in fact, the court in which I used to sit, the U.S. District Court for the Southern District of New York—and to bring another group headed by a man named Nashiri, as well, and to try them in a military commission stateside at a place that is yet undisclosed.

I still plan to follow, to a certain extent, the format that I had intended to follow and to start with some positive news. But obviously, I want to deal to some extent with the decision to bring these detainees to the United States. This is a decision that I consider to be not only unwise, but based on a refusal by this administration to face the fact that we are involved in a war with people who follow a religiously based ideology that calls on them to kill us. Yet, the administration wants to return instead to the mindset that prevailed before September 11, 2001, that acts such as the first World Trade Center bombing and the bombing of our embassies in East Africa can and should be treated as conventional crimes and tried in conventional courts.

But first: the good news that I promised you. The first category has to do with intelligence gathering. Although there was actually an incipient move in Congress to repeal the authorities that were put in place under the Foreign Intelligence Surveillance Act, and amendments were passed in 2008, much of the intelligence-gathering authorities have remained in place. To what extent they are being used, and how, is something I obviously cannot speak to now because I am not privy to that; even if I were, considerations of security would not permit that to be discussed in a forum like this. However, I can tell you, based on a report from somebody who was there, that at a meeting during which representatives of the Department of Homeland Security were presenting to foreign security officials the current procedure for tracing money transfers through what is known as the SWIFT system, the foreign officials responded that the procedure was the same as the one that had been in place under the prior administration. The U.S. Homeland Security official who was present agreed and pointed out that this was continuity that you can believe in. Now, that is actually reassuring for two reasons. The first, of course, is continuity, and the second is that there is somebody at Homeland Security who has a sense of humor.

The same appears to be true, at least for the moment, as to procedures that we at the Department of Justice put in place to allow the FBI intelligence gathering to continue and to be subsumed into its already existing crime-solving functions. We put those procedures into effect in December 2008, after more than a year of consideration and review. Despite pressures to roll back those procedures, they have been left in place, at least for the moment, and the department has indicated that it intends to allow them to work for a reasonable time before making any changes; all in all, an encouraging, if not surprising, conclusion.

Finally, the administration has said that it will continue to recognize the state secrets privilege when litigation threatens to disclose national security information and to bring such litigation to an end even when the government is not a party to it. The current administration professes to have a somewhat narrower view of that privilege than we did under the prior administration, but it is in place nonetheless.

The record is less encouraging when it comes to the detention and apprehension of prisoners on the battlefield; or the gathering of intelligence from those who may be in possession of it; or prosecuting those who can be charged with war crimes; and detaining others who cannot be but who nonetheless should be detained as unlawful combatants because, for example, they were captured while engaged in combat with the United States and allied troops, or while targeting civilians, or while engaged in other unlawful activities, and were obviously too dangerous to be released.

That change of attitude seems to have followed sweeping proclamations announced in January 2009 that suggested, at least implicitly, that the prior administration had sanctioned torture and had been bent on holding detainees at Guantánamo without proper treatment or access to legal proceedings. The administration ordered us to abandon harsh interrogation techniques, which were loosely characterized as torture, and to close the detention facility at Guantánamo within a year. What has followed seems, in many instances, to be a system in which policy is fashioned to fit antecedent rhetoric rather than being thought out in advance, with arguments then formulated in support of it.

With respect to interrogations carried on in the past, because of the implicit suggestion that the prior administration had sanctioned torture, the Department of Justice declassified memoranda that described the limits to which trained CIA personnel could engage in coercive questioning, along with the legal reasoning underlying how those limits are set. The result is that our enemies are now aware of precisely the legal and factual limits of how they can be treated if captured, and to train accordingly. Before now, our enemies were training to the Army Field Manual, which described less coercive techniques that can be used by soldiers in the field and was generally available on the Internet.

When he was a candidate, Obama was quoted as saying that it would be absurd to contemplate giving Miranda warnings to those captured on the battlefield. Since then, the armed forces have been directed to provide such warnings to those captured on the battlefield in Afghanistan.

In addition, this administration has reopened previously dropped cases that involved claims that CIA personnel acted unlawfully in the course of interrogating prisoners, but were found insufficient to justify prosecution. Before decisions to drop a case are made, career prosecutors in the Justice Department investigate all facts alleged, interview subjects of the investigations, and then summarize the reasons for not prosecuting a case in prosecutive memoranda. Now, the Attorney General has directed a second investigation of the subjects, even though there is no claim that new facts have been discovered or developed, and even though, judging from all reports, the Attorney General who ordered the second review did not himself read the prosecutive memoranda.

And there is this morning's disclosure that the government intends to try several defendants charged with planning and participating in the September 11, 2001 attack—including the self-proclaimed mastermind of that attack, Khalid Sheikh Mohammed, as well as a principal organizer of the operation, Ramzi bin al-Shibh—in the U.S. District Court of New York. In addition, as I mentioned, another detainee named Nashiri and potentially three or four others associated with him are to be brought here and tried in military courts.

President Bush attempted by executive order to authorize military commissions to try these and other terrorists, and the Supreme Court said he could not do so absent congressional authorization. So Congress passed the Military Commissions Act to provide authorization. Thus, the military commissions are fully authorized by law and indeed the trials were to have already begun. You may recall that Khalid Sheikh Mohammed and others attempted to plead guilty and to achieve their martyr's reward during one of their appearances before the military tribunal that was supposed to have begun to try them. But now, that procedure is to be short-circuited (actually, long-circuited would be more accurate) so that they could be brought to this country and tried in a civilian court.

We should all be aware that those cases were scheduled already to have begun. So they will now have to start from scratch with the filing of indictments, the customary motions addressed to them, and the like. Whether Khalid Sheikh Mohammed will duplicate the demand here that he be permitted to plead guilty to what he did—about which he has already boasted on several occasions on Al Jazeera and in a letter to his wife—I do not know. But if not, he can avail himself of the full array of procedural steps, including discovery and public presentation of evidence, that can turn a criminal proceeding into both a cornucopia of information for those still at large and a circus for those in custody.

The tribunal and the facility at Guantánamo were put together for the explicit purpose of handling trials involving classified information and the presentation of evidence of that kind in controlled circumstances using special rules of evidence. Those special rules have as the touchstone for admissibility whether the evidence is reliable and relevant, and not whether it conforms to all of the requirements of the Federal Rules of Evidence.

You should recall that, unlike the case of a man named Ahmed Ghailani, who was recently brought here from Guantánamo to stand trial on the embassy bombings case, the cases against the defendants whose arrival here was announced today were not investigated—nor was evidence gathered—on the assumption that they would be presented in a federal court with evidence and witnesses secured in conformity with the rules of federal court. This is only a hint of the difficulties presented by this step, and does not even touch on the security issues that would be raised by trying to confine and try prisoners who present risks of the sort presented by prisoners like this, including security for the courthouses and jails involved, security for the judge and jurors involved, and the like.

This step appears to have resulted simply from a commitment to close Guantánamo within a year because, regardless of the reality on the ground, it has a poor image and apparently a desire to exceed what the law requires in order to show the world that we can do not only what the law requires, but more. That a military trial at Guantánamo, a facility that I have visited and one that is actually less harsh than most medium-security facilities in this country (forget maximum-security facilities), might actually be seen by the American public and the rest of the world as both fair and successful appears not to have occurred to anyone in authority.

If I thought that I or my family or my fellow citizens had three lives to live, I suppose I could be persuaded that we should live one of them as a social experiment to see whether the result here is one that we'd want to live with. But I don't, and they don't, and you don't. It would take a whole lot more credulousness than I have available to be optimistic about the outcome of this latest experiment.

access to justice in the "war on terror"

ANTHONY D. ROMERO

I n the decade following the attacks of September 11, 2001, the Bush administration, followed by the Obama administration, and often with the cooperation of Congress and the courts, have restricted access to justice for victims of civil liberties and human rights violations and have limited the availability of effective remedies for these violations. These efforts have denied victims of human rights violations their day in court and shielded responsible officials and corporations from liability.

A strong judiciary is fundamental to the protection of our liberties. It stands as a crucial arbiter among and between the desires of powerful institutions in and out of government, the rights of individuals and groups, and the politics and prejudices of the moment. Over the past ten years, on matters of civil liberties and national security, power has shifted away from the judiciary toward the executive branch, which has tended to prioritize politics and power over liberty and justice.

Access to justice is an absolute precondition to justice. Attempts to limit access are serious attacks not only on individual liberties, but on the judiciary itself. Diminished access to justice means diminished confidence in justice, which emboldens the other branches of government to seize greater power. For eight years, the Bush administration sought to diminish access to justice in order to shift power to itself. It frequently invoked national security concerns and the discredited unitary executive theory as reasons why the courts' reach should not extend to the Oval Office or to other, undisclosed locations.

In the course of seizing greater power for itself, the executive branch has often sought—and received—the cooperation of Congress to emasculate the judiciary. Perhaps most surprisingly, federal courts have largely been willing accomplices in limiting their own power. A series of decisions in recent years has chipped away at access and placed a tremendous and often insurmountable burden on plaintiffs. Consequently, entire classes of people are not only denied access to justice, but may not even be aware of the injustices to which they are subject.

On January 22, 2009—his second full day in office—President Obama signed a series of executive orders that prohibited torture and limited all interrogations to techniques authorized by the Army Field Manual; outlawed the CIA's practice of secret detention and shut down the CIA's overseas secret prisons; and mandated the closure of the Guantánamo Bay prison complex within one year. These were important steps to restoring America's commitment to justice and the rule of law.

Since that day, however, the Obama administration's record on access to justice in matters involving national security has been mixed, at best. Consistent with our nation's history that the executive branch—regardless of the party in control—tends to seize opportunities to expand its own power, President Obama has largely taken the baton from President Bush on a range of issues including military commissions, detention, state secrets, surveillance, and targeted killings.

MILITARY COMMISSIONS

In November 2001, President Bush created a legal black hole when he established a military commission system to prosecute individuals, whom he deemed to be "enemy combatants," detained at Guantánamo Bay. This creation of a separate system of detention and trial for terrorism suspects was an audacious assertion of executive power that severely diminished access to justice for hundreds of men.

Military commissions are nothing like the federal criminal trials governed by our Constitution or the long-established courts martial of the Uniform Code of Military Justice. The Bush administration scrapped both time-tested systems of justice and made its own rules. It ignored the tenets of due process and set up an unjust system to convict detainees based on secret evidence, hearsay evidence, and confessions extracted by torture.

In June 2006, the Supreme Court held in *Hamdi v. Rumsfeld* that the military commission system established by the Bush administration was unconstitutional.[1] Just a few months later, Congress approved and President Bush signed the Military

Commissions Act, which revived the commissions and incorporated many of their most egregious flaws into federal law.[2] The act undercut the role of the courts and stripped individual detainees of important legal avenues to challenge their imprisonment.

While campaigning for the presidency, then-Senator Obama made cogent arguments against military commissions on both principled and pragmatic grounds. His subsequent embrace of commissions has been a major disappointment. Instead of calling a permanent halt to the fatally flawed system, the Obama administration encouraged an effort to redraft the Military Commissions Act and signed that bill into law. The reformed Act contains some improvements, but still the danger that defendants might be convicted and sentenced to death on the basis of hearsay evidence obtained coercively from other detainees who will not be available for cross-examination.

Fundamentally, a second-class system of justice undermines the prosecution of terrorism suspects. Civilian courts are well-equipped to handle even the most complicated and sensitive terrorism cases. There have been hundreds of successful terrorism trials in the federal courts, before and after 9/11. So long as the government can choose between two systems of justice, one fairer than the other, both systems will be tainted. The government likely will use the federal courts only when conviction seems virtually assured, and resort to military commissions for cases with weaker evidence or where there are credible allegations that the defendants were abused while in U.S. custody.

DETENTION

Over the last decade, there has been a serious erosion in the ability of individuals detained by the U.S. government on suspicion of terrorist activity to use the writ of habeas corpus—the legal instrument by which an individual can challenge the lawfulness of his or her imprisonment. There also has been a dangerous increase in military detentions without charge or trial of terrorism suspects captured far from any battlefield.

In the years following 9/11, the Bush administration sought to deny detainees access to justice by imprisoning them overseas at Guantánamo Bay; Bagram, Afghanistan; and secret "black sites" around the world. Not until the *Hamdan* ruling did President Bush finally acknowledge the existence of the secret, CIA-run prisons. The Military Commissions Act then eliminated the right of habeas corpus for detainees at Guantánamo and elsewhere.

A series of Supreme Court decisions rebuked the Bush administration's expansive detention power. In 2004, the Court held in *Hamdi v. Rumsfeld* that the executive branch could not indefinitely detain a U.S. citizen designated as an "enemy combatant" without access to basic due process protections and judicial review.[3] The Court also ruled in *Rasul v. Bush* that non-citizens held at Guantánamo had the right to challenge their detention in U.S. courts.[4] In 2008, in *Boumediene v. Bush*, the Court held unconstitutional the Military Commissions Act's elimination of Guantánamo detainees right to habeas corpus.

Despite early signs of change, attempts to deny detainees access to justice largely continue under the Obama administration. While campaigning for the presidency, then-Senator Obama rejected "detaining thousands without charge or trial" and promised to close Guantánamo if elected. Shortly after inauguration, President Obama abandoned the Bush administration's dubious legal argument that lawful U.S. resident (and ACLU client) Ali al-Marri could be detained indefinitely. After spending nearly six years in solitary confinement in a naval brig within the continental United States, al-Marri was finally criminally indicted in

February 2009 and transferred to civilian custody. He pled guilty to conspiracy to provide material support to al-Qaeda and was sentenced to eight years.

It was a promising beginning. But years later, over 170 individuals remain imprisoned at Guantánamo. President Obama deserves credit for the release of more than sixty Guantánamo detainees; however, his administration has continued to oppose the release of numerous detainees against whom it has scant evidence of wrongdoing. The administration's decision to halt all detainee releases to Yemen—even when the detainees have been cleared—has been a major factor in the prison's continued existence, because a majority of the remaining detainees are Yemeni.

Of greater significance is the Obama administration's embrace of the theory that the military can detain—without charges or trials—terrorism suspects captured far from a conventional battlefield. In May 2009, President Obama stated that Guantánamo detainees whom the administration deemed dangerous, but who "could not be prosecuted" because of a lack of reliable evidence, would be held indefinitely without trial. The administration subsequently revealed that forty-eight detainees had been designated for indefinite detention.

In December 2010, credible press reports emerged that the Obama administration is considering an executive order that would institutionalize the indefinite detention of those 48 detainees—albeit with periodic administrative review (at the time of this writing, the specifics of the contemplated order have not been made public). Executive branch review is no substitute for criminal charges and trials. An executive order that allows any President to hold suspects captured far from any battlefield without charges or trials is fundamentally un-American. Such a premise violates core American principles such as "innocent until proven guilty" and the right to confront one's accusers and rebut evidence of wrongdoing in court. It threatens to enshrine the theory that America is engaged in a global armed conflict without end, in which the entire world is a battlefield and suspected enemies can be detained—or even killed—based solely on the President's say-so. Any effort to resort to indefinite detention without charge or trial in the terrorism context is sure to be the proverbial "slippery slope" that will expand to other areas, such as organized crime and drug trafficking. The exception would swallow the time-tested rule of guaranteeing access to justice.

Perhaps the most troubling iteration of the Obama administration's sweeping theory of its detention authority occurred in legal proceedings in which it opposed judicial review for detainees at Bagram, Afghanistan. In response to habeas petitions filed by prisoners who had been captured outside of Afghanistan and transferred there by the Bush administration, the Obama administration argued that the courts lacked jurisdiction even to hear the prisoners' challenges because the prison is in a war zone. This was disingenuous bootstrapping: the prisoners were transferred to Afghanistan by the government; the government thereafter used their presence in Afghanistan to avoid judicial scrutiny. The D.C. Circuit Court of Appeals nonetheless sided with the administration.[5] Obama administration officials have reportedly debated using Bagram to imprison—without any access to justice—individuals captured anywhere in the world.

STATE SECRETS

The state secrets privilege, when properly invoked, permits the government to block the release of evidence in a lawsuit that, if disclosed, would cause harm to national security. The Bush administration used the privilege not only to restrict discovery but to quash entire lawsuits without having to demonstrate the validity of its claims to a judge. Lamentably, the Obama administration has continued that abuse of power.

The U.S. government has intervened in cases alleging forced disappearance and torture to assert the state secrets privilege. It has even moved to have these cases dismissed without any consideration of unclassified, publicly available information. Courts have largely accepted the government's assertions. The government's abuse of the privilege has short-circuited judicial scrutiny and has denied victims of torture and secret detention access to justice. Due to the government's overly broad use of the state secrets privilege, not a single victim of the Bush administration's torture program has had his day in an American court to date.

For example, the government invoked the state secrets privilege to squelch an ACLU lawsuit on behalf of German citizen Khaled el-Masri. On December 31, 2003, el-Masri was abducted while on holiday by Macedonian officials and turned over to CIA agents. He was detained and tortured in the notorious "Salt Pit" prison in Afghanistan for nearly five months—long after the CIA realized it was a case of mistaken identity. In May 2004, el-Masri was led out of his cell and flown to Albania, where—without explanation—he was abandoned on a hillside at night. He was never charged with a crime.

In response to the ACLU lawsuit, the CIA claimed that merely holding a judicial hearing would jeopardize state secrets, despite widespread media reports of el-Masri's rendition, many of them based on the accounts of government officials. In 2006, a judge accepted the CIA's claim and dismissed the case; the Fourth Circuit Court of Appeals upheld the dismissal. In what the *New*

York Times called a "Supreme Disgrace," the Supreme Court refused to review the case.

The government invoked the state secrets privilege in another ACLU lawsuit, *Mohamed v. Jeppesen Dataplan, Inc.*, filed in 2007 on behalf of five survivors of the CIA's rendition program. The suit charged that Jeppesen, a subsidiary of Boeing Company, knowingly provided flight planning and support services to aircraft and crews used by the CIA to detain and torture these men.

The Bush administration asked the district court to dismiss the case on state secrets grounds, and in February 2008 the court did so. The ACLU appealed, while the Obama administration defended the dismissal. After a three-judge panel sided with the ACLU in April 2009, the administration asked the full Ninth Circuit to reconsider the decision. In September 2010, an *en banc*, eleven-judge panel reversed the 2009 decision by a 6 to 5 vote and dismissed the case.[6] The ACLU filed a cert petition with the Supreme Court in December 2010.

As *Jeppesen* illustrates, there has been no significant difference between the Bush and Obama administrations on state secrets, even though the latter has instituted a more rigorous process in deciding when to advance a state secrets argument. Despite this higher level of review, the Obama administration has continued to invoke the privilege to extinguish lawsuits brought by torture survivors and other victims of abusive government programs, parroting arguments pioneered by the Bush administration.

SURVEILLANCE

During the past ten years, Congress has repeatedly deferred to the executive branch in constraining access to justice, particularly with regard to government surveillance.

Just six weeks after 9/11, after virtually no debate, Congress passed the USA Patriot Act. The act was a wholesale overhaul of federal surveillance laws that vastly expanded the government's power to spy on Americans and diminished judicial oversight and the ability to challenge government spying in court. It gave the government the power to search a home without informing its resident that a warrant was issued; collect information from personal records—medical, financial, library, etc.—without probable cause of a crime; and monitor private emails and Internet activity.

A few of the most egregious provisions have been modified. For example, in *Doe v. Mukasey*, the ACLU won a challenge to the constitutionality of the provision that all recipients of National Security Letters (NSLs)—government demands for records or data issued without judicial oversight—could be permanently prohibited from disclosing that such a letter was issued.[7] Nevertheless, most of the powers authorized in 2001 remain in force in 2011. There is little evidence that the Patriot Act has made America safer, but it is quite clear that the government has abused its virtually unchecked powers under the act and violated the privacy rights of countless people. An audit by the Department of Justice Inspector General revealed that the FBI under-reported its use of NSLs to Congress and used NSLs to collect private information about individuals who were not subjects of FBI investigations.

Another major surveillance power grab took place in the months following 9/11, unbeknownst to the public and without the approval of Congress. In December 2005, the *New York Times* reported that President Bush had secretly authorized the NSA to eavesdrop on international telephone calls and to monitor the international email messages of people inside the United States, without a warrant. The ACLU sued, and in August 2006, a federal district court ruled that the NSA program violated the Constitution and federal law. The Bush administration appealed, and in July 2007, the Sixth Circuit dismissed the case, ruling the plaintiffs lacked standing to sue because they could not state with certainty that they had been wiretapped by the NSA.[8] Since it would be nearly impossible for anyone to meet that burden, the ruling effectively insulated warrantless government spying from judicial review.

Congress further reduced the courts' role as a check against unlawful government spying in 2008 by passing the Foreign Intelligence Surveillance Act of 1978 Amendments Act, which permits the government to obtain annual court orders that can capture all communications coming into or leaving the United States. This staggering and virtually unchecked collection of Americans' private communications continues under the Obama administration. The ACLU filed a lawsuit challenging the constitutionality of this law in July 2008. In August 2009, the district court dismissed the suit—also on standing grounds. The ACLU's appeal is pending before the Second Circuit.

The Obama administration has been reluctant to yield any of the expansive surveillance powers claimed by the Bush administration. It has pushed for the reauthorization of some of the Patriot Act's most problematic surveillance provisions. It has sought to expand the NSL statute to allow the FBI to obtain Americans' Internet activity records without court approval or even suspicion of wrongdoing. And it has continued to insist that the FISA Amendments Act is effectively immune from judicial review. Individuals can challenge the statute's constitutionality, the administration has proposed, only if they can prove that their own communications were monitored. Since the administration refuses to disclose whose communications have been monitored, the statute cannot be challenged.

TARGETED KILLING

Of all the national security policies introduced by the Obama administration, none presents access to justice and human rights concerns as grave as those raised by the so-called "targeted killing" program. The program contemplates the killing of suspected terrorists—including U.S. citizens—located far from zones of actual armed conflict.

The entire world is not a war zone. Outside of armed conflict, lethal force may be used only as a last resort, and only to prevent imminent attacks that are likely to cause death or serious physical injury. An extrajudicial, bureaucratized killing program under which names are added to CIA and military "kill lists" through a secret executive process and stay there for months at a time is plainly not limited to imminent threats. As applied to U.S. citizens, it is a grave violation of constitutional due process.

In August 2010, the ACLU and the Center for Constitutional Rights (CCR) sued on behalf of Nasser al-Aulaqi and his son Anwar al-Aulaqi—a U.S. citizen in hiding in Yemen, whose name is on the "kill list"—challenging the Obama administration's asserted power to target the younger Aulaqi for summary execution.

Before the ACLU and CCR could file the substantive lawsuit, the groups had to sue officials at the Treasury Department for permission. In July 2010, the Treasury Department's Office of Foreign Asset Control (OFAC) froze Mr. Aulaqi's assets; those rules also made it illegal for any attorney to provide "legal services" on his behalf without first obtaining a license. That meant that the

ACLU and CCR were not allowed to challenge the targeted kill-ing program until they obtained a license from OFAC. In August, the ACLU and CCR sued, charging that the government could not constitutionally require uncompensated attorneys to obtain a license in order to challenge government conduct, or to represent a particular client in court. OFAC granted the groups a license one day after they filed their lawsuit. The ACLU and CCR vol-untarily dismissed the case after OFAC made significant changes to the attorney licensing scheme.

When the ACLU and CCR presented the case, the federal district court judge acknowledged that it presented "fundamental questions of separation of powers involving the proper role of the courts in our constitutional structure." But he dismissed the case on procedural grounds without addressing the merits.

CONCLUSION

In a nation driven by spectacular partisan rivalries, marked by a massive and well-earned distrust of major institutions, and beset by serious questions about civil rights and civil liberties, there is a fundamental need for individual access to an institution that delivers justice.

A vigorous democracy demands checks and balances. When judicial oversight is weakened and access to the courts is dimin-ished, other institutions—particularly the executive branch—are strengthened, and the delicate system of checks and balances is disrupted.

The last decade has seen systematic efforts to limit access to justice by the executive, Congress, and the courts themselves in the name of national security. While each individual case, law, or executive order may seem by itself isolated or limited, the cumulative effect threatens to undermine the fundamental values of this nation and shift power in ways that will inevitably lead to a less just society.

There is no doubt that the Obama administration inherited a legal and moral morass, and that in important respects it has endeavored to restore the nation's historic commitment to the rule of law. But if the administration continues to limit access to justice and to assert broad, virtually unchecked power on issues of national security, there is a great danger that the Obama administration will enshrine within the law policies and practices that support a dangerous notion that America is in a permanent state of emergency and that core liberties must be surrendered forever.

problematic post-9/11 judicial inactivism: immunizing executive branch overreaching

NADINE STROSSEN[1]

INTRODUCTION

Political conservatives have deployed the term "judicial activism" to stigmatize the courts' fundamental power—and responsibility—to invalidate government measures that violate the U.S. Constitution or laws. These critics contend that, by actively exercising this core power, courts unduly oversee and overturn decisions that instead lie within the discretion of elected officials. Unfortunately, there has been less vocal concern about the less obvious but greater dangers to our democracy that flow from the opposite phenomenon, which I will label "judicial inactivism" or "judicial passivism": the courts' failure even to review—and, consequently, their failure to remedy—serious constitutional and statutory violations by elected officials.

The dangers of judicial inactivism are not obvious because they are couched in rulings that do not substantively address the violations at issue, let alone expressly reject the legal challenges on the merits. Instead, the rulings invoke various justiciability doctrines that preclude the courts from resolving the claims. The result is that plaintiffs' complaints are simply dismissed, which has the same practical impact as a negative ruling on the merits: the plaintiffs receive no relief, the defendants are free to proceed with their challenged conduct, and no judicial sanction deters. The justiciability doctrines are judicially created, defined by vague criteria, and unpredictably and inconsistently applied. Critics— including Supreme Court Justices—complain that judges can too easily invoke these doctrines to reject substantively disfavored claims without having to rule on the merits.[2]

Post-9/11, judicial passivism has blocked review of compelling claims of gross violations of fundamental human rights, including the rights to be free from torture, forced disappearance, and targeted killing.[3] Judicial inactivism has also effectively licensed the government to engage in sweeping secret surveillance of our telephone calls and emails without any basis to believe that we are engaging in any illegal activity, let alone terrorism.[4] The Supreme Court and lower courts have reviewed and struck down some important post-9/11 measures that unduly expanded government power and restricted individual freedom. Nonetheless, the courts have held in too many other cases that challenges are non-justiciable, thus permitting serious government abuses. The Supreme Court has compounded the

230

problem by declining to review challenges to lower courts' non-justiciability rulings.

Under both the Bush and Obama administrations, the government has regularly pressed several non-justiciability arguments to close the courthouse door to compelling claims. It has argued that plaintiffs lacked standing because they could not show that they personally suffered a particular type of injury—even though the plaintiffs had demonstrably suffered severe injuries, thereby warranting judicial redress.[5] The government also has argued that plaintiffs' claims have become moot because the government had voluntarily ceased the complained-of conduct—even though the government maintained the option of resuming it.[6] Finally, and most regularly, the government has argued that many cases cannot be litigated without an undue risk of revealing "state secrets" that will endanger national security—even when there is ample publicly available information to substantiate the claims and defenses.[7]

CHECKS AND BALANCES: VIGOROUS JUDICIAL REVIEW OF INVIGORATED EXECUTIVE POWER

Throughout history, during war or other national security crises, the executive branch has consistently exceeded the outer bounds of its constitutional power in order to protect our nation's security. Presidents have asserted the power to take any steps they deem necessary, including steps that violate civil liberties. This pattern has repeated regardless of political party. After all, it was no less a liberal icon than Franklin Roosevelt who authorized the internment of 120,000 Japanese-American citizens during World War II. Likewise, both post-9/11 Presidents, despite their partisan and ideological differences, have asserted executive power to trammel individual rights in the service of national security.[8]

Even assuming that a national crisis can justify the executive branch's most vigorous exercise of its power to protect the nation, the judicial branch would then have a countervailing duty to exercise its judicial review power with corresponding vigor, to ensure that the executive branch does not overstep its power or violate individual rights. In one of the earliest post-9/11 judicial rulings about competing claims of executive branch power and civil liberties, federal judge Gladys Kessler stressed these complementary roles of our government's executive and judicial branches:

> The Court fully understands and appreciates that the first priority of the executive branch in a time of crisis is to ensure the physical security of its citizens. By the same token, the first priority of the judicial branch must be to ensure that our Government always operates within the statutory and constitutional constraints which distinguish a democracy from a dictatorship.[9]

The Supreme Court's 1944 *Korematsu* decision has been resoundingly repudiated because the majority of the Justices uncritically accepted the government's unsubstantiated assertion that the internment of Japanese-American citizens was necessary to protect national security. Justice Jackson's dissent stressed that the Court's passive deference did even greater damage to liberty, equality, and justice than the unconstitutional executive action. As Justice Jackson concluded: "A military commander may overstep the bounds of constitutionality, and it is an incident. But if we review and approve, that passing incident becomes the doctrine of the Constitution."[10]

Likewise, if the Court does *not* review a lower court decision that in turn has not reviewed constitutional overstepping by military or executive officials, such overstepping approaches constitu-

232

tional doctrine. Conduct that the courts do not halt may proceed unimpeded. Moreover, some Justices and others have argued that accepted practices, even if not affirmatively upheld by the courts, could in some circumstances "be treated as a gloss on 'executive Power'" that the Constitution vests in the President.[11] In short, the *Korematsu* majority's judicial passivity, in exercising an unduly deferential form of judicial review, greatly damaged constitutional principles. The even more extreme judicial passivity that this essay discusses, involving no judicial review at all, likewise greatly damages constitutional principles.

THE SUPREME COURT'S MIXED POST-9/11 RECORD

After the 9/11 terrorist attacks, civil libertarians anxiously awaited indications of how actively or passively the Supreme Court would assert judicial review over claims of overreaching by the executive branch and violations of individual rights. Now that a decade has passed, with substantial Supreme Court action and inaction, the Court's record is mixed.

On the one hand, in almost all of the major post-9/11 cases that the Court has decided on the merits, it has consistently curbed the government's excesses, subjecting them to meaningful scrutiny and stressing not only the individual rights at stake, but also the essential role of judicial review.[12] The Court set the tone for its robust judicial review of the executive branch in one of the first of these cases, *Hamdi v. Rumsfeld*, in 2004. In ringing language, Justice Sandra Day O'Connor's plurality opinion declared:

> [A] state of war is not a blank check for the President when it comes to the rights of the Nation's citizens. Whatever power the United States Constitution envi-

sions for the Executive in its exchanges with other nations or with enemy organizations in times of conflict, it most assuredly envisions a role for all three branches when individual liberties are at stake.[13]

Especially when contrasted with *Korematsu*, these positive actions by the Court are cause for celebration.

On the other hand, since 9/11, the Court has also provided cause for consternation through its inaction. Specifically, the Court has declined to review a dozen important cases in which lower courts had rejected challenges to post-9/11 measures that unjustifiably expand government power and violate fundamental rights.[14] Although the Justices' decision not to review a case does not constitute a ruling on the merits, its practical impact is similar.

Of greatest concern is the Court's failure to review lower court decisions that have rejected challenges to post-9/11 abuses not on the merits, but rather on various justiciability grounds, concluding that there should be no judicial forum for such claims. When the Supreme Court lets these lower court rulings stand, it is not only declining to exercise its own judicial review power; it is also authorizing lower courts to continue to deny *any* judicial recourse. In short, these cases constitute major exceptions to Justice O'Connor's bracing words in *Hamdi*: they do give the executive branch "a blank check . . . when it comes to the rights of the nation's citizens" (and non-citizens).

Of particular concern, the Court has declined to review—and has thereby effectively authorized—lower courts' failures to review compelling claims of serious abuses of fundamental rights, including torture, abduction, forced disappearance, prolonged incommunicado detention in inhumane conditions, the indefinite military detention of a lawful U.S. resident without criminal charge or trial, sweeping surveillance of the electronic communications of U.S. citizens, blanket denial of public and press access to important court proceedings, and retaliation against internal whistleblowing by an FBI employee about security breaches and espionage within the FBI's counterterrorism programs.

THE INCREDIBLY EXPANDING STATE SECRETS PRIVILEGE

One variant of the non-justiciability theory that has done the greatest damage is the distorted state secrets evidentiary privilege that both post-9/11 Presidents have regularly pressed. However, as the term "privilege" signifies, state secrets do not give rise to a non-justiciability doctrine, and hence should never be invoked to dismiss a case outright. Rather, along with other evidentiary privileges such as the privilege against self-incrimination or the attorney-client privilege, the state secrets privilege is properly invoked to shield specific evidentiary items from being used in the lawsuit.[15] Nevertheless, this privilege (rarely invoked pre-9/11) has been invoked by both the Bush and Obama administrations with increasing frequency and success as an automatic, door-closing non-justiciability doctrine. The lower-court rulings on point have been divided and inconsistent, underscoring the rampant confusion about the state secrets doctrine, which the Supreme Court should dispel.

Some courts have dismissed lawsuits that challenge serious government overreaching even before discovery takes place, based only on the government's broad, speculative assertions that the general subject matter involves state secrets. In those cases, the courts did not ask the government to identify specific documents, or even categories of documents, as to which the privilege should apply. Nor did the courts assess whether the parties could present their claims and defenses through non-privileged material, or whether special procedures—such as conducting portions of the litigation *in camera* or *ex parte*, i.e., confidential proceedings involving only the judge and the government—could be utilized to safeguard sensitive material.

The Supreme Court has directly discussed the state secrets privilege in only one case, in 1953: *United States v. Reynolds.* The Court held that the privilege was "not to be lightly invoked" and that its misuse could lead to "intolerable abuses." The Court also warned that "judicial control in a case cannot be abdicated to the caprice of executive officers."[16]

The *Reynolds* Court considered only whether a specific document could be excluded from the litigation because the government insisted that this document would reveal state secrets. Although the Court accepted the government's argument that the document should be excluded, the Court stressed that plaintiffs should be able to establish their case through other government-provided evidence. The Court remanded the case so it could proceed based on this other evidence.

Specifically, *Reynolds* was a tort action brought by the widows of three civilians who had been killed in the crash of an Air Force plane. The government declined to produce the official accident report, claiming that the plane was engaged in a "confidential mission" to test "confidential equipment."[17] Although the Supreme Court excluded the report, it concluded that plaintiffs could prove their case through the testimony of the surviving crew-members, which the government offered to provide. The Court stressed that the greater the need for any allegedly privileged material in a particular lawsuit, the more a "court should probe in satisfying itself that the occasion for invoking the privilege is appropriate."[18] Accordingly, had the Court believed that the accident report was central to the plaintiffs' claims, it might well have required the government to produce it. Following the Supreme Court's remand, the *Reynolds* litigation did proceed and ultimately was resolved via a negotiated settlement. *Reynolds* provides no support for the government's and lower courts' recasting of the state secrets privilege into a non-justiciability, executive immunity doctrine.

The misapplication of the *Reynolds* evidentiary privilege has apparently resulted from confusing it with a separate, narrow non-justiciability doctrine that applies only to a particular type of lawsuit involving a particular type of secret evidence: a lawsuit to enforce a clandestine espionage agreement with the government. The Court has enforced this limited non-justiciability doctrine in only two cases: *Totten v. United States*[19] in 1875 and *Tenet v. Doe*[20] in 2005. In *Tenet*, the Court reaffirmed that the "sweeping holding in *Totten*," rendering the case non-justiciable and hence subject to dismissal at the outset, applies only to suits "where success depends on the existence of [the plaintiff's] secret espionage relationship with the government."[21] The *Totten* non-justiciability rule flows from the law of contracts that is the legal basis for the lawsuits at issue. It reflects the contracts law premise that a secret employment contract is implicitly conditioned on an agreement to forego litigation to enforce it. This highly specific rule is wholly inapplicable to any other types of lawsuits involving any other types of state secrets.

Even though *Reynolds* emphasized that "judicial control . . . cannot be abdicated to . . . executive officers,"[22] it did evince undue judicial inactivism in one key respect. The Court passively accepted the government's assertions that the accident report contained state secrets, without independently assessing the report. Decades later, when the report was declassified, it turned out not to reveal the asserted "details of any secret project the plane was involved in," but instead what one historian decried as "a horror show of [governmental] incompetence, bungling and tragic error."[23]

As Justice Douglas observed in the landmark Pentagon Papers case, government officials regularly engage in the "widespread practice" of invoking national security concerns to achieve the "suppression of embarrassing information."[24] The *Reynolds* case illustrates the government's general tendency to exaggerate the national security benefits of secrecy, while overlooking the significant ways in which an assertion of government secrecy can actually undermine national security, as well as due process, accountability, and other essential democratic values. For example, the bipartisan commission that analyzed the intelligence failures that contributed to the 9/11 attacks criticized excessive government secrecy as one factor.[25]

Post-*Reynolds* developments underscore not only that maintaining secrecy is not always beneficial to national security interests, but also that courts are fully capable of identifying and safeguarding materials whose disclosure would pose genuine national security risks. Since 1953, several important federal statutes—the Freedom of Information Act, the Foreign Intelligence Surveillance Act, and the Classified Information Procedures Act[26]—have laid out procedures for confidential judicial evaluation of materials that the government resists disclosing on national security grounds. In enforcing these statutes, courts have permitted disclosure when appropriate and ensured secrecy when appropriate, including in high-profile terrorism prosecutions.

In four post-9/11 cases, the ACLU has asked the Supreme Court to review lower court decisions that dismissed serious civil liberties claims based on a distorted version of the state secrets privilege. The most recent such request was filed in December 2010, in *Mohamed v. Jeppesen Dataplan.*[27] The Court had not yet ruled at the time this essay was completed. In the three prior cases, the Court denied review.[28]

The *Jeppesen* case powerfully demonstrates the misuse of the state secrets evidentiary privilege to foreclose judicial review and immunize executive abuses. It also underscores lower court judges' confusion about this issue. A bare majority of the Ninth Circuit supported the government's generalized assertion that "the very subject matter of this case is a state secret."[29] The dissenters correctly concluded that the privilege would warrant dismissal "if and only if specific privileged evidence is itself indispensable to establishing either the truth of the plaintiffs' allegations or a valid defense that would otherwise be available to the defendants."[30]

The five plaintiffs in this case were forcibly kidnapped and flown to foreign sites where they were tortured and detained incommunicado in inhumane conditions. Jeppesen organized the flights at the direction of the CIA. The Ninth Circuit dissent summarized 1,800 pages of "the voluminous public record materials submitted by Plaintiffs in support of their claims."[31]

CONCLUSION

The lower courts have inappropriately invoked non-justiciability doctrines to decline to review many cases challenging post-9/11 government abuses, and the Supreme Court in turn has declined to review those rulings. This double-layered judicial passivism has adversely affected not only many victims of gross human rights violations, but also our system of checks and balances. Ironically, these severe costs were stressed even by the narrow majority of the Ninth Circuit judges who misapplied the state secrets doctrine in *Jeppesen*:

> Denial of a judicial forum based on the state secrets doctrine poses concerns at both individual and structural levels. For the individual plaintiffs . . . our decision forecloses . . . judicial remedies. . . . At a structural level, terminating the case eliminates further judicial review . . . one important check on alleged abuse by government officials and . . . contractors.[32]

The Supreme Court should use the pending *Jeppesen* case to reinvigorate the judicial review power to curb post-9/11 abuses by reaffirming that the state secrets evidentiary privilege is not a non-justiciability doctrine. This would be an important step toward curbing undue judicial passivism.

the guantánamo mess[*]

THE HONORABLE
A. RAYMOND RANDOLPH

have drawn the title of my essay from a well-known passage
in *The Great Gatsby*:

They were careless people, Tom and Daisy—they
smashed up things and creatures . . . and let other people
clean up the mess they had made. . . .

* This essay is an edited version of a Joseph Story Distinguished Lecture delivered by Judge Randolph at the Heritage Foundation in Washington, D.C., on
October 20, 2010.

In 2008, in *Boumediene v. Bush*, a five-Justice majority of the U.S. Supreme Court declared that habeas corpus jurisdiction extended beyond the shores of the United States.[1] This, it said, was a matter of American constitutional law. The *Boumediene* ruling was unprecedented, not just in this country in modern times, but in the entire ancient history of habeas corpus jurisprudence. *Boumediene* ripped up centuries of settled law, leaving in its wake the title of my essay—a legal mess.

Ben Wittes, Robert Chesney, and Rabea Benhalim, in their comprehensive study for the Brookings Institution, wrote that "it is hard to overstate the resulting significance" of the lower court cases that are following in the wake of *Boumediene*.[2] Indeed it is.

Since *Boumediene*, those decisions have attracted little public attention. But the Guantánamo habeas cases march on, hundreds of them, case by case in our court and in the district court. Law is made; precedents set; judicial standards declared. Soldiers capturing combatants in the field may have to comply with judicially prescribed evidentiary requirements. Questioning of prisoners may have to adhere to some sort of judicial norm. Exclusionary rules may be enforced. Modes of questioning may not exceed proper bounds as judges see them. Evidence may have to be handled and preserved in certain judicially approved ways.

The short of it is that, in the peace and quiet of the federal courthouse at Third and Constitution Avenue, Washington, D.C., federal judges are making law—law that potentially affects the actions of our soldiers in the battlefields of the world now and in the future, all in the name of the Constitution. As Wittes, Chesney, and Benhalim say, these habeas corpus cases are the vehicles for an unprecedented wartime lawmaking exercise with broad implications for the future. The law established in these cases will in all likelihood govern not merely the Guantánamo detentions themselves but any other detentions around the world over which American courts acquire habeas jurisdiction. What's more, to the extent that these cases establish substantive and procedural rules governing the application of law-of-war detention powers in general, they could end up impacting detentions far beyond those immediately supervised by the federal courts.

In this essay, I will focus on the *Boumediene* majority opinion and where it has moved us to this point. I will be blunt. Supreme Court opinions command compliance. But Supreme Court opinions do not command agreement.

To begin, I should survey some history. Under English common law, alien enemies captured abroad had no right to habeas corpus—period. In the mid-1700s Blackstone wrote: "alien enemies have no rights, no privileges, unless by the king's special favour, during the time of war."[3] Until *Boumediene*, American law reflected these time-honored precepts.

During World War II the Allies captured and held two million prisoners. The German prisoners were the most litigious. Before the war ended, two hundred of them had filed petitions for writs of habeas corpus directly in the Supreme Court of the United States. The Court denied each petition, but only eight Justices voted. Justice Robert Jackson did not participate. While on the Supreme Court, he had taken a leave of absence to serve as chief counsel at the Nazi War Crime Trials in Nuremberg.

When Jackson returned to the Supreme Court, a case arose in a setting that did not require him to step aside. After Germany's surrender on May 8, 1945, but before the surrender of Japan, twenty-one German nationals in China assisted Japanese forces fighting against the United States. The U.S. Army captured the Germans and tried and convicted them before a military commission in Nanking. The U.S. Army then transferred the prisoners to a prison in Bavaria, Germany—the Landsberg Prison.

Landsberg was already famous. In 1924 Adolf Hitler was imprisoned there for treason. It was in his thirteen months at Landsberg that Hitler began writing *Mein Kampf* ("My Struggle")—a treatise Churchill called "the new Koran of faith and war."[4] The U.S. Army took over the Landsberg fortress in 1945 and ran it for thirteen years. Not until 1958 did the Army release the last of those imprisoned there. At one point there were more than 1,500 Germans at Landsberg. The Allies executed nearly 300 of them.

After the German prisoners from Nanking arrived at Landsberg, they filed habeas corpus petitions—not in the Supreme Court, but in the United States District Court in Washington, D.C. They claimed violations of the Fifth Amendment to the Constitution. Their cases, consolidated for decision, led to the Supreme Court's opinion in *Johnson v. Eisentrager*, handed down in 1950.[5]

This case should have settled the controversy that arose years later in the Guantánamo habeas cases. The issue was the same: Did the writ of habeas corpus reach alien enemies captured abroad during war and held beyond the sovereign territory of the United States?

Justice Jackson wrote the Court's opinion, which held that "the privilege of litigation" in federal court had not been extended to the German prisoners. At no time had these prisoners been "within any territory over which the United States is sovereign, and the scenes of their offense, their capture, their trial and their punishment were all beyond the territorial jurisdiction of any court of the United States." Moreover, habeas corpus "trials would hamper the war effort and bring aid and comfort to the enemy." Witnesses, including military officials, might have to travel to the United States from overseas.

All of this would engender "conflict between judicial and military opinion," "diminish the prestige of" any field commander as he was called "to account in his own civil courts" and "divert his efforts and attention from the military offensive abroad to the legal defensive at home."

Justice Jackson also held for the Court that the Constitution did not confer rights upon the German prisoners. As he put it:

> If the Fifth Amendment confers its rights on all the world . . . [it] would mean that during military occupation irreconcilable enemy elements, guerrilla fighters, and "werewolves" could require the American Judiciary to assure them freedoms of speech, press, and assembly as in the First Amendment, right to bear arms as in the Second, security against "unreasonable" searches and seizures as in the Fourth, as well as rights to jury trial as in the Fifth and Sixth Amendments.[6]

Eisentrager became a leading opinion. The Supreme Court relied on it again and again, as did the D.C. Circuit, in deciding that various constitutional rights were not held by aliens who were outside the sovereign territory of the United States. And so matters stood on the morning of September 11, 2001. In the aftermath of the attacks, neither President George W. Bush nor his legal advisors could possibly have anticipated what would come as a result of using the U.S. Naval Base at Guantánamo Bay, Cuba, to hold some of the prisoners captured in Afghanistan and elsewhere.

The first wave of Guantánamo habeas cases reached the D.C. Circuit in late 2002. The issue was statutory, not constitutional: Did the federal habeas statute give the district court jurisdiction? The habeas statute was basically the same as the habeas statute existing at the time of *Eisentrager*. Matters seemed pretty clear-cut. I have always believed that the first principle of jurisprudence is to treat like cases alike. Without that principle we are not governed by the rule of law.

We compared the cases. The U.S. Army controlled the Landsberg Prison. The U.S. Navy controlled Guantánamo. Neither area was part of the sovereign territory of the United States. Sovereignty is a purely political question. And Congress has declared that Guantánamo—which we lease from Cuba—is not part of the United States. We write a check to our landlord each year, but Cuba refuses to cash it. That's their problem.

The Guantánamo prisoners also had much in common with those held at Landsberg. They were aliens; they were captured during military operations; they were in a foreign country when captured; they were now abroad; they were in the custody of the American military; and they had never been in the United States.

Relying on *Eisentrager*, the D.C. Circuit held that the Guantánamo detainees were not entitled to habeas relief in the courts of the United States. I wrote the opinion for our court.[7] The Supreme Court reversed.[8] The Court's opinion, by Justice Stevens, used a rationale neither party had bothered to argue, a rationale that to my mind was indefensible. I will not go into it. The dissent in the case dismantles it.

Congress also thought that Justice Stevens' opinion was profoundly mistaken and overruled the Supreme Court. The Detainee Treatment Act of 2005 stated that no court, judge, or justice shall have jurisdiction to hear habeas cases from Guantánamo. In place of habeas, the act substituted judicial review in the D.C. Circuit of the decisions of a military tribunal—the Combat Status Review Tribunal—finding the detainee to have been an enemy combatant. (Each detainee at Guantánamo has now gone through such a hearing.)

Then a second wave of habeas cases arrived in our court. Again I wrote the opinion. We held, as the Detainee Treatment Act stated, that there was no jurisdiction. Again the Supreme Court reversed, this time on the ground that the act applied only to cases filed after Congress enacted it, not to habeas cases already pending.[9]

This too struck me as profoundly mistaken—the statute was clear as a bell. Once again Congress agreed and overruled the Supreme Court. The Military Commissions Act of 2007 made crystal clear that the jurisdictional bar against habeas applied to all future and pending cases "without exception." It was as if Congress slammed its fist on the table and shouted to the Supreme Court, "we really mean it!"

The stage was thus set for *Boumediene*, the third case in the Guantánamo trilogy and the focus of my comments. Again I wrote the opinion for our court.[10] The issue in *Boumediene* was whether the Military Commission Act and the Detainee Treatment Act—which clearly abolished jurisdiction over Guantánamo habeas actions—violated the Suspension Clause of the Constitution.

The Suspension Clause reads: "The Privilege of the Writ of Habeas Corpus shall not be suspended, unless when in Cases of Rebellion or Invasion the public Safety may require it." The clause is a riddle: it limits the instances when Congress may suspend the writ yet it does not seem to guarantee that the writ will ever exist. The Supreme Court, in my view, has done a poor job of solving the riddle, but I want to focus on a different problem.

The problem deals with the Court majority's ostensible—and I use the word ostensible intentionally—use of originalism in the first half of its opinion and the Court's total abandonment of that mode of analysis in the second half.

As to the first part of the opinion, all nine Justices accepted the proposition that the Suspension Clause at least preserved the common law writ of habeas corpus as it existed in 1789. The historical question addressed in the first part of *Boumediene* was therefore of a geographical nature: how far did the writ of habeas corpus reach in 1789? If the writ did not extend beyond the nation's sovereign territory, Congress had not suspended the writ when it barred petitions from the Guantánamo detainees. As I have said, Guantánamo is not now and never has been part of this country's sovereign territory.

With every theory of constitutional interpretation there is always a catch. And so it is with originalism. The catch is this: To interpret the Constitution in light of history—which is what originalism amounts to—you have to interpret history. How well you perform the task of the historian will determine how valid your interpretation of the Constitution will be. This should be an obvious point, but too little has been made of it.

I remember working at home on the geographical-scope issue. The language of the Suspension Clause seemed to contemplate a writ confined to United States sovereign territory. It struck me that I ought to look at the lectures on English law Sir Robert Chambers gave at Oxford between 1767 and 1773. (Pretty contemporary, I thought.) It just so happened that I had the Chambers lectures in my home library. You might wonder why. The reason is that I am somewhat of a Johnsonian, as they say. In the summer of 1767 Chambers took over the law lectureship at Oxford from Blackstone. But writer's block grabbed him. Chambers begged his friend Samuel Johnson—who was not a lawyer—to come help him prepare the lectures. Johnson obliged and Chambers graciously acknowledged Johnson's assistance in his published volumes.

I pulled the Chambers lectures off the shelf and cracked open Volume Two to a discussion directly on point. Chambers instructed his law students at Oxford that the writ of habeas corpus did not extend beyond the King's dominions. Among other authorities, he relied on an opinion of Lord Chief Justice Mansfield and on the Habeas Corpus Act of 1679. Lord Mansfield—the greatest lawyer of eighteenth-century England—delivered a lengthy opinion in 1759 stating that the writ of habeas corpus did not extend beyond England's sovereign territories. Like Sir Robert Chambers, he explained that the Habeas Corpus Act—which Blackstone described as the bulwark of English liberties—provided just that.

For at least a generation leading up to the adoption of our Constitution, English lawyers educated at Oxford were instructed that the writ of habeas corpus did not reach beyond the King's dominions. I thought it legitimate to rely on Chambers in my opinion in *Boumediene* even though the lectures were not published in this country until 1986, and even though I did not know whether any of the Framers had even heard of his lectures. Of course I also relied on Lord Mansfield, along with other historical material, to hold for our court that the constitutional writ did not extend to Guantánamo.

Justice Jackson wrote in *Eisentrager* in 1950: "We are cited to no instance where a court, in this or any other country where the writ [of habeas corpus] is known, has issued it on behalf of an alien enemy who, at no relevant time and in no stage of his captivity, has been within its territorial jurisdiction." Until the Supreme Court decision in *Boumediene*, Justice Jackson's statement of law was clearly correct.

When *Boumediene* reached the Supreme Court, dozens of amicus briefs were filed by the leading lights of academia, all in favor of the Guantánamo detainees. Yet not one of them was able to come up with a single case or any contemporary commentary indicating that habeas reached beyond a nation's sovereign terri-tory. The historical evidence was overwhelming, and it was all the other way. I gave a few speeches at law schools about the *Boume-diene* case while it was pending in the high Court. I said there was no getting around this history. I was wrong.

One of the classic books on historical research and analysis is David Hackett Fischer's *Historians' Fallacies: Toward a Logic of Historical Thought*, published in 1970. Professor Fischer lists 112 common fallacies in historical scholarship. The majority opinion in *Boumediene* managed to commit many of them.

To illustrate, the Court's opinion states: "Lord Mansfield can be cited for the proposition that, at the time of the found-ing [1789], English courts lacked the 'power' to issue the writ to Scotland" or other regions beyond England's sovereign territory, which Lord Mansfield "referred to as 'foreign.'" Note the Court's wishy-washy phrasing—"can be cited for the proposition." How about "establishes" the proposition? Mansfield was, after all, not the average man on the street. He was the Lord Chief Justice of England.

Anyway, the Supreme Court majority then purports to blunt this powerful history by noting "the possibility" that the English courts were "motivated" by "prudential concerns" rather than "formal legal constructs." And, the Court adds, Scotland was not really a foreign country vis-à-vis England when Lord Mansfield wrote his opinion.

These few lines are critical to the entirety of the Court's his-torical analysis in the first part of *Boumediene*. Yet they contain no less than four different historians' fallacies. The Court then rounds off this short but crucial discussion with a whopper—a gross error of historical fact.

I will deal with the fallacies first. Perhaps the most obvious is the fallacy of the metaphysical question. In framing the issue in terms of the real "motivations" of the judges of the Court of King's Bench in mid-eighteenth-century England, the *Boumediene* majority set up an impossible inquiry. What were the motives of English judges 250 years ago? How can anyone know this today? (Indeed, how could they back then?) We do not even know the real motivations of the five Justices who signed on to the *Boumediene* opinion.

The Court's next misstep was subscribing to the fallacy of the false dichotomy, a mistake, Professor Fischer writes, so serious that it "deserves to be singled out for special condemnation." The Court's statement assumes there are only two possibilities: either the English courts were motivated by formal legal constructs (whatever that means) or they were motivated by prudential concerns (whatever that means). But there is another explanation, a conclusive one I believe: As Lord Mansfield recognized, the English courts limited their habeas jurisdiction to sovereign territory in compliance with the Habeas Corpus Act of 1679. That does not strike me as a formal legal construct or a prudential concern.

Another fallacy in the quoted passages is the fallacy of the negative proof. As Professor Fischer explains, this occurs "whenever the historian declares that 'there is no evidence that X is the case,' and then proceeds to affirm or assume that not-X is the case." The *Boumediene* majority suggests that there is no evidence that Lord Mansfield or the other judges of the Court of King's Bench were applying the requirements of the law. Hence, they must have been doing something else.

This is a clear "attempt to sustain a factual proposition merely by negative evidence." "[N]ot knowing that a thing exists," Professor Fischer tells us, "is different than knowing that it does not exist." One is reminded of Alice and the King in *Through the Looking Glass*:

"I see nobody on the road," said Alice.

"I only wish *I* had such eyes," the King remarked in a fretful tone. "To be able to see nobody! And at that distance too!"

The Court's fourth mistake in this short passage embraced the fallacy of the possible proof. This particular blunder infects much of the *Boumediene* opinion. "Valid empirical proof," Professor Fischer writes, "requires not merely the establishment of possibility, but an estimate of probability." The Court mentions the "possibility" that Lord Mansfield was mistaken about the scope of habeas, but does not bother to assess the probability. In fact, there is no evidence to support the Court's "possibility," and the overwhelming historical evidence is that habeas corpus did not reach beyond England's sovereign territory.

This brings me to the Court's massive error of fact. Lord Mansfield's mid-1700s opinion stated that the writ was geographically confined and did not extend to Scotland because Scotland was a foreign country. In order to disprove this, the Supreme Court majority charged Lord Mansfield with having made a mistake of law—Scotland, the *Boumediene* majority said, was not then "foreign." Professor Philip Hamburger in a thoroughly researched article in the *Columbia Law Review* explains why the error was the Supreme Court's, not Lord Mansfield's.[11] I must add one fact. Of all the legal authorities in eighteenth-century England, Lord Chief Justice Mansfield would have known better than anyone else the status of Scotland. Why? He was not merely the greatest lawyer of his time, but—obviously unknown to the *Boumediene* majority—Lord Mansfield was himself a Scot.

At the end of its historical inquiry the *Boumediene* majority said that the "conception of sovereignty does not provide a comprehensive or altogether satisfactory explanation for the general understanding that prevailed when Lord Mansfield considered issuance of the writ outside England." Not an "altogether satisfactory explanation for the general understanding"? Satisfactory to whom? It was surely satisfactory to the English barristers and judges of the eighteenth century. So what are we to make of the Supreme Court's remark? Maybe the Court was engaging in literary criticism. It certainly was not engaging in objective historical analysis.

The Court majority's final point in this section of its opinion is stranger still. The Court says it cannot reach a conclusion about the geographical scope of habeas because the historical record is not complete. And it is not complete because not all eighteenth-century habeas proceedings were reported. If one took this rationale seriously, originalism would be a dead letter. The historical record is never complete.

With the deck thus cleared, the majority declares the original meaning of the Suspension Clause ambiguous. Even if this were true—which it decidedly is not—it should not have led to the Court's ruling. If the Court had been faced with an ambiguous statute interpreted by an administrative agency, the Court would have recognized that the choice of meanings was a policy choice and would therefore defer to the agency. Why then did the Court refuse to defer to Congress's choice—a choice clearly resting on foreign policy considerations and judgments about the security of the nation? Do Supreme Court Justices have any expertise in these subjects? The question answers itself.

No matter. The *Boumediene* majority plunged ahead with what it termed a functional analysis to resolve the perceived ambiguity. In doing so, it distorted *Johnson v. Eisentrager* beyond recognition. The case was directly on point, and obviously so, which is why President Bush relied on *Eisentrager* in deciding to use Guantánamo for some of those captured in the Afghan war. The *Boumediene* Court stated that it was not overruling *Eisentrager*, just distinguishing it—on grounds Justice Scalia called "patently false." Nonetheless, the Court decided that the common law writ of habeas, as it existed in 1789, reached beyond the nation's sovereign territory and could be invoked by alien enemies captured and held overseas during wartime. Thus ended part one of the Court's opinion.

But now another question loomed. What did this constitutional habeas for enemy combatants entail? What is the nature of these proceedings? What is their content? What rights do the detainees have? The Court had to face these questions in order to determine whether the acts of Congress violated the Suspension Clause. The writ of habeas corpus is not suspended if Congress has provided a sufficient alternative procedure for testing the legality of detention. And so the question came down to whether that alternative—review of the military tribunal's judgment in the D.C. Circuit—was an adequate substitute for habeas.

Here again, the question was novel, a question the Supreme Court had never before considered. (Our court did not reach it because we had decided that habeas did not extend to the Guantánamo detainees in the first place.) In trying to answer the question, one would have expected the Court to proceed as it had in the first part of the opinion—that is, by consulting history to determine the original meaning of habeas corpus as used in the Suspension Clause. The Solicitor General assumed the Court would follow this approach and put the government's arguments in those terms.

Of course the Court faced a rather severe historical problem. There was no history—none at all—of providing habeas review to alien enemies captured and held abroad during military operations. There was no history because the first part of the Court's opinion was unprecedented and, in my view, flat wrong. The closest cases in this country dealt with review of criminal judgments during World War II. Take for instance, *Ex parte Quirin*, involving the German saboteurs captured in the United States during World War II, tried at the Department of Justice before a military commission and then executed.[12]

In cases like *Quirin*, habeas was *limited* to determining whether the military tribunal had jurisdiction. For the *Boumediene* majority that narrow—yet historically accurate—view of habeas would not do. And so, in stark contrast to the first part, the second part of the majority opinion dealing with the content of habeas corpus all but ignores original meaning. Instead we are treated to a general discussion of the law of "traditional" habeas corpus. Never mind that none of the cases and authorities that the Court cites in this part has anything to do with wartime or with enemies captured on the battlefield, or with aliens held abroad. Instead of seeking to discover the content of the common law writ as it existed in 1789, the Court talks about the development of statutory habeas corpus from the mid-1800s through the twentieth century.

This is the philosophy of the living Constitution in a not very good disguise.

Even after surveying these authorities, the Court pulls back and states that it will leave it up to the district court and our court to decide the content of constitutional habeas for the Guantánamo detainees. I am reminded of what John Hart Ely wrote in his critique of *Roe v. Wade*. The second part of *Boumediene* "is bad because it is bad constitutional law, or rather because it is *not* constitutional law and gives almost no sense of an obligation to try to be."[13]

If, as the *Boumediene* Court essentially holds, the scope of constitutional habeas is not determined by the content of the writ as it existed in 1789, what determines it? The Court gave no answer, and this is precisely what has led to the Guantánamo mess. The Court simply pronounced that the solution of Congress—review of military tribunals in the D.C. Circuit—was inadequate. The Court then stated that the district court judges and the judges of our court had discretion to decide what habeas involved.

The open-ended nature of the second part of *Boumediene* is what led Wittes, Chesney, and Benhalim to describe the Court's action as a massive grant of legislative power to our court and to the district court—an odd but accurate way of describing the judicial function in these cases. The *Boumediene* Court did say that the habeas proceedings should be "meaningful." This statement comes out of the blue. It has no context. "Meaningful" as compared to what? Habeas corpus in 1789? Habeas corpus under modern statutes? Habeas for illegal aliens facing deportation? For convicted criminals? For criminal defendants awaiting trial?

In 2011, there are more than 200 Guantánamo habeas cases pending in our court and in the district court. In consolidated proceedings our court is scheduled to hear 45 lead cases. These figures give only an abstract picture of what is at stake. Let me give you a glimpse of the factual settings in which the cases arise.

I issued an opinion in a case that raised several unsettled issues. Here is the opening paragraph:

In the summer of 2001, a thirty-nine year-old Yemeni security guard took a six-month leave of absence from his job to move to Afghanistan. Leaving his wife and two children, he stayed at the Kandahar home of his brother-in-law, a close associate of Usama bin Laden. Twice he met personally with bin Laden. From Kandahar he moved to a guesthouse used as a staging area for al-Qaida recruits. He then attended the al-Qaida's Al Farouq training camp, where many of the September 11th terrorists had trained. He traveled between Kabul, Khost, and Kandahar while American forces were launching attacks in Afghanistan. Among other explanations for his movements, he claimed that he had decided to take a vacation. After sustaining injuries requiring his hospitalization, he crossed the Pakistani border on a bus carrying wounded Arab and Pakistani fighters. This man, Mohammed Al-Adahi, who is now a detainee at the Guantánamo Bay Naval Base, admits all of this but insists he was not a part of al-Qaida and never fought against the United States. Others identified him as a [redacted]. On his petition of a writ of habeas corpus, the district court ordered him released. We reverse.[14]

This case, and more than 200 others, present fundamental issues about the scope of habeas corpus. It is up to my colleagues and me, and the district judges, to fill in the blanks.

Consider one of the most basic issues: who bears the burden of proof? Must the government show that it is properly holding the detainee? Or is it up to the detainee to show that he is being held improperly? *Boumediene* contains language that seems to support both positions. On the one hand, the Court said that habeas "entitles the prisoner to a meaningful opportunity to demonstrate that he is being held pursuant to 'the erroneous application or interpretation' of relevant law." This sounds like the ball is in the detainee's court.

But a few pages later we find the Court stating that the "extent of the showing required of the Government in these cases is a matter to be determined." This seems to contemplate some sort of showing required of the government. Assume that to be the case—as several of our cases do and as have the district judges. The question remains: what exactly is the nature of the government's burden? Reading and rereading *Boumediene* will not give you an answer. So how does a court go about resolving the question?

Here are some options. The burden of proof could be beyond a reasonable doubt, as in criminal cases. It could be clear and convincing evidence. Perhaps the standard is a preponderance of the evidence. Or maybe it is probable cause, which is all the police need to arrest and hold someone suspected of a crime. Or maybe the proof required of the government is merely some evidence. For decades that was the standard in deportation cases.

Again, how does a court choose among these options? What legal principles govern? Some of the judges of the district court have followed a case management order that puts the burden on the government to show by a preponderance of evidence that the detainee is part of al-Qaeda or the Taliban. Yet if you consulted the common law writ of habeas as it existed in 1789, you would find no case in which the Crown had to prove by a preponderance that it was justifiably holding the prisoner.

In this country, even in a statutory regime, the government only had to produce "some evidence" in habeas cases challenging selective service decisions, and in cases challenging orders of deportation. In *Boumediene*, the Solicitor General pointed out—actually quoted from Supreme Court opinions—that in traditional habeas proceedings in this country well into the twentieth century the courts did not review factual determinations made by the executive in detaining individuals. That was certainly true in the military context. In habeas cases seeking review of courts martial, the government only had to show that the soldier received full and fair consideration of his claims.

Other issues, just as fundamental as the burden of proof, are working their way through our courts. For instance, is the detainee entitled to engage in discovery? If so, what sort of discovery? May he depose field commanders, CIA agents, and other government officials? May he or his attorney examine intelligence reports and other government documents? Is there a *Brady* rule—that is, does the government have to provide the detainee with exculpatory evidence? What sort of evidentiary search and production does the government have to make in response to discovery requests, if these are allowed? Must records in the field be reviewed? CIA records? NSA? The Pentagon?

To give you an idea of the enormity of what's involved, we had a Guantánamo case pending while the Court was considering *Boumediene*. A panel of our court decided to order the government to produce all documents bearing on whether the detainee was properly held. Affidavits from the CIA, NSA, DoD, FBI and other agencies predicted that for each detainee this sort of blanket discovery would amount to hundreds of thousands of documents, many of which were classified.

That is far from all. If there is an evidentiary hearing in the habeas proceedings, what sort of evidence can the government use in satisfying its burden, if it has one? Can it introduce hearsay? May it rely on classified intelligence reports? Must it show such reports to the detainee or his counsel? What of confidential informants? Should the government be required to disclose the informant's identity, produce the individual for questioning, give the detainee all of the statements the informant has made to the military or to the CIA?

Parts of the al-Qaeda training manual have been introduced in several of the habeas cases. The manual instructs those who are captured to lie to their captors, to make up stories and to claim they have been tortured. How should the district court treat claims of torture? Whose burden is it? What exactly constitutes torture? Must all statements from the detainee during torture be excluded? What about statements in the weeks and months and years after those events?

One might suppose that at least some of these procedural and evidentiary questions, and others, could be decided by referring to the body of law that has grown up around the Fifth Amendment or the Sixth Amendment or other constitutional provisions. But recall Justice Jackson's reasoning in *Eisentrager*. He denied that constitutional protections extended beyond the United States to aliens who never had any presence in this country. The law of the D.C. Circuit is the same—these constitutional provisions do not extend to aliens who have no property or presence in the United States.

The Guantánamo cases raise many other enormously important issues. I will mention just two more. Late last spring a panel of our court overruled a district court decision extending the writ of habeas corpus to prisoners being held at the Bagram Air Force Base in Afghanistan.[15] The United States was occupying Bagram as a lessee. One way of looking at the case is that our court had to choose between *Eisentrager* and *Boumediene*. Was the military's lease and occupation of Bagram more like the Army's control of Landsberg Prison in Bavaria or was it more like the Navy's lease of Guantánamo from Cuba? As I said, our court came down on the side of *Eisentrager* and held that habeas did not extend to Afghanistan. No certiorari petition has yet been filed. The case is back in the district court, at least for the moment.

The second issue came up in the case of *Salahi v. Obama*.[16] The detainee in the case admits having sworn an oath of allegiance or "*bayat*" to bin Laden. One question in the case is who bears the burden of proving that the detainee quit al-Qaeda—which Salahi says he did—when there is no dispute that the detainee had been part of the organization?

What I have described is but a glimpse of the Guantánamo mess created by the Supreme Court. I have barely scratched the surface. Where all of this will lead and what effect it will have on future military conflicts is anyone's guess. Justice Scalia in his *Boumediene* dissent predicts that the majority opinion in the case will make the war on terror "harder on us. It will almost certainly cause more Americans to be killed." I hope he is wrong. But I do not know.

I am, however, certain of one thing. It is easy to distort history. Professor Fischer lists 112 ways to do it, and there are many more. And I am certain too that George Orwell was right. "Who controls the past controls the future: who controls the present controls the past."

our fighting faith, ten years later

CHARLES R. KESLER

O n the afternoon of September 11, 2001, when I could no longer bear to watch the awful images from New York City and Washington, D.C., I went to my office and hurriedly wrote a few paragraphs for *National Review Online*. The brief article was posted on the *National Review* website at 7:30 p.m., Eastern Time, and so probably qualifies as one of the earliest editorial reactions to the day's savage attacks. Here is an excerpt:

The first thing that Americans must do when confronting the moral implications of the attacks . . . is to stop calling them a "tragedy." The word is inadequate, having been cheapened by overuse, and strictly speaking it is inapt. In the original sense, a tragedy is not simply a dreadful event or terrible calamity but one that befalls a great man as the result of his own flaw, the effect on the audience being to elicit pity and terror. But our enemies today did not aim for a catharsis. They meant to terrorize America, to dispirit us by fear, to leave us stupefied and paralyzed.

The consequences of these attacks are tragic, of course, in the broad contemporary sense of the term, but that sense is so broad as to be morally neutral. If the World Trade Center towers had collapsed due to an earthquake we would be calling that event tragic, too. Granted, it's hard to tear oneself away from the terrible human toll, but to take a proper . . . view of the attacks we must focus not merely on their consequences but on the intentions behind [them]. These were wicked acts: savage, cruel, and evil.[1]

I concluded the piece with a prediction: "Our enemies underestimate American courage, forgetting that American democracy has ever been a fighting faith."

Ten years later, we pause to remember and take stock. How goes that fight, and that faith? Let me comment on three aspects of our evolving reaction to the attacks—the language with which we came to grips with them; the repercussions for our domestic political opinions; and the new emphasis on the export—or at least the spread—of democracy abroad.

After a decade, we have found no better way to refer to the massacres of that day than as "9/11." Battles are usually named after a nearby city or geographical feature, but this was less a battle than a slaughter, and in not one but two cities (though apparently there had been some planning for a third blow, against Los Angeles), thus ruling out a single place name like Bull Run or Pearl Harbor. So it seems likely we shall continue to know the sneak attack as "September 11," no year necessary. Probably the only other date burned so indelibly into the national memory is July 4, but it is called more grandly the Fourth of July and has an official designation, Independence Day, which 9/11 lacks. Many Americans will never forget Franklin D. Roosevelt's magnificent declamation of "Yesterday, December 7, 1941, a date which will live in infamy . . . ," but I fear quite a few have forgotten it or, in the days of YouTube, never heard of it. Besides, George W. Bush, despite giving several very good speeches in the wake of 9/11, never managed a phrase as memorable as Roosevelt's. We are stuck with a name based on the date—usually expressed entirely in Arabic numerals, no less, because of the coincidence with 9-1-1, the emergency number.

Identifying the attacks with their date suggests the arbitrariness of it all: it is as though suddenly, on this date, for no assignable reason, "everything changed," as the phrase had it. Or conversely, the date may imply that a kind of terrible fate befell America, an existential stroke of doom not unlike what the false prophets had predicted for Y2K. In any case, the day's images were difficult to believe, and compelled repeated showings from multiple angles. Over and over and over again, against the perfect sky, those shimmering airplanes crashed into the Twin Towers, but the association of cause with effect still seemed impossible to take in. The country reeled in shock, disbelief, and fear.

But the American character reasserted itself more quickly than the jihadist commandoes had figured. Up smoke-filled stairwells and in melting corridors, firemen and policemen did their jobs courageously, unstintingly. Aboard United Flight 93, the passengers assumed responsibility for a task that was no one's clear responsibility, because it could hardly have been imagined before takeoff. It was, in its own spontaneous yet deliberate way, a quintessential American moment: after saying a prayer and taking a vote together, the passengers launched their own revolution, rushing the cockpit and sacrificing their lives to save their countrymen in the nation's capital. That moment came naturally to those brave men and women because it struck, somewhere in their souls, the mystic chords of memory connecting them to generations of praying, voting, and fighting Americans stretching back to Bastogne, Gettysburg, and Valley Forge.

In the days and months afterward, New York Mayor Rudy Giuliani's and President George W. Bush's words and deeds were vital to the larger recovery of American self-confidence. Their words were deeds, and their deeds had an eloquence of their own. Still, President Bush's fine speech on September 20 yielded pride of place to Todd Beamer, a passenger on United 93, whose words Bush adopted when a few weeks later he led the nation to war in Afghanistan: "Let's Roll." For a while this functioned as a kind of national slogan. As a watchword, it had obvious limitations compared to, say, "Remember Pearl Harbor" or "Remember the Lusitania." It did not directly engage our memory and conscience, for one thing, though it appealed to them indirectly, of course. I recall, at the time, wondering why "Remember 9/11" or something similar had not become a byword. Perhaps the footage of the collapsing towers was sufficiently raw in the national consciousness that nothing additional was necessary. It did not take long, however, before that footage began to disappear from television, and within a year or so it was effectively banished. No common words then recorded the sacred vow of vengeance or justice the public had presumably taken after September 11, and as time passed it became easier to forget why and where we were rolling. Victory loses its luster, and its urgency, when rescinded from the reasons we fight. "Let's Roll" easily faded into *Mission Accomplished*, an "ending" out of a Hollywood action movie, leaving much unfinished business to be treated in the sequel.

At home, one of the most striking features of the reaction to 9/11 was the outpouring of religious sentiment and ceremony. Millions of prayers rose heavenward on that day, and for months afterward the churches and synagogues were packed. (The mosques, too, as the President observed several times, insisted that the terrorists had attempted, unsuccessfully, to hijack their own peaceful religion.) The formerly naked public square was suddenly and richly clothed. On the evening of the attack, Democratic and Republican congressmen gathered on the steps of the Capitol to sing "God Bless America." A few days later, President Bush led an ecumenical prayer service at the National Cathedral. New Yorkers gathered to pay tribute at a memorial service in Yankee Stadium, and similar ceremonies were convened in churches and town halls across the country. Face-to-face with evil, even the ACLU blinked. No lawsuits were filed challenging the use of public property for religious purposes or seeking to enjoin firemen and policemen from praying on the job.

Founded to secure its citizens' rights to life, liberty, and the pursuit of happiness, a polity like the United States is in some respects peculiarly vulnerable to acts of mass terrorism. When the customs and laws protecting our rights and guaranteeing their peaceful exercise are suddenly and violently disrupted, the government's principal reason for being is called into question. Fear—not the Hobbesian fear of your neighbor but the Lockean fear felt by a community suddenly unprotected against violent assault, abandoned to "force without right"—asserts itself powerfully, though in the American case only momentarily. Courage and righteous indignation swelled, too, aided by religion's steadying focus on our duties here and now, the God who loves justice, and the consolations of the world to come. A polity founded, at least partly, to observe an unprecedented separation of church and state has always found fertile ways to connect religion and politics.

Yet the resurgence of religious expression on 9/11 and afterward marked more of a ceasefire than a victory in the contemporary battle over the public place of religion. Soon the federal judiciary roused itself. In 2002, a three-judge panel of the U.S. Court of Appeals for the Ninth Circuit ruled that voluntary recitation by California schoolchildren of the phrase "under God" in the Pledge of Allegiance created an unconstitutional establishment of religion, and forbade public teachers to lead their students in the Pledge.[2] The U.S. Supreme Court overturned the decision two years later on a technicality, holding that the plaintiff lacked standing to sue.[3] So soon after 9/11, and so close to the 2004 elections, a contrary decision would have been theological and political dynamite. Happily, the Court also avoided the embarrassment of affirming the Pledge on the grounds it had staked out in recent Establishment Clause cases: that public expressions of religious sentiments pass constitutional muster insofar as they are purely ceremonial, that is, religiously insignificant.

Alongside the temporary religious bloom, the revival of patriotism was the most startling change in public opinion wrought by 9/11. The two were connected, as the Pledge case showed. Most Americans thought the republic eminently worthy of allegiance. In fact, their emotional solidarity after the attacks imbued the American flag and the Pledge with renewed meaning—one nation, under God, indivisible, with liberty and justice for all. We were all in this together, God help us. The faith that united us was a reasonable faith, anchored in the self-evident truths of human equality, liberty, and self-government; truths that helped define a moral community spanning the American past, present, and future. Although 9/11 revived that faith, it did not and could not overcome its doubters and critics who therefore saw in the American past mostly moral hypocrisy, or worse; those doubters saw a country that has cultivated a progressive faith in a future of ever more moral, rational, and cosmopolitan governance, quite different from the old republic. The lines in American politics were softened but not erased or redrawn by 9/11. And yet, though the impassioned flag-waving eventually subsided, the patriotic sensitivity endured.

Consider Barack Obama's experience. As a candidate for President in fall 2007, then-Senator Obama not only declined to wear a flag pin routinely on his lapel, but also defended his decision on grounds of high principle. "The truth is that right after 9/11, I had a pin," he said in Cedar Rapids, Iowa, on October 3. "Shortly after 9/11, particularly as we're talking about the Iraq war, that became a substitute for, I think, true patriotism, which is speaking out on issues that are of importance to our national security. I decided I won't wear that pin on my chest. Instead I'm going to tell the American people what I believe will make this country great and hopefully that will be a testimony to my patriotism."[4] The second stage of his defense was to suggest that people who wear the lapel pin are compensating, as the Freudians say, for their own inadequate patriotism. On October 4, he explained, "After a while, you start noticing people wearing a lapel pin, but not acting very patriotic. Not voting to provide veterans with resources they need. Not voting to make sure that disability payments were coming out on time."[5] By early 2008, as his campaign took off, Obama arrived at stage three: wearing the flag pin almost daily.

Though a small incident in a long decade, Obama's handling of the issue (Pingate?) nicely recapitulates the arc through which contemporary liberalism has moved in regard to patriotism. The problem began in the 1960s. Middle-class and working-class Americans found it hard to forget—or forgive—the zeal with which campus protesters and anti–Vietnam War marchers burned the American flag. It seemed it was not the war they were objecting to, but the country waging it, the America (sometimes spelled with a "k") trying to contain communism. An enmity grew between large numbers of ordinary Americans and the then long-haired, now balding, academic left. The enmity naturally spread to the Democratic Party, which could not shake its affection for the cultural and academic left. Obama's first stance reflected his wariness of reopening the quarrel. He had worn the pin, after all, in tribute to the fallen of 9/11. Yet he did not want that kind of gesture, which would appeal to policemen and firefighters and other middle-class types, to be mistaken for the "true patriotism" that would appeal to artists and professors. He chose to abjure the middle-class rituals: "I decided I won't wear that pin on my chest." Instead, he would "tell the American people what I believe will make this country great. . . ."[6] In other words, this was not a great country, but it could be—with the right President.

Sensing he may have gone too far, yet unwilling to repudiate his own convictions, Obama moved the following day to a second line of argument. True patriotism, which he emphasized now included administering and expanding the "resources" and "disability payments"[7] of the welfare state, ought to appeal to the *interests* of the middle class, even if their false or unenlightened patriotism could not acknowledge America's endemic flaws—its racism, sexism, and other sins much dwelled on by the cultural left and, it turned out, by his pastor of twenty years, the Reverend Jeremiah Wright. Obama stuck to this position through the fall and winter.

In Philadelphia, in March, 2008, President Obama had to deliver his much lauded speech on race, separating himself not only from the Reverend Wright's condemnation of America as a racist nation, guilty of heinous sins at home and abroad, but also from Wright's charge that 9/11 had been divine retribution for those sins, especially America's support for Israel, a case of our "chickens coming home to roost." But that was not the end of the matter. In a Pittsburgh-area town-hall meeting a month later, a veteran handed Obama a pin and asked him to wear it, which he did for a day, leading to what *Time* magazine called "a much-ridiculed question on the issue at a much-ridiculed ABC debate later that week." At that debate, Obama told the questioner, remarkably, "I have never said that I don't wear flag pins or refuse to wear flag pins."[8] And so as the campaign and then his presidency proceeded, the flag pin became more or less a staple of his wardrobe, a capitulation to the spirit of 9/11 and to the sensibility of the patriotic middle- and working-class voters whose support he needed.

Not much time had to be spent explaining to Americans why the massacres of 9/11 were evil. Yet a further explanation of the "freedom" the terrorists had attacked, of the principles of the Declaration of Independence, and the purposes of our own form of government and way of life, might have illuminated the way forward better than allowing 9/11 to spark "our mission and our moment," as Bush put it to a joint session of Congress on September 20, 2001. By far the largest consequence of the new "moment" was a foreign policy mission that shifted gradually from retaliating for 9/11, to waging a decade-long war in Afghanistan and Iraq. The moral focus changed, almost necessarily, from the specific evil of 9/11 to future evils that might be prevented and future goods that might be obtained. When Osama bin Laden was finally killed by U.S. forces on May 2, 2011—President Obama wore a flag pin when he made the announcement—Americans rejoiced but understood that the al-Qaeda head's death closed a chapter in the war but not the war itself, which had become something much larger and more diffuse than anyone had anticipated.

At the heart of the Bush administration's case for this "long war" was the so-called Bush Doctrine. Originally an endorsement of punitive war against the sponsors of the 9/11 atrocities as well as the states that harbored or abetted them, it soon expanded to include preemptive and even preventive war. The doctrine's final provision, the commitment to the global advance of democracy, emerged partly as an inference from the willingness to wage preemptive and preventive war. Regimes that might pass along weapons of mass destruction (WMD) to terrorists simply could not be permitted to possess such weapons. In the interim these regimes had to be denied dangerous technology, but in the long run they had to be changed into peaceful, commercial democracies, which would presumably exchange their WMD for ploughshares. Alongside this "realist" argument for democratization, Bush also advanced an "idealistic" one, discovering the imperative to spread democracy in America's own founding principles, or at least in a twentieth-century Wilsonian version of them.

The Second Inaugural Address represents the Bush Doctrine's high-water mark. Harking back to 9/11, the "day of fire," the President explained:

We have seen our vulnerability—and we have seen its deepest source. For as long as whole regions of the world simmer in resentment and tyranny—prone to ideologies that feed hatred and excuse murder—violence will gather, and multiply in destructive power, and cross the most defended borders, and raise a mortal threat. There is only one force of history that can break the reign of hatred and resentment, and expose the pretensions of tyrants, and reward the hopes of the decent and tolerant, and that is the force of human freedom. We are led, by events and common sense, to one conclusion: The survival of liberty in our land increasingly depends on the success of liberty in other lands. The best hope for peace in our world is the expansion of freedom in all the world. . . . So it is the policy of the United States to seek and support the growth of democratic movements and institutions in every nation and culture, with the ultimate goal of ending tyranny in our world.[9]

The problem is President Bush wanted to be both idealistic (he used that term or a variant of it nine times in the speech) and prudent at the same time. He wanted to take credit for proclaiming the lofty, breathtaking moral imperative (to end tyranny everywhere), which is breathtaking precisely because it is stubbornly opposed to experience, and insists that duty requires maximum striving for the impossible dream precisely because it seems impossible. That's idealism. (He went even further at the National Cathedral service after 9/11: "Just three days removed from these events, Americans do not yet have the distance of history. But our responsibility to history is already clear: to answer these attacks and rid the world of evil." A world not merely without tyranny, but without evil!) Yet at the same time Bush always wanted to be sober, responsible, and popular. He wanted to foster democracy everywhere and extinguish tyranny anywhere— though not immediately, nor by our efforts alone, and not at the expense of local customs and traditions, nor at the risk of our authoritarian allies, nor by force except in rare cases. These are all sensible limitations, of course, but what, then, is left of the idealistic imperative that made the blood race and the head swoon?

Bush's inability to bring these two projects into focus affected his discussions of 9/11, as well. In his speech on the fifth anniversary of 9/11, he declared, "on 9/11, our nation saw the face of evil." He implied that Mohammed Atta and the other mass murderers were not to be pitied or excused from their evildoing because they had poor education, exiguous exposure to political freedom, or too little midnight basketball. Atta and most of the others had had advanced education and had resided in the West, enjoying plenty of exposure to democratic freedom and opportunity. Their joyful adherence to what Bush rightly condemned as "a totalitarian ideology," a "perverted version of Islam," was as much a protest against liberal democracy as against Middle Eastern despotism.[10] In fact, they favored a much more thoroughgoing regime of despotism than any ever devised by the region's secular tyrants.

At the same time, Bush blamed the United States for contributing to the surge of radical Islam in the Middle East because for decades—for the sake of stability—we supported the region's undemocratic governments (the only kind that existed, incidentally, except in Israel). As a result, a generation of young Muslims, beset by "stagnation and despair," grew up "with little hope to improve their lives, and many fell under the sway of radical extremism." He explained at the American Legion's national convention, "the lack of freedom in the Middle East made the region an incubator for terrorist movements." September 11 really was a kind of tragedy, then, with the United States as the flawed hero. The only solution, he concluded, was to democratize the region, beginning with Iraq. "Dissidents with the freedom to protest around the clock are less likely to blow themselves up during rush hour," he averred.

Bush left us, and perhaps himself, wondering: do Islamic terrorists long for civil freedom, or for tyranny? Is evil the result of material and political deprivation, or of the excessive or insatiable desire for honor and pleasure? Is tyranny a temporary detour from history, which is hurtling towards global democracy and progress, or a permanent temptation of human nature, certain to be around, in some form, as long as politics is?

I do not mean to deny what President Bush called the "global appeal of liberty," rooted in a genuine "longing of the soul"; and there is wisdom in his remark (also from the Second Inaugural Address) that "Americans, of all people, should never be surprised by the power of our ideals." But freedom is not the only human longing, nor is it always the most powerful; and not every revolution is based on "our ideals," even if the revolutionaries call loudly for democracy. Thus, even as we cheer the lengthening roster of democracies in the world, we should wish for them, and for our own fighting faith, the self-control that keeps liberty a blessing and not a curse. Our principles are sometimes more demanding than we realize. This, too, is a lesson that looms larger a decade after 9/11.

Conclusion

JOHN YOO

Germany's Iron Chancellor, Otto von Bismarck, reportedly observed on his deathbed that Heaven held "a special providence for drunkards, fools, and the United States."[1] As President Barack Obama nears the end of his first term in office, he has come to depend on Bismarck's quip for his greatest responsibility: protecting America's national security.

Only the bravery of individual passengers and the flight crew stopped Umar Farouk Abdulmutallab from blowing up Northwest Airlines Flight 253 over Detroit on Christmas Day 2009. Janet Napolitano, the secretary of the Department of Homeland Security, bizarrely claimed, "the system worked."[2] Another terrorist, Faisal Shahzad, almost succeeded in exploding a car bomb in New York City's crowded Times Square in May 2010. Lives were spared because the al-Qaeda agent unwittingly failed to construct the bomb properly.

But it was not simply a lucky roll of the dice that brought al-Qaeda to the brink of more spectacular bombings. Abdulmutallab and Shahzad almost succeeded because of the White House's loss of focus on national security priorities—all too ironic coming from a candidate who campaigned asserting that President George W. Bush had neglected the real counterterrorist fight in Afghanistan for the distraction of Iraq. The Obama administration's reversal of the presidency's constitutional priorities has triggered national security policy inattention, which has led to strategic drift and tactical mistakes that have reduced security for little gain.

CONSTITUTIONAL PRIORITIES

Throughout his first years in office, Obama has placed national security second to his ambitious plan to remake the American economy and society. Even while the wars in Afghanistan and Iraq raged on, he concentrated on the nationalization of the health care industry, the billion-dollar bailouts of AIG, Citibank, GM, and Chrysler, the massive overhaul of the financial services and banking industries, the regulation of greenhouse gas emissions, and the remaking of the American energy industry. Bailouts and stimulus spending will drive the budget deficit to almost $1.5 trillion in 2011, the largest in U.S. history. According to the

Congressional Budget Office, the deficit will constitute 9.8 percent of GDP, a figure not seen since World War II.

Even as Obama delayed a decision on whether to surge 30,000 troops to Afghanistan, he retreated from his predecessor's aggressive strategy against al-Qaeda. He remains intent on closing the detention facility at Guantánamo Bay, Cuba, despite the fact that released jihadists have rejoined al-Qaeda (at a rate of 25 percent by 2010, according to the Pentagon)[3] and were linked to the Christmas Day bombing attempt. He ended the tough interrogation of al-Qaeda leaders that had yielded crucial intelligence on their plans, and he attempted to transfer the trial of Khalid Sheikh Mohammed (KSM) and other 9/11 plotters from specially created military tribunals to federal civilian court in New York.

President Obama's State of the Union addresses nicely sum up his topsy-turvy approach to the presidency. He has pressed for new jobs bills, more domestic spending, and health care nationalization. He attributed his political setbacks not to broad opposition to his domestic ambitions but to the American people's "deficit of trust—deep and corrosive doubts about how Washington works that have been growing for years."[4] National security amounted to an afterthought. In his 2010 State of the Union, Obama devoted one paragraph each—out of the approximately 110 paragraphs in the speech—to Iraq, Afghanistan, and terrorism. His 2011 address similarly relegated these three ongoing wars to a few brief paragraphs at the very end of his speech.[5] It is as if Lincoln had spent most of his inaugural addresses praising the transcontinental railroad and the Homestead Act.

Obama believes the President should lead a revolution in society, the economy, and the political system, but defer national security and foreign policy to the other branches of government. This upends the Framers' vision of the presidency: they thought the chief executive's powers would expand broadly to meet external challenges while playing a modest role at home.

The latest Democratic President is repeating the mistake of the first. When Thomas Jefferson entered office 210 years ago, Chief Justice John Marshall warned that Jefferson would "embody himself in the House of Representatives."[6] This would "increase his personal power," Marshall predicted, but it would lead to the "weakening of the office of the President."[7] The Chief Justice meant that his political rival (and distant cousin) would gain power by joining forces with his party's legislative majorities. But the combination would soon realize the Framers' fear that Congress would come to dominate the executive branch.

Marshall's observation explains much about Obama's first term. By associating himself so closely with congressional Democrats, Obama became responsible for their every misstep. Their reckless overspending and earmarks became his. Their corrupt deal to buy Senator Ben Nelson's support for nationalized health care became his sordid bargain. Their command-and-control approach to global warming, which would set nationwide limits on energy use and industrial production, became his socialist program.

Putting the President's fortune in Congress's hands not only makes for poor politics, it also runs counter to the Framers' plans for the office. The Framers saw Congress, not the presidency, as the main threat to the people's liberties. In a democracy, James Madison wrote in *The Federalist Papers*, "The legislative authority, necessarily, predominates" because it has access to the "pockets of the people." He warned, "it is against the enterprising ambition" of Congress "that the people ought to indulge all their jealousy and exhaust all their precautions."[8]

The Framers expected the presidency to counterbalance the "impetuous vortex" of Congress. A vigorous executive, Alexander

Hamilton wrote in *Federalist No. 70*, would protect against those "irregular and high-handed combinations which sometimes interrupt the ordinary course of justice" and provide security against "enterprises and assaults of ambition, of faction, and of anarchy" which would emanate from the "humours of the legislature."[9] The great threat to the Constitution, Hamilton wrote, was the "propensity of the legislative department to intrude upon the rights and absorb the powers of other departments" such as the executive branch, the courts, and the states.[10] The President's veto would not only protect the executive's constitutional rights from Congress, he wrote, it would also furnish "an additional security against the enaction of improper laws" and allow the President "to guard the community against the effects of faction, precipitancy, or of any impulse unfriendly to the public good."[11]

The power to regulate the domestic economy and society—limited as it originally was meant to have been—rested with Congress. The President was to restrain the legislature when it favored party or special interests over the public good. This was no easy job. To give it institutional backbone, the Framers clothed the presidency with independent election, consistent pay, the veto, and control over the execution of the laws. Still, Hamilton could only hope in *Federalist No. 71* that when the legislature gave in to demagogues or temporary passions, the President would "be in a situation to dare to act his own opinion with vigor and decision."[12]

Obama has inverted the presidency in domestic affairs by transforming it from a check into a facilitator of Congress. The American people's response has been the political version of shock and awe. Public approval of Obama's job performance fell from 76 percent in February 2009 to 48 percent in early 2010, the largest drop on record for a first-year President. Obama's stimulus program received no Republican votes, nor did his health care or global warming bills. Public approval of his party's control in Congress collapsed in tandem, with the result that Republicans won sweeping gains in the 2010 midterm elections in the House of Representatives, the Senate, state governorships, and state legislatures.

NATIONAL SECURITY AND THE PRESIDENCY

Obama's political fortunes have fallen so sharply because he is straining to burst the Framers' original intentions for the presidency. The presidency was meant to be weak at home and strong abroad. Obama's second and even more significant reversal of the presidency's constitutional position is his hesitance toward—and even retreat from—its core role as the protector of the nation's security.

As Hamilton wrote in *Federalist No. 70*, the presidency was to be the one part of government that could respond with "decision, activity, secrecy, and dispatch" to unforeseen crises, especially war.[13] Borrowing liberally from John Locke, Hamilton argued in *Federalist No. 74* that the central function of the executive was to be a branch of the government always in being, one that could respond swiftly to emergencies. War would make the most demands on the presidency. "Of all the cares or concerns of government," Hamilton wrote, "the direction of war most peculiarly demands those qualities which distinguish the exercise of power by a single hand."[14]

The dependence of executive power on these circumstances was not lost on early observers of the American system. In *Democracy in America*, Alexis de Tocqueville stated that the presidency would grow with the United States: "The President of the United States possesses almost royal prerogatives, which he has no opportunity of exercising; and the privileges that he can at present use are very circumscribed. The laws allow him to be strong, but circumstances keep him weak." That would change, Tocqueville predicted, as America became a great nation. It is in foreign relations "that the executive power of a nation finds occasion to exert its skill and its strength." If the security of the country "were perpetually threatened, if its chief interests were in daily connection with those of other powerful nations," Tocqueville continued, "the executive government would assume an increased importance in proportion to the measures expected of it and to those which it would execute."[15]

Obama, by contrast, has steered the presidency in exactly the opposite direction. He wants the executive to be a domestic strongman who can speedily dismiss opposition to his health care and economic ambitions. But his decisions to try KSM in federal court and to place the Christmas bomber in FBI custody represent an unprecedented effort to leave critical wartime decisions—here, final decisions on the disposition of enemy combatants—up to the other branches of government.

Obama only started to turn things around with his decision to send 30,000 troops to Afghanistan and to stick with the Iraq drawdown timetable. He has become what he campaigned against—a decisive, "unilateral," President. Obama did not conduct extensive consultations with congressional leaders on the Afghanistan surge. Obama did not go back to Congress for authorization, but instead pointed to the 2001 approval of the use of force in response to the 9/11 attacks. In speeches in Oslo and West Point, Obama defended America's unilateral right to use force to defend itself and its interests. He is beginning to mature, just as Kennedy's early setbacks with the Bay of Pigs and the Berlin Wall prepared the way for his unilateral leadership during the Cuban Missile Crisis.

TERRORISM TACTICS

Obama's inversion of the presidency's constitutional priorities has led, nonetheless, to a loss of coherence in military and intelligence tactics against al-Qaeda. In one of his first acts upon taking office, President Obama ordered the shutdown of Guantánamo. He issued executive orders halting all military commission trials for terrorists and limiting the CIA's authority to interrogate al-Qaeda leaders. Obama pledged to reduce terrorism to a problem for law enforcement without any loss in security. America can "reject as false the choice between our safety and our ideals," he proudly announced in his inaugural address.[16]

For almost a decade, the anti-war left portrayed the naval base at Guantánamo Bay as a twenty-first-century Bastille, to be stormed by a throng of left-wing lawyers, journalists, and human rights activists (some of whom now work in the Obama administration). Wearing an orange jumpsuit became a radically chic protest against the Bush administration.

Barack Obama fed these fantasies. As a presidential candidate, Senator Obama declared: "it's time to show the world . . . we're not a country that runs prisons which locks people away without ever telling them why they're there or what they're charged with."[17] President Obama not only ordered Guantánamo closed within a year, but he seems to have ended snatch-and-grab operations. Even as al-Qaeda has redoubled its attacks on the U.S. homeland, the Obama administration did not capture a single high-ranking al-Qaeda leader. In even its greatest victory in the war, the Obama administration chose to kill rather than capture Osama bin Laden despite the unique intelligence in his possession.

The Guantánamo myth also drove the Justice Department's headstrong push to prosecute al-Qaeda leaders in U.S. civilian courts. Nowhere else did the Obama administration more clearly display its view of terrorism as a problem for law enforcement. The near-acquittal of Ahmed Ghailani, the al-Qaeda operative who facilitated the bombing of the USS *Cole*, by a New York jury in late 2010 has clearly revealed that path as a dead end—even if Attorney General Holder remains in denial. The simple alternative to such prosecutions is to continue detentions at Guantánamo. Detention is consistent with the rules of war, which allow captured combatants to be held indefinitely without requiring criminal charges to be filed against them. It also keeps our troops and agents in the field focused on finding and killing the enemy, not collecting evidence and interviewing witnesses.

By now, even the Obama Girl must concede that her hero isn't one to keep his promises. Guantánamo, still open for business, holds about 170 suspected terrorists. The administration acknowledges its authority to hold them indefinitely, and it has halted the release of detainees after learning that at least one quarter of the ones previously released have returned to terrorism. The White House has suspended Attorney General Eric Holder's high-profile decision to try KSM and other 9/11 plotters in New York City. In January 2011, Pentagon sources revealed that the military would soon restart its commissions to try terrorists, after Congress banned the transfer of any detainees from Guantánamo to the United States.

Our military and intelligence officers can't be blamed for experiencing a disorienting sense of déjà vu beyond detention operations. Obama has continued the broad filtering of normal electronic communications to search for terrorists. He has stepped up the use of unmanned Predator drones to kill al-Qaeda leaders, including those who happen to be American citizens.

Obama most resembles not John F. Kennedy, but Dwight Eisenhower. Eisenhower criticized the Truman administration's containment policy toward an expansionist Soviet Union and campaigned for the "rollback" of communism. Once in office, however, he essentially adopted the main principles of the Truman strategy, including the acceptance of a Soviet sphere in Eastern Europe. Similarly, once he faced the reality of the terrorism threat and bore responsibility for the nation's security, President Obama has dropped his criticism and continued much of his predecessor's strategy and tactics in the war on terror.

But there are important differences within this broad analogizing framework, just as there were between Truman and Eisenhower. Obama has weakened the nation's fight against al-Qaeda by drying up our primary source of intelligence on the enemy. It is no coincidence that the enemy has redoubled its efforts to launch unconventional attacks on the U.S. homeland. Near misses like the Christmas Day and Times Square bombings inevitably flow from Obama's naïve desire to close the terrorist detention facility at Guantánamo Bay.

Apparently convinced by the anti-war left's irresponsible allegations of widespread abuse and torture at Guantánamo, Obama was convinced that his decision would help our anti-terrorism efforts. Closing Guantánamo would make the United States more popular abroad and remove an al-Qaeda recruitment narrative. Neither Congress nor the American people bought this story of terrorist radicalization, and by the end of 2010 Congress used its power of the purse to keep the base open and to prevent the transfer of enemy prisoners to the United States.

Despite Congress's move to keep Guantánamo open, Obama has stubbornly prohibited the military from bringing any more detainees to Cuba. This creates a strong incentive, if not command, to the troops in the field not to return with any terrorists. Our soldiers will simply kill more of the enemy and capture fewer—far easier than collecting evidence, taking witness statements, and even risking prosecution by Attorney General Holder, who continues to investigate CIA agents who interrogated high-ranking al-Qaeda leaders in the months after 9/11. Not only does this mean that we kill more terrorists (how's that for a violation of human rights?), but we lose the opportunity to question them about al-Qaeda's future plans of attack.

This mistake is only compounded by the Obama administration's overreliance on drone warfare. CIA Director Leon Panetta calls it "the only game in town." Drones don't take prisoners. They sometimes kill civilians nearby. And they cannot interrogate the dead or decipher blown-up hard drives. Firing missiles from afar cannot substitute for the capture and interrogation of al-Qaeda leaders for intelligence. (The real question now is whether CIA agents will decline to interrogate prisoners, fearing Holder's criminal investigations into Bush policies.) As long as no one is sent to Guantánamo, the Obama administration will leave itself only two options: killing terrorists or catch-and-release. Obama's drone-heavy policy means that more people will die, including not only al-Qaeda and Taliban fighters, but also innocent Afghan and Pakistani civilians. Choosing to kill from afar rather than capture in person deprives the United States of yet another opportunity to gather intelligence.

Gaining the information in the heads of terrorist leaders remains the most effective means for stopping terrorist attacks on the U.S. homeland. Our enemy has no territory, population, or regular armed forces. It operates covertly, concealing its movements and communications within everyday economic traffic, and aims to launch surprise attacks on innocent civilian targets. Conventional military tactics have limited success against this new breed of enemy. Only by learning al-Qaeda's plans can we preempt its attacks on the U.S. homeland. It is this irreplaceable source of information that the Obama administration has cast aside as it pursues its Guantánamo obsession.

Even the Obama administration's greatest victory in the war on terror—the killing of Osama bin Laden—reflects these shortcomings in policy. As the operation put so vividly on display, President Obama would rather kill al-Qaeda leaders—whether by drones or Special Ops teams—than wade through the difficult questions raised by their detention. This may have dissuaded Mr. Obama from sending a more robust force to attempt a capture.

News reports were conflicted, but it appears that bin Laden was not armed. He did not have a large retinue of bodyguards—only three other people, the two couriers and bin Laden's adult son, were killed. Special Forces units using nonlethal weaponry might have taken bin Laden alive, as happened with other senior al-Qaeda leaders before him.

If true, one of the most valuable intelligence opportunities since the beginning of the war slipped through American hands. Some claim that bin Laden had become a symbol, or that al-Qaeda had devolved into a decentralized terrorist network with more active franchises in Yemen or Somalia. Nevertheless, bin Laden was still issuing instructions and funds to a broad terrorist network and would have known where and how to find other key al-Qaeda players. His capture, like Saddam Hussein's in December 2003, would have provided invaluable intelligence and been an even greater example of U.S. military prowess than his death.

White House counterterrorism advisor John Brennan said after the bin Laden operations that the SEAL team had orders to take the al-Qaeda leader alive "if he didn't present any threat," though he correctly dismissed this possibility as "remote." This is hard to take seriously. No one could have expected bin Laden to surrender without a fight. And capturing him alive would have required the administration to hold and interrogate bin Laden at Guantánamo Bay, something that has given this President allergic reactions bordering on a seizure.

President Obama deserves credit for ordering the mission that killed bin Laden. But he should also recognize that he succeeded despite his urge to disavow Bush administration policies. Perhaps one day he will acknowledge his predecessor's role in making the dramatic success possible. More importantly, he could end the ongoing criminal investigation of CIA agents and restart the interrogation program that helped lead American forces to bin Laden.

CONCLUSION

We can only hope that Obama will have the courage to pursue a more serious counterterrorism policy in the rest of his term. His decision to surge troops to Afghanistan, and at least maintain some of the Bush security policies, hints at a maturing disregard for the triumphalist press on the 2008 election. Democrats mistook Obama's election for a massive political realignment of the kind ushered in by Franklin D. Roosevelt and Ronald Reagan. The political tectonic plates have shifted so drastically only in 1800, 1828, 1860, 1932, and 1980. These shifts created years of dominance of the political system by one party and its general set of political ideas. Despite hopes by some, that didn't happen in 2008. Even California—the bluest of blue states—which elected Obama by an unprecedented 61–37 margin, also banned gay marriage, added a crime victims' rights amendment to the state constitution, and continues to prohibit affirmative action.

Obama's election, like Eisenhower's, reflected personal popularity more than an ideological sea change in the electorate. It is hard to believe now, but Obama sold himself within the Reagan framework. He promised to kill and capture terrorists, opposed gay marriage, promised to balance the budget, and wanted the death penalty for child rapists. Nixon and Clinton similarly misread their elections as political realignments, which led to similar overreaching and ultimately failure despite their re-elections. Obama risks the same failure with his partisan push for health care without the electorate's support.

Obama should take a cue from his political hero and the last truly great Democratic President, Franklin D. Roosevelt. If World War II had not come, FDR might have become an average President at best. His New Deal, we now know, did not end the Great Depression, and he wrecked his own political party in the process. But FDR joined the pantheon of Washington and Lincoln as one of our three greatest Presidents by foreseeing and preparing for the existential threat posed by Hitler and the Axis powers. As FDR himself said, "Dr. New Deal" had to give way to "Dr. Win the War."[18]

To save his presidency, Obama should follow the real lesson of FDR and our other great Presidents and turn away from the failures of health care reform and nationalization of the economy. Obama will be remembered favorably if he follows through in Iraq, pursues al-Qaeda with the restoration of aggressive measures, and wins victory in Afghanistan. If he loses in war in favor of nationalization at home, he will take his place in presidential history alongside Jimmy Carter or Lyndon Johnson, rather than FDR or Reagan.

AUTHOR BIOGRAPHIES

Professor John D. Ashcroft   Professor Ashcroft is currently Distinguished Professor of Law and Government at Regent University, and chairman of the Ashcroft Consulting Group, LLC. He served as Attorney General of the United States from 2001 to 2005. Professor Ashcroft was previously a U.S. Senator from Missouri, 1995–2001, and the Governor of Missouri, 1985–1993.

Bob Barr   Bob Barr is a former federal prosecutor and a former member of the U.S. House of Representatives. From 1995 to

2003, he represented Georgia's 7th congressional district. While in Congress, Mr. Barr served as a senior member of the Judiciary Committee, as vice chairman of the Government Reform Committee, and as a member of the Committee on Financial Services and the Committee on Veterans' Affairs. He was also one of the leaders of the Clinton impeachment trial. Prior to serving in Congress, Mr. Barr was appointed by President Ronald Reagan in 1986 to serve as a U.S. Attorney for the Northern District of Georgia, a position he held until 1990. He was an official with the CIA from 1971 to 1978. In 2008, Mr. Barr was the Libertarian Party nominee for President of the United States. Today, he practices law with the Law Offices of Edwin Marger, and runs a consulting firm, Liberty Strategies, Inc., headquartered in Atlanta, Georgia. He is also a member of the Constitution Project's Initiative on Liberty and Security.

Michael Chertoff Mr. Chertoff was the second U.S. Secretary of Homeland Security under President George W. Bush, from 2005 to 2009. Prior to being appointed to that position, he served as a federal judge on the U.S. Court of Appeals for the Third Circuit and Assistant Attorney General for the Criminal Division of the U.S. Department of Justice, a position in which he oversaw the department's investigation of the 9/11 terrorist attacks and during which time he co-authored the USA Patriot Act. Mr. Chertoff also spent more than a decade as a federal prosecutor, including service as an Assistant U.S. Attorney for the Southern District of New York, First Assistant U.S. Attorney for the District of New Jersey, and U.S. Attorney for the District of New Jersey. From 1995 to 1996, he served as Special Counsel for the U.S. Senate Whitewater Committee. Since leaving government service, he has worked as senior of counsel at the law firm of Covington & Burling in Washington, D.C. He also founded the Chertoff Group, a risk management and security consulting firm.

Professor Alan Dershowitz   Professor Dershowitz is the Felix Frankfurter Professor of Law at Harvard Law School, where in 1967 he became the youngest full professor of law in the school's history. He has taught and lectured on subjects ranging from history to criminal law, and philosophy to mathematics. Professor Dershowitz clerked for Judge David L. Bazelon of the U.S. Court of Appeals for the District of Columbia Circuit and for Justice Arthur Goldberg of the Supreme Court of the United States. He has published over a hundred articles in magazines and journals such as the *New York Times Magazine*, the *Washington Post*, the *Wall Street Journal*, and the *New Republic*, as well as numerous legal journals. He has also authored twenty-seven fiction and nonfiction works.

Professor Viet D. Dinh   Professor Viet Dinh is currently professor of law and co-director of Asian Law and Policy Studies at the Georgetown University Law Center, and founder and principal of Bancroft PLLC. He served as Assistant Attorney General for the Office of Legal Policy from 2001 to 2003 under the presidency of George W. Bush. He was one of the chief authors of the USA Patriot Act. Professor Dinh also served as Associate Special Counsel to the U.S. Senate Banking Committee for the Whitewater Investigation and as Special Counsel to U.S. Senator Pete V. Domenici for the impeachment trial of President Clinton. Previously, Professor Dinh clerked for Judge Laurence H. Silberman of the U.S. Court of Appeals for the District of Columbia Circuit and for Justice Sandra Day O'Connor of the U.S. Supreme Court. He has authored a number of articles on topics including corporate governance and economic development.

Professor Richard A. Epstein   Professor Richard Epstein is
the Laurence A. Tisch Professor of Law at New York University
Law School, a position he has held since 2010. Prior to joining
the faculty at NYU, he was the James Parker Hall Distinguished
Service Professor Emeritus of Law and senior lecturer at the
University of Chicago Law School, where he was a director of
the John M. Olin Program in Law and Economics from 2001 to
2010. Professor Epstein has served as the Peter and Kirstin Bed-
ford Senior Fellow at the Hoover Institution at Stanford University since 2000. He has authored countless books and articles on
a wide range of legal and interdisciplinary subjects and teaches
courses ranging from constitutional law to health law and policy.
Professor Epstein began his teaching career at the University of
Southern California, from 1968 to 1972.

Dr. Victor Davis Hanson   Dr. Hanson is a military historian,
columnist, political essayist, and the Martin and Illie Anderson
Senior Fellow at the Hoover Institution. He was formerly a clas-
sics professor at California State University, Fresno, where he
inaugurated a program in classical languages. Dr. Hanson has
authored or edited twenty books, and has written over 150 articles, book reviews, and newspaper editorials on Greek, agrarian,
and military history, as well as essays on contemporary culture.
He has won a number of awards, including the Eric Breindel
Award for opinion journalism (2002), the National Humanities
Medal (2007), and the Bradley Prize (2008), and has served as a
commentator on modern warfare and contemporary politics for
National Review and other media outlets.

Dr. Arthur Herman   Dr. Herman is a prolific American historian, author, and lecturer, and currently a visiting scholar at the
American Enterprise Institute. He is known principally for his

works on British history, most notably his 2001 *New York Times* bestseller on the Scottish Enlightenment, *How the Scots Invented the Modern World*. His most recent book, *Gandhi and Churchill: The Epic Rivalry That Destroyed an Empire and Forged Our Age*, was a finalist for the Pulitzer Prize in 2009. Dr. Herman has taught at Sewanee: The University of the South, George Mason University, Georgetown University, and The Catholic University of America. He is a regular contributor to *National Review* and *Commentary*, among other publications.

Dr. Charles R. Kesler   Professor Charles Kesler is a senior fellow of the Claremont Institute, editor of the *Claremont Review of Books*, and a professor of government at Claremont McKenna College. From 1989 to 2008, he was the director of Claremont McKenna's Henry Salvatori Center for the Study of Individual Freedom in the Modern World, and from 2000 to 2001 he served as vice chairman of the Advisory Committee to the U.S. Congress's James Madison Commemoration Committee. He has written extensively on American constitutionalism and political thought, and his edition of *The Federalist Papers* is the best-selling edition in the country. Dr. Kesler's articles on contemporary politics have also appeared in the *Washington Times, Policy Review, National Review*, and the *Weekly Standard*, among other journals.

Andrew C. McCarthy   Mr. McCarthy is a former Chief Assistant U.S. Attorney for the Southern District of New York. Among his most notable cases, he led the 1995 prosecution against the jihad organization of Sheikh Omar Abdel-Rahman, in which a dozen Islamic militants were convicted of the bombing of the World Trade Center in 1993 and of planning a series of attacks against New York City landmarks. Mr. McCarthy also contributed to the prosecution of terrorists who bombed U.S. embassies in Kenya and Tanzania, and supervised the Justice Department's command post near Ground Zero after 9/11. He is currently a senior fellow at the National Review Institute and a contributing editor at *National Review*. He is the author of two *New York Times* bestsellers, *Willful Blindness: A Memoir of the Jihad* and, most recently, *The Grand Jihad: How Islam and the Left Sabotage America*.

Edwin Meese III   Mr. Meese served as the 75th Attorney General of the United States from 1985 to 1988, under President Ronald Reagan. Prior to being appointed to that position, he held the position of Counselor to the President from 1981 to 1985 and functioned as President Reagan's chief policy advisor. He also served President Reagan in a number of capacities, including Chief of Staff, when he was Governor of California from 1967 to 1974. In 2006, Mr. Meese was named to the Iraq Study Group, a special presidential commission dedicated to examining the best resolutions for America's involvement in Iraq. He currently holds fellowships and chairmanships with several public policy councils and think tanks. He holds the Ronald Reagan Chair in Public Policy at the Heritage Foundation and is the chairman of Heritage's Center for Legal and Judicial Studies. He is also a Distinguished Visiting Fellow at the Hoover Institution, and he lectures, writes, and consults throughout the country on a variety of subjects.

Michael B. Mukasey   Mr. Mukasey served as Attorney General of the United States under President George W. Bush from 2007 to 2009. Prior to being appointed Attorney General, he served as an Assistant U.S. Attorney for the Southern District of New York, and then became a federal district court judge for the Southern District of New York from 1988 to 2006, including as Chief Judge from 2000 to 2006. While on the federal bench, he presided over numerous high-profile terrorist prosecutions, including the criminal prosecution of Omar Abdel-Rahman and El Sayyid Nosair, whom he sentenced to life in prison for plotting to blow up the United Nations and other New York City landmarks. Mr. Mukasey is currently a partner at the law firm of Debevoise & Plimpton.

Theodore B. Olson   Ted Olson was the Solicitor General of the United States from 2001 to 2004. He was appointed to that position by President George W. Bush. He also served as Assistant Attorney General of the United States during the Reagan administration, from 1981 to 1984. Mr. Olson served as private counsel to President Ronald W. Reagan during the Iran-Contra affair. He has twice been awarded the U.S. Department of Justice's Edmund J. Randolph Award, which is the highest award for public service and leadership, and has also received the Department of Defense's highest civilian award for his advocacy in the courts of the United States. Mr. Olson is currently a partner at the law firm of Gibson, Dunn & Crutcher LLP. He is one of the nation's premier appellate and U.S. Supreme Court advocates and has argued more than fifty cases before the Supreme Court.

Judge A. Raymond Randolph   Judge Raymond Randolph was appointed by President George H. W. Bush to the U.S. Court of Appeals for the District of Columbia Circuit in 1990 and assumed senior status in 2008. He has authored a number of important opinions in the national security area, including *Hamdi v. Rumsfeld* and *Boumediene v. Bush*. After graduating *summa cum laude* from the University of Pennsylvania Law School, he clerked for Judge Henry J. Friendly of the U.S. Court of Appeals for the Second Circuit. Judge Randolph served as Assistant to the U.S.

Solicitor General from 1970 to 1973, and as a Deputy Solicitor General from 1975 to 1977. From 1979 to 1980, he was Special Counsel to the Ethics Committee of the U.S. House of Representatives. He has also served as Special Assistant Attorney General for Utah, Montana, and New Mexico. Prior to his appointment to the bench, Judge Randolph was a partner at the firm of Pepper, Hamilton & Scheetz. A Distinguished Professor of Law at George Mason Law School, he has also taught numerous courses at Georgetown University Law Center, and has served on the U.S. Judicial Conference's Codes of Conduct Committee as a member (1992–1995) and as chairman (1995–1998).

Dean Reuter Mr. Reuter is Vice President and director of Practice Groups at the Federalist Society for Law and Public Policy, where he has been employed since 2001. He served as Deputy Attorney General and Counsel to the Inspector General at the federal Corporation for National and Community Service from 1998 to 2001, immediately prior to which he was the Student Division director of the Federalist Society. From 1991 to 1997, he was an attorney in private practice in Maryland and Virginia. He served in the Legal Services Corporation from 1984 to 1991, conducting compliance oversight of federal grants. Mr. Reuter is a graduate of Hood College (1983) and the University of Maryland School of Law (1986), after completing his studies at Northwestern University School of Law.

Anthony D. Romero Anthony D. Romero is the executive director of the American Civil Liberties Union, a position he has held since 2001. In this capacity he has been involved in opposition to several policies pursued by the Bush and Obama administrations with respect to civil liberties and national security. In 2005, Mr. Romero was named one of *Time* magazine's 25 Most

Influential Hispanics in America. He has received dozens of public service awards and an honorary doctorate from the City University of New York School of Law. In 2007, he co-authored, along with NPR correspondent Dina Temple-Raston, the book *In Defense of Our America: The Fight for Civil Liberties in the Age of Terror*.

Paul Rosenzweig Mr. Rosenzweig is the founder of Red Branch Consulting PLLC, a homeland security consulting company, and formerly served as Deputy Assistant Secretary for Policy in the Department of Homeland Security. In 2011 he will be a Medill Carnegie National Security Journalism Fellow at the Medill School of Journalism at Northwestern University. He also serves as a professorial lecturer in law at George Washington University, a senior editor of the *Journal of National Security Law and Policy*, and a visiting fellow at the Heritage Foundation. Mr. Rosenzweig is a *cum laude* graduate of the University of Chicago Law School. He has an M.S. in chemical oceanography from the Scripps Institution of Oceanography and a B.A. from Haverford College. He served as a law clerk to the Honorable R. Lanier Anderson III of the United States Court of Appeals for the Eleventh Circuit. He is the co-author (with James Jay Carafano) of *Winning the Long War: Lessons from the Cold War for Defeating Terrorism and Preserving Freedom* and author of the forthcoming book *Cyberwarfare: How Conflicts in Cyberspace Are Challenging America and Changing the World*.

Judge Laurence H. Silberman Judge Laurence Silberman is a senior judge on the U.S. Court of Appeals for the District of Columbia Circuit. He was appointed to the federal bench in 1985 by President Ronald Reagan and took senior status in 2000. In 2008, Judge Silberman was named a recipient of the Presidential Medal of Freedom, the highest civilian honor granted by the government of the United States. Prior to being appointed to the bench, he worked as a partner at the law firms of Moore, Silberman & Schulze in Honolulu, and Morrison & Foerster and Steptoe & Johnson in Washington, D.C. Judge Silberman has held numerous government positions, including attorney in the National Labor Relations Board's appellate section, Solicitor of the Department of Labor, Undersecretary of Labor, Deputy Attorney General of the United States (1974–1975), and Ambassador to Yugoslavia (1975–1977). From 1981 to 1985, he served on the General Advisory Committee on Arms Control and Disarmament and on the Department of Defense Policy Board. Chief Justice William Rehnquist appointed him to the Foreign Intelligence Surveillance Court's Review Panel (1996–2003). Judge Silberman also served as co-chairman of the President's Intelligence Commission (2004–2005). He has taught at New York University, at Harvard, and at Georgetown University Law Center, where he has held the title of "Distinguished Visitor from the Judiciary" since 2000.

Professor Nadine Strossen   Since 1988, Nadine Strossen has been a professor at New York Law School, specializing in constitutional law, civil liberties, and international human rights. From 1991 to 2008, Professor Strossen served as president of the American Civil Liberties Union. She was the first woman to head the organization and still retains leadership positions with the ACLU as a member of its National Advisory Council and as co-chair of its Campaign for the Future. The *National Law Journal* has twice named Professor Strossen one of "The 100 Most Influential Lawyers in America." Her writings have been published in numerous scholarly and general interest publications, and her book, *Defending Pornography: Free Speech, Sex, and the Fight for*

Women's Rights, was named by the *New York Times* as a "Notable Book" of 1995. Before becoming a law professor, she practiced law for nine years in Minneapolis and New York City.

Marc Thiessen   Marc Thiessen served as chief speechwriter for President George W. Bush and before that for Secretary of Defense Donald Rumsfeld. He spent six years (1995–2001) on Capitol Hill as spokesman and senior policy advisor to Sen. Jesse Helms (R-NC), chairman of the Senate Foreign Relations Committee. Mr. Thiessen is currently a visiting fellow at the American Enterprise Institute and a weekly columnist for the *Washington Post*. He is the author of the 2010 *New York Times* bestseller *Courting Disaster: How the CIA Kept America Safe and How Barack Obama Is Inviting the Next Attack*.

Professor Jonathan Turley   Professor Turley is the J.B. and Maurice Shapiro Professor of Public Interest Law at The George Washington University Law School, where he started teaching in 1990, and in 1998 became the youngest chaired professor in the school's history. He is the founder and executive director of the Project for Older Prisoners and heads a public interest litigation project at George Washington. Previously, he taught at Tulane Law School. Professor Turley has served as a consultant on homeland security and constitutional issues, and is a frequent witness before the U.S. Senate and House of Representatives on constitutional and statutory issues. He has served as lead counsel in a variety of national security and terrorism cases, and has been ranked as one of the top lawyers handling military cases. His often-cited constitutional cases range from his 2010 impeachment defense of Judge Thomas Porteous before the U.S. Senate to his representation of five former U.S. Attorneys General during the Clinton impeachment controversy. Professor Turley has published more than three dozen academic articles in leading law journals and recently completed a three-part study of the historical and constitutional evolution of the military system. He frequently appears in the national media as a commentator on many subjects, and has written hundreds of legal and policy columns for various national publications, including *USA Today*, where he is on the board of contributors. His award-winning blog, www. jonathanturley. org, is ranked among the most visited legal websites in the world.

Professor John Yoo   Professor Yoo has taught law at the University of California at Berkeley School of Law (Boalt Hall) since 1993, and is a visiting scholar at the American Enterprise Institute. From 2001 to 2003, Professor Yoo served as a Deputy Assistant Attorney General in the Office of Legal Counsel of the U.S. Department of Justice, where he worked on issues involving foreign affairs, national security, and the separation of powers. He served as general counsel of the U.S. Senate Judiciary Committee from 1995 to 1996, advising on constitutional issues and judicial nominations. Professor Yoo clerked for Judge Laurence H. Silberman of the U.S. Court of Appeals for the District of Columbia Circuit and for Justice Clarence Thomas of the U.S. Supreme Court. He is the author of *Crisis and Command: A History of Executive Power from George Washington to George W. Bush* (2010), *War by Other Means* (2006), and *The Powers of War and Peace* (2005). He has contributed to the opinion pages of national newspapers including the *Wall Street Journal*, the *New York Times*, the *Washington Post*, the *Los Angeles Times*, and the *Philadelphia Inquirer.*

ACKNOWLEDGMENTS

The editors wish to acknowledge, with much gratitude, the contributors to this volume. Their time and talent transformed this project from an idea into a book that will make a lasting contribution to our thinking on one of the most important events of our new century.

Our thanks to Christopher Bowen for his keen eye on cite checking, and Meng Xi for her editing prowess and helpful suggestions. We are also grateful to Beverly Moore, who assembled and edited the author biographies.

For reading and commenting on early drafts, we wish to thank Roy Reuter, Ellen Reuter, and John Malcolm. It was truly an extraordinary benefit to have their insights and suggestions. Lynn Chu, once again, proved herself to be an agent and editor without peer. Emily Pollack of Encounter Books steadily managed this book from manuscript to printed volume with good cheer.

Professor Yoo thanks Dean Christopher Edley, Jr. of Berkeley Law School (Boalt Hall), University of California Berkeley, for generous institutional support, and Jesse Choper for his wise counsel.

Professor Yoo would also like to thank his wife, Elsa Arnett, for her constant love, warmth and encouragement that makes all of his work possible.

Dean Reuter would like to thank his wife, Lou Anne, and his children, Taylor and Hannah, for their unwavering support.

ENDNOTES

INTRODUCTION

1. Abraham Lincoln, President of the United States, Annual Message to Congress, Dec. 1, 1862, in *Abraham Lincoln: Speeches and Writings 1859–1865*, ed. Don E. Fehrenbacher (Library of America, 1989), 415.

9/11 IN ITS HISTORICAL CONTEXT

1. George Washington, Farewell Address to the People of the United States, Sept. 17, 1796, in Felix Gilbert, *To the Farewell Address: Ideas of Early American Foreign Policy* (Princeton University Press, 1961), 144–45.

2. *John Quincy Adams and American Continental Empire: Letters, Speeches, and Papers*, ed. Walter LaFeber (Quadrangle, 1965), 45.

3. Quoted in Henry Kissinger, *Diplomacy* (Simon & Schuster, 1994), 39.

4. A. J. P. Taylor, *The Origins of the Second World War* (Touchstone, 1961), 185.

5. Nicholas Spykman, *America's Strategy in World Politics: The United States and the Balance of Power* (Harcourt, Brace & Co., 1942), at 447; Arnold Wolfers, "'National Security' as an Ambiguous Symbol," *Political Science Quarterly* 67 (1952), reprinted in *Discord and Collaboration: Essays on International Politics*, ed. Arnold Wolfers (Johns Hopkins, 1962), 150–51, n. 6.

6. Spykman, *America's Strategy in World Politics*, 447.

7. Quoted in Fred Kaplan, *The Wizards of Armageddon* (Simon & Schuster, 1983), 22.

WAR V. CRIME

1. See, e.g., Foreign Intelligence Surveillance Act of 1978, § 102, 92 Stat. 1783 (1978) (current version at 50 U.S.C. § 1802 (2010); § 106 (current version at 50 U.S.C. § 1806); Exec. Order No. 12,333, 46 Fed. Reg. 59,441, 59,949 (Dec. 4, 1981); Exec. Order No. 12,036, 43 Fed. Reg. 3,674, § 2–202 (Jan. 24, 1978).

2. Use of Army and Air Force as Posse Comitatus, 18 U.S.C. § 1385 (2010) (formerly Posse Comitatus Act, Law of June 18, 1878, ch. 263, § 15, 20 Stat. 152); Insurrection Act, 10 U.S.C. § 331 (2010).

3. National Commission on Terrorist Attacks Upon the United States, The 9/11 Commission Report (2004), at 78–80; *In re Sealed Case*, 310 F.3d 717, 730 (FISA Ct. Rev. 2002). *See* USA Patriot Act of 2001, § 203(b), 18 U.S.C. § 2517 (2010).

4. *See*, 9/11 Commission Report.

5. *Compare* Ex Parte Milligan, 71 U.S. 2, 128–129 (1866) (permitting United States citizen to be held as a prisoner of war does not forfeit constitutional protections) *with* Ex Parte Quirin, 317 U.S. 1, 44 (1942) (denying United States citizen held as enemy combatant right to jury trial).

6. *See* Press Release, U.S. Department of Justice, "United States Charges 50 Leaders of Narco-Terrorist FARC in Columbia with Supplying More Than Half of the World's Cocaine," March 22, 2006, http://www.justice.gov/usao/nys/pressreleases/March06/farcindictmentpr.pdf.

7. *See, e.g.*, Ex Parte Quirin, 317 U.S. 1, 44 (1942).

8. Boumediene v. Bush, 553 U.S. 723, 723–24 (2008) (describing background of military commissions and Military Commissions Act, 28 U.S.C. § 2241 (2006)); Rasul v. Bush, 542 U.S. 466, 470–71 (2004) (describing detention of foreign terrorist combatants prior to Military Commissions Act).

9. Hamdi v. Rumsfeld, 542 U.S. 507 (2004).

10. United States v. Lindh, 212 F. Supp. 2d 541 (E.D. Va. 2002).

11. United States v. Padilla, No. 04-cr-60001, 2007 WL 2349148 (S.D. Fla. Aug. 16, 2007) (jury verdict finding Padilla guilty); United States v. Al-

Marri, No. 09-cr-10030, 2009 WL 6498890 (C.D. Ill. October 20, 2009) (plea agreement and sentencing memorandum).

A UNIFIED DEFENSE AGAINST TERRORISTS

1. Less controversially, our Presidents have also twice reorganized the White House, first creating a Homeland Security Council (HSC) to operate parallel to the National Security Council (NSC), and then, under President Obama, disbanding the HSC and merging its functions into a separate directorate of the NSC. As we note with respect to the DHS and the IC, every reorganization saps energy from the institution that is being reorganized. Fortunately, the White House reorganizations were achieved with greater alacrity and less controversy than attended the other reorganizations—at least in part because the President was able to act unilaterally when it comes to White House organization, thereby avoiding much of the politicization of the other efforts we discuss.

2. Homeland Security Act of 2002, Pub. L. 107–296, 116 Stat. 2135 (2002).

3. National Security Act of 1947, Law of July 26, 1947, ch. 343, § 2, 61 Stat. 496 (1947) (codified at 50 U.S.C. § 401 et seq.).

4. Intelligence Reform and Terrorism Prevention Act of 2004, Pub. L. 108–458, 118 Stat. 3638 (2004).

5. IRTPA § 102(a) (codified at 50 U.S.C. § 403(1)).

6. Intelligence Reform and Terrorism Prevention Act of 2004, Pub. L. 108–458, § 1013, 118 Stat. 3638 (2004).

7. Authorization for Use of Military Force Against Terrorists, Pub. L. 107–40, 115 Stat. 224 (2001).

8. To cite but one example, it should trouble every American that the executive's decision to target a known al-Qaeda affiliate, Anwar al-Aulaqi, has become the subject of litigation simply because he prosecutes the war from his home in Yemen rather than on the traditional battlefield. Nobody should welcome the prospect of a federal district court judge micromanaging the launch of a kinetic attack. Al-Aulaqi v. Obama, 727 F. Supp. 2d 1 (2010).

9. Katz v. United States, 389 U.S. 347 (1967).

10. Now codified at 18 U.S.C. §§ 2510–22.

11. Piracy, after all, was one of the domains of responsibility explicitly given to Congress in the Constitution. U.S. Const. art. I, § 8, cl. 10.

12. Portions of this section are based upon an earlier work, see Paul Rosenzweig, "Civil Liberties and the Response to Terrorism," *Duquesne Law Review* 42 (2004), 663–723.

13. *See* Uniting and Strengthening America by Providing Appropriate Tools Required to Intercept and Obstruct Terrorism Act of 2001 (USA Patriot Act), Pub. L. 107–56, 115 Stat. 272 (2001).

14. *See generally* John Yoo, *The Powers of War and Peace: The Constitution and Foreign Affairs after 9/11* (University of Chicago Press, 2005).

15. Letter from Thomas Jefferson to E. Carrington, May 27, 1788, reprinted in *The Founders' Almanac*, ed. Matthew Spalding (Heritage Foundation, 2002), 157.

16. John Locke, *Two Treatises of Government*, ed. Peter Laslett (Cambridge University Press, 1988), 305–6.

REFORMING THE INTELLIGENCE COMMUNITY

1. Karl Rove, *Courage and Consequence: My Life as a Conservative in the Fight* (Threshold, 2010).

THE IMPERFECT RECONCILIATION OF LIBERTY AND SECURITY

1. Pub. L. No. 95–511, 92 Stat. 1783 (1978) (codified at 50 U.S.C. §§ 1801 et seq.).

2. FISA Amendments Act of 2008, Pub. L. No. 110–261, 122 Stat. 2436 (to be codified in scattered sections of 50 U.S.C.).

3. U.S. Const. amend. IV.

4. U.S. Const. amend. V.

5. U.S. Const. art. I, § 9, cl. 2.

6. Pub. L. No. 109–366, 120 Stat. 2600 (2006) (codified at 10 U.S.C. §§ 948 et seq.), *invalidated in part by* Boumediene v. Bush, 553 U.S. 723 (2008).

7. 548 U.S. 557 (2006).

TORTURE AND DEMOCRATIC ACCOUNTABILITY

1. Although I am personally opposed to torture as a normative matter (see Alan M. Dershowitz, "Tortured Reasoning," in *Torture: A Collection*, 2004), my views have been repeatedly distorted by commentators and bloggers alike. I feel no need to name names, but I entreat anyone inclined to summarize or summarily dismiss my views to peruse them first.

2. Quoted in Alan M. Dershowitz, "Torture and Accountability: 'Torture Warrants' Are a Necessary Evil—Even Bill Clinton Agrees with Me Now," *Los Angeles Times*, Oct. 17, 2006, B13.

3. Quoted in W. L. Twining and P. E. Twining, "Bentham on Torture," *Northern Ireland Legal Quarterly* 24 (1973), 305–356, at 345.

4. Matthew Brzezinski, "Bust and Boom: Six Years Before the September 11 Attacks, Philippine Police Took Down an al Qaeda Cell That Had Been Plotting, Among Other Things, to Fly Explosive-Laden Planes into the Pentagon—and Possibly Some Skyscrapers," *Washington Post*, Dec. 30, 2001, W9.

5. It is in my view dishonest, though politically correct, to claim as an empirical matter that torture *never* works—that it *never* produces reliable and useful real-time information that could save lives. It can certainly be argued, though subject to empirical testing, that torture *rarely* works, that it generally

produces false information, that there are better ways to secure such information, or that on balance any good it accomplishes is more than offset by the evil it produces. All of these are reasonable statements. But it defies history, science, common sense, logic, and what we know about human behavior to deny that under *some* circumstances, *some* people will produce *some* useful and truthful information that could in fact save lives. We are not talking about seeking to use the fruits of torture to convict someone of a crime based on his own confession. Nor are we talking about the verbal pronouncements of a person under torture. What we are talking about is the torturer who insists that his victim take him to where the bomb is hidden or to take some other action that is self-proving. So many brave men and women—in the French Resistance and other such organizations—have disclosed the location of friends, loved ones, even relatives under torture, that its effectiveness under some circumstances cannot be denied.

6. United States v. Lefkowitz, 285 U.S. 452, 464 (1932).

7. It is, of course, possible to believe that torture and the death penalty are both morally wrong. *See* Charles Fried and Gregory Fried, *Because It Is Wrong: Torture, Privacy and Presidential Power in the Age of Terror* (W. W. Norton, 2010), 76–80. Gregory Fried has told me that he believes torture is a greater evil than the death penalty.

8. Korematsu v. United States, 323 U.S. 214, 245–46 (1944) (Jackson, J., dissenting).

9. Glenn Greenwald, "Lawsuit Challenges Obama's Power to Kill Citizens Without Due Process," *Salon*, Aug. 30, 2010.

NUREMBURG REVISITED AND REVISED

1. Convention Against Torture and Other Cruel, Inhuman or Degrading Treatment or Punishment, art. 1, para. 1, Dec. 10, 1984, 108 Stat. 382, 1465 U.N.T.S. 85.

2. Geneva Convention Relative to the Treatment of Prisoners of War, art. 3, Aug. 12, 1949, 6 U.S.T. 3316, 75 U.N.T.S. 135.

3. *See* Memorandum from Steven G. Bradbury, Assistant Attorney General, Office of Legal Counsel, U.S. Department of Justice, to John Rizzo, Senior Deputy General Counsel, CIA 15, at 37 (May 30, 2005).

4. 630 F.2d 876, 890 (2d Cir. 1980).

5. Jonathan Turley, "A Tortured Defense," *USA Today*, Feb. 27, 2008, A11.

6. See United States v. Lee, 744 F.2d 1124 (5th Cir. 1984).

7. Geneva Convention for the Amelioration of the Condition of the Wounded and Sick in Armed Forces in the Field, Aug. 12, 1949, 6 U.S.T. 3114, 75 U.N.T.S. 31; Geneva Convention for the Amelioration of the Condition of Wounded, Sick and Shipwrecked Members of Armed Forces at Sea, Aug. 12, 1949, 6 U.S.T. 3217, 75 U.N.T.S. 85; Geneva Convention Relative

to the Treatment of Prisoners of War, art. 3, Aug. 12, 1949, 6 U.S.T. 3316, 75 U.N.T.S. 135; Geneva Convention Relative to the Protection of Civilian Persons in Time of War, Aug. 12, 1949, 6 U.S.T. 3516, 75 U.N.T.S. 287.

8. Convention Against Torture and Other Cruel, Inhuman or Degrading Treatment or Punishment, Dec. 10, 1984, 108 Stat. 382, 1465 U.N.T.S. 85.

9. *See* International Committee of the Red Cross, Report on the Treatment of Fourteen "High Value Detainees" in CIA Custody (2007), http://www.nybooks.com/icrc-report.pdf.

10. U.S. Department of Justice, Office of Professional Responsibility, Investigation into the Office of Legal Counsel's Memoranda Concerning Issues Relating to the Central Intelligence Agency's Use of "Enhanced Interrogation Techniques" on Suspected Terrorists 11 (2009), http://judiciary.house.gov/hearings/pdf/OPRFinalReport090729.pdf.

11. *Id.*

12. Long after his administration withdrew the memos, President Bush still relied on the now-ridiculed advice given by his lawyers to justify the legality of his actions. In his new memoir, *Decision Points*, Bush writes that "Department of Justice and CIA lawyers conducted a careful legal review" and came up with an "enhanced interrogation program." *See* "In Memoir, Bush Defends Waterboarding, Admits Mistakes," CNN Politics, Nov. 9, 2010.

13. United States v. Defries, 129 F.3d 1293, 1308–09 (D.C. Cir. 1997).

14. Convention Against Torture and Other Cruel, Inhuman or Degrading Treatment or Punishment, art. 4–8, Dec. 10, 1984, 108 Stat. 382, 1465 U.N.T.S. 85. Prosecutions are supposed to occur "in the same manner as in the case of any ordinary offense of a serious nature under the law of that State." *Id.* at art. 7.

15. Not only did Bush admit to ordering waterboarding, but Cheney appeared to brag that he was a "big supporter of waterboarding" despite later views that it constituted torture. *See* R. Jeffrey Smith, "Bush Says in Memoir He Approved Waterboarding," *Washington Post*, Nov. 4, 2010, A2.

16. It would have been a larger group, but two lawyers committed suicide before trial. Those lawyers convicted included Adolf Georg Thierack, former minister of justice; Carl Westphal, a ministerial counselor; Herbert Klemm, former minister of justice, director of the ministry's Legal Education and Training Division; Oswald Rothaug, prosecutor and later a judge; Wilhelm von Ammon, a justice official in occupied areas; Guenther Joel, advisor to the Ministry of Justice and later a judge; Curt Rothenberger, a legal advisor at the Ministry of Justice and deputy President of the Academy of German Law; Wolfgang Mettgenberg, a representative of the Criminal Legislation Administration Division of the Ministry of Justice; and Ernst Lautz, chief public prosecutor of the People's Court.

17. Jan Crawford Greenburg et al., "Sources: Top Bush Advisors Approved 'Enhanced Interrogation,'" ABC News, April 9, 2008.

18. Jonathan Turley, op-ed, "Rights on the Rack: Alleged Torture in Terror War Imperils U.S. Standards of Humanity," *Los Angeles Times*, March 6, 2003, 17.

STOPPING THE TERRORISTS

1. Greg Miller et al., "Stepped-Up Search for al-Qaeda; But Using Predators to Fire Missiles Presents Its Own Risks," *Washington Post*, Nov. 8, 2010, A1.

2. Press Release, U.S. Department of Justice, "Virginia Man Pleads Guilty to Providing Material Support to a Foreign Terrorist Organization and Encouraging Violent Jihadists to Kill U.S. Citizens," Oct. 20, 2010, http://www.justice.gov/opa/pr/2010/October/10–nsd-1174.html.

3. Karen DeYoung and Joby Warrick, "Under Obama, More Targeted Killings Than Captures in Counterterrorism Efforts," *Washington Post*, Feb. 14, 2010, A1.

4. *Id.*

INTERROGATION

1. National Commission on Terrorist Attacks Upon the United States, The 9/11 Commission Report (2004), at 161.

2. *Id.* at 145.

3. Most of the details of the formation and execution of the 9/11 attacks are directly attributed in the 9/11 Commission Report's text and footnotes to their interrogations. See the note on Detainee Interrogation Reports, *id.* at 146.

4. Kevin Johnson et al., "Arrest of 9/11 Suspect Yields 'Lots of Names, Information,'" *USA Today*, March 3, 2003, A1.

5. *See, e.g.,* Seymour Hersh, *Chain of Command: The Road from 9/11 to Abu Ghraib* (HarperCollins, 2004).

6. Susan Schmidt, "Ashcroft Refuses to Release '02 Memo," *Washington Post*, June 9, 2004, A1.

7. Evan Thomas and Michael Hirsh, "The Debate over Torture," *Newsweek*, Nov. 21, 2005, 26.

8. S. Treaty Doc. No. 100–20, at 4–5 (1988). The Reagan administration listed acts of torture that were encompassed in the OLC's August 2002 memo: the definition of torture "is usually reserved for extreme, deliberate and unusually cruel practices, for example, sustained systematic beatings, application of electric currents to sensitive parts of the body, and tying up and hanging in positions that cause extreme pain." S. Exec. Rep. No. 101–30, at 14 (1990).

9. S. Treaty Doc. No. 100–20, at 4. The George H. W. Bush administration eventually submitted to the Senate a more extensive definition of severe physical and mental pain that became the 1994 criminal statute. State and Justice Department officials testified before the Senate that there was no

difference between the Reagan and George H. W. Bush understandings of the treaty, but rather that the Bush administration sought to make the Reagan understanding more specific. *See* Convention on Torture: Hearing Before the Senate Committee on Foreign Relations, 101st Cong. 10 (1990) (statement of Abraham Sofaer, Legal Advisor, Department of State); *id.* at 13–14 (statement of Mark Richard, Deputy Assistant Attorney General, Criminal Division, Department of Justice).

10. 18 U.S.C. § 2340(1). As the Senate attached this language to its advice and consent to the CAT in 1994, and the Clinton administration attached it to its document ratifying the treaty, it also defines the United States' international legal obligations under the treaty. S. Exec. Rep. No. 101–30, at 36 (1990), 1830 U.N.T.S. 320 (Oct. 21, 1994).

11. The difference between "specific" intent and general intent is a difficult one to understand, and it has been only imperfectly explained by the Supreme Court. *Compare* United States v. Ratzlaf, 510 U.S. 135, 141 (1994); United States v. Carter, 530 U.S. 255, 269 (2000); United States v. Bailey, 444 U.S. 394, 405 (1980).

12. *See*, e.g., *Webster's New International Dictionary*, 2nd ed. (1935), 2295; *American Heritage Dictionary of the English Language*, 3rd ed. (1992), 1653; *Oxford English Dictionary*, vol. 9 (1978), 572.

13. 42 U.S.C. § 1395w-22(d)(3)(B).

14. Congress here had adopted an understanding of the CAT recommended by the George H. W. Bush administration. The Reagan administration had not submitted an extensive definition of mental pain and suffering.

15. In sending the treaty to the Senate, the Reagan administration said: "Torture is thus to be distinguished from lesser forms of cruel, inhuman, or degrading treatment or punishment, which are to be deplored and prevented, but are not so universally and categorically condemned as to warrant the severe legal consequences that the Convention provides in case of torture." S. Treaty Doc. No. 100–20, at 3.

16. *Id.* at 15 (discussing Case of X v. Federal Republic of Germany).

17. *Id.* at 15–16.

18. Ireland v. United Kingdom, 2 Eur. Ct. H. R. 25, para. 167 (1978).

19. Supreme Court of Israel, Judgment Concerning the Legality of the General Security Service's Interrogation Methods, 38 I.L.M. 1471 (1999) (H.C. 5100/94, Pub. Comm. Against Torture in Israel v. Gov't of State of Israel, 53(4) P.D. 817).

20. Jeremy Waldron, "Torture and Positive Law: Jurisprudence for the White House," *Columbia Law Review* 105 (2005), 1681–1750, at 1701.

21. The most well known was a symposium on the Landau Commission Report published in *Israel Law Review* 23 (1989). There have been a number of collections published since 9/11, such as *Torture: A Collection*, ed. Sanford Levinson (2004).

22. Model Penal Code section 3.02; Wayne R. LaFave and Austin W. Scott, 1 Substantive Criminal Law section 5.4, at 627 (1986); United States v. Bailey, 444 U.S. 394, 410 (1980).

23. Michael Moore, "Torture and the Balance of Evils," *Israel Law Review* 23 (1989), 280–344.

24. *In re* Neagle, 135 U.S. 1 (1890).

25. Convention Against Torture and Other Cruel, Inhuman or Degrading Treatment or Punishment, Dec. 10, 1984, S. Treaty Doc. No. 100–20, 1465 U.N.T.S. 85, art. 2.2.

26. For a more extensive discussion of this point, see John Yoo, *Crisis and Command: A History of Executive Power from George Washington to George W. Bush* (Kaplan, 2010).

27. Alliance for Justice, Lawyers' Statement on Bush administration's Torture Memos (Aug. 2004), http://www.sfcityattorney.org/Modules/Show-Document.aspx?documentid=507.

28. 343 U.S. 579 (1952).

29. Regulation of domestic production, Justice Black wrote for the Court, "is a job for the Nation's lawmakers, not for its military authorities." *Id.* at 587.

30. *Id.* at 637 (Jackson, J., concurring).

31. Memorandum from Walter Dellinger, Assistant Attorney General, Office of Legal Counsel, U.S. Department of Justice, to Abner J. Mikva, Counsel to the President, Presidential Authority to Decline to Execute Unconstitutional Statutes, 18 Op. OLC 999 (Nov. 2, 1994).

32. Placing of United States Armed Forces under United Nations Operational or Tactical Control, 20 U.S. Op. OLC 182, 1996 WL 942457 (May 8, 1996). *Cf.* H. Jefferson Powell, *The President's Authority over Foreign Affairs* (Carolina Academic Press, 2002).

33. Waldron, "Torture and Positive Law," *supra* note 20, at 1715.

34. Philip Heymann, *Terrorism, Freedom, and Security: Winning Without War* (MIT Press, 2003), 109–11.

35. Marc Thiessen, *Courting Disaster* (Regnery, 2010).

36. Henry Shue, "Torture," *Philosophy and Public Affairs* 7 (1977), 124–143, at 141; Heymann, *Terrorism, Freedom, and Security*, at 110.

37. Heymann, at 112.

38. Waldron, "Torture and Positive Law," *supra* note 20.

39. Oren Gross, "Are Torture Warrants Warranted? Pragmatic Absolutism and Official Disobedience," *Minnesota Law Review* 88 (2007), 1481, at 1507–09; Seth F. Kreimer, "Too Close to the Rack and the Screw: Constitutional Constraints on Torture in the War on Terror," *University of Pennsylvania Journal of Constitutional Law* 6 (2003), 278–325; Mordechai Kremnitzer, "The Landau Commission Report—Was the Security Service Subordinated to the Law or the Law to the 'Needs' of the Security Service?" *Israel Law Review* 23 (1989), 216–279, at 254–57, 261–62.

40. Frederick Schauer, "Slippery Slopes," *Harvard Law Review* 99 (1985), 361–383; Eugene Volokh, "The Mechanisms of the Slippery Slope," *Harvard Law Review* 116 (2003), 1026–1137.

41. Eric A. Posner and Adrian Vermeule, "Should Coercive Interrogation Be Legal?" *Michigan Law Review* 104 (2006), 671–707.

FEAR

1. *The Federalist* No. 51 (James Madison).

2. Marbury v. Madison, 1 Cranch (5 U.S.) 137, 166–67 (1803).

3. Act of June 18, 1798, c. 54, 1 Stat. 566; Act of June 25, 1798, c. 58, 1 Stat. 570; Act of July 6, 1798, c. 66, 1 Stat. 577; Act of July 14, 1798, c. 74, 1 Stat. 596.

4. "Transcript of Frost-Nixon Interview," *New York Times*, May 20, 1977, A16.

5. The term "USA Patriot Act" is the acronym created by the legislation's proponents in the Department of Justice during the early debate on the measure in the fall of 2001. The full title of the legislation is Uniting and Strengthening America by Providing Appropriate Tools Required to Intercept and Obstruct Terrorism Act of 2001 (USA Patriot Act), Pub. L. No. 107–56, 115 Stat. 272 (2001). The acronym was a stroke of public relations and political genius, effectively casting every opponent as "un Patriotic" and every supporter as " Patriotic."

6. Pub. L. No. 104–132, 110 Stat. 1214 (1996).

7. *See, e.g.*, USA Patriot Act of 2001, Pub. L. No. 107–56, 115 Stat. 272 (2001).

8. *See* FISA, 50 U.S.C. §§ 1801–1811 (2002 & Supp. 2007), *as amended by* FISA Amendments Act of 2008, Pub. L. No. 110–261, 122 Stat. 2436 (2008).

9. In 2009, for example, Missouri's fusion center, the Missouri Information Analysis Center (MIAC), noted on its website (before being forced to remove it) that "suspicious" activity might include vehicles sporting bumper stickers in support of Bob Barr (the 2008 Libertarian Party nominee for President), Ron Paul (a Republican candidate for President in 2008), or Ralph Nader (2008 independent candidate for President).

10. Following the 1989 fall of the Berlin Wall, Western authorities were amused to find among the files and archives of the dreaded East German secret police a large collection of articles in sealed containers supposed to permit the authorities to identify suspects by smell. At the time, this was viewed as evidence of a police state run amok.

11. Privacy International, The 2007 International Privacy Ranking: Leading Surveillance Societies in the EU and the World, http://www.privacyinternational.org/article/leading-surveillance-societies-eu-and-world-2007; *see also*, the U.S.-based Electronic Privacy Information Center

(EPIC), which similarly publishes results of surveys and studies on privacy and surveillance.

12. "2010 Privacy Trust Study of the United States Government," Ponemon Institute, June 2010.

13. *See, e.g.*, John Yoo, *Crisis and Command: A History of Executive Power from George Washington to George W. Bush* (Kaplan, 2010), 410–23; Handschu v. Special Servs. Div., 273 F. Supp. 2d 327, 337–38 (S.D.N.Y. 2003) (decreasing restrictions on police within a consent decree in light of September 11, 2001 and the threat of terrorism); Adrian Vermeule, "Emergency Lawmaking After 9/11 and 7/7," *University of Chicago Law Review* 75 (2008), 1155–1190, at 1155 (arguing that libertarian and legislative responses to emergency legislation prevent the executive branch from aggregating threatening amounts of power).

14. *See, e.g.*, "Gonzalez Says the Constitution Doesn't Guarantee Habeas Corpus," *San Francisco Chronicle*, Jan. 24, 2007, A1.

15. *The Federalist* No. 49 (James Madison).

LIBERTY, SECURITY, AND THE USA PATRIOT ACT

1. Edmund Burke, Speech to the Electors of Bristol, Nov. 3, 1774, quoted in Robert H. Bork, *Slouching Towards Gomorrah: Modern Liberalism and American Decline* (ReganBooks, HarperCollins, 1996), 64.

2. USA Patriot Act of 2001, Pub. L. 107–56, 115 Stat. 272 (2001).

3. In May 2001, Deputy Attorney General Larry Thompson cautioned investigators regarding the paralytic effects of the wall, warning the FBI not to underestimate its potentially harmful consequences. John Ashcroft, *Never Again: Securing America and Restoring Justice* (Hachette Book Group, 2006), chap. 10.

4. USA Patriot Act of 2001, Pub. L. 107–56, § 218, 115 Stat. 272 (2001) (codified at 50 U.S.C. § 1823).

5. *In re* Sealed Case, 310 F.3d 717 (FISA Ct. Rev. 2002).

6. *Id.* at 735.

7. USA Patriot Act of 2001, Pub. L. 107–56, § 220, 115 Stat. 272 (2001).

8. U.S. Department of Justice, Office of Inspector General, A Review of the Federal Bureau of Investigation's National Security Letters, March 2007, http://www.justice.gov/oig/special/s0703b/final.pdf.

9. Pub. L. 109–177, § 106(f)(2), 120 Stat. 198 (2006) (adding new 50 U.S.C. § 1861(f)(1)).

10. The so-called "roving wiretap," "business records," and "lone wolf" provisions.

PROTECTION OF OUR NATIONAL SECURITY—REVISITED

1. Alex Kingsbury, "Declassified: The Secret Soviet Documents of a Leading CIA Spy," *U.S. News & World Report*, Dec. 16, 2008.

2. Charlie Savage, "Terror Verdict Tests Obama's Strategy on Trials," *New York Times*, Nov. 18, 2010.

3. Dexter Filkins and Pir Zubair Shah, "After Arrests, Taliban Promote a Fighter," *New York Times*, March 24, 2010.

4. "Counterterrorism Advisor Defends Jihad as Legitimate Tenet of Islam," FOX News, May 27, 2010.

5. *Id.*

6. "Counterterrorism Czar Brennan Draws Fire for Comments on Guantanamo Recidivism," ABC News, Feb. 14, 2010.

7. Ex parte Quirin, 317 U.S. 1, 30–31 (1942).

8. James Cole, op-ed, *Legal Times*, Sept. 9, 2002, quoted by William Kristol, "Just 'a Prosecutor Fighting Crime,'" *Weekly Standard*, Dec. 30, 2010.

ACCESS TO JUSTICE IN THE "WAR ON TERROR"

1. Hamdi v. Rumsfeld, 548 U.S. 557, 575–76 (2006).

2. Military Commissions Act of 2006, 120 Stat. 2600 (2006) (codified at 10 U.S.C. § 948 (2006)).

3. Hamdi v. Rumsfeld, 542 U.S. 507, 507 (2004).

4. Rasul v. Bush, 542 U.S. 466, 480–81 (2004).

5. Al Maqaleh v. Gates, 605 F.3d 84, 87 (D.C. Cir. 2010).

6. Mohammed v. Jeppesen Dataplan, Inc., 614 F.3d 1070, 1086 (9th Cir. 2010) (en banc).

7. Doe v. Mukasey, 549 F.3d 861, 880–81 (2d Cir. 2008).

8. American Civil Liberties Union v. Nat'l Sec. Agency, 493 F.3d 644, 674–75 (6th Cir. 2007) *rev'g* 438 F. Supp.2d 754 (E.D. Mich. 2006).

PROBLEMATIC POST-9/11 JUDICIAL INACTIVISM

1. The author gratefully acknowledges the research assistance of New York Law School students Staesha Rath and Joseph N. Schneiderman.

2. Erwin Chemerinsky, *Constitutional Law: Principles and Policies*, 3rd ed. (2006), 50–53.

3. *See, e.g.,* Mohamed v. Jeppesen Dataplan, Inc., 614 F.3d 1070, 1075–76, 1084 (9th Cir. 2010) (en banc); El-Masri v. United States, 479 F.3d 296, 299–300 (4th Cir. 2007), *cert. denied*, 552 U.S. 947 (2007); Al-Aulaqi v. Obama, 727 F. Supp.2d 1, 8, 54 (D.D.C. 2010).

4. *See, e.g.,* ACLU v. Nat'l Sec. Agency, 493 F.3d 644, 661–62 (6th Cir. 2007), *cert. denied*, 552 U.S. 1179 (2008).

5. See, e.g., ACLU v. Nat'l Sec. Agency, 493 F.3d 644, 648–49 (6th Cir. 2007), *cert. denied*, 552 U.S. 1179 (2008); Al-Aulaqi v. Obama, 727 F. Supp.2d 1, 8, 54 (D.D.C. 2010).

6. *See, e.g.,* ACLU v. Nat'l Sec. Agency, 493 F.3d 644, 711–13 (6th Cir. 2007), *cert. denied*, 552 U.S. 1179 (2008); *see also* N. Jersey Media Group v.

Ashcroft, 205 F. Supp. 2d 288, 292–295 (D.N.J 2002), *rev'd on other grounds*, 308 F.3d 198 (3d Cir. 2002), *cert. denied*, 538 U.S. 1056 (2003).

7. *See, e.g.*, Mohamed v. Jeppesen Dataplan, Inc., 614 F.3d 1070, 1095 (9th Cir. 2010) (Hawkins, J., dissenting); ACLU v. Nat'l Security Agency, 493 F.3d 644, 653–54 (6th Cir. 2007) (Batchelder, J., writing for the majority); *cert. denied*, 552 U.S. 1179 (2008); El-Masri v. United States, 479 F.3d 296, 311 n.5 (4th Cir. 2007), *cert. denied*, 552 U.S. 947 (2007); Edmonds v. United States, 161 Fed. Appx. 6 (D.C. Cir. 2005) *aff'g* 323 F.Supp.2d 65, 69 (D.D.C. 2004), *cert. denied*, 546 U.S. 1031 (2005).

8. *See, e.g.*, ACLU, Establishing a New Normal: National Security, Civil Liberties and Human Rights Under the Obama Administration (July 2010).

9. Ctr. for Nat'l Sec. Studies v. Dep't of Justice, 215 F. Supp. 2d 94, 96 (D.D.C. 2002), *rev'd in part*, 331 F.3d 918 (D.C. Cir. 2003), *cert. denied*, 540 U.S. 1104 (2004).

10. Korematsu v. United States, 323 U.S. 214, 246 (1944) (Jackson, J., dissenting).

11. Youngstown Sheet & Tube Co. v. Sawyer, 343 U.S. 579, 611 (1952) (Frankfurter, J., concurring).

12. Boumediene v. Bush, 553 U.S. 723, 732 (2008); Hamdi v. Rumsfeld, 548 U.S. 557, 567 (2006); Hamdi v. Rumsfeld, 542 U.S. 507, 509–10 (2004); Rasul v. Bush, 542 U.S. 466, 480–81 (2004). *But see* NASA v. Nelson, 131 S. Ct. 746, 761 (2011); Holder v. Humanitarian Law Project, 130 S. Ct. 2705, 2720–21 (2010).

13. 542 U.S. 507, 536 (2004) (plurality opinion).

14. Mayfield v. United States, 599 F. 3d 964, 972–73 (9th Cir. 2010), *cert. denied*, 131 S Ct. 503 (2010); Milner v. Nat'l Sec. Agency, 592 F. 3d 60, 75, 77–78 (2d Cir. 2009), *cert. denied*, 131 S Ct. 387 (2010); Arar v. Ashcroft, 585 F.3d 559, 569–70 (2d Cir. 2009), *cert. denied*,130 S. Ct. 3409 (2010); Al-Marri v. Pucciarelli, 534 F. 3d 213, 216 (4th Cir. 2008) (en banc), *cert. granted*, 129 S Ct 680 (2008), *vacated and remanded as moot sub nom* Al-Marri v. Spagone, 129 S Ct 1545 (2009); ACLU v. Nat'l Security Agency, 493 F. 3d 644, 653–54 (6th Cir. 2007), *cert. denied*, 552 U.S. 1179 (2008); El-Masri v. United States, 479 F.3d 296, 313 (4th Cir. 2007), *cert. denied*, 552 U.S. 947 (2007); United States v. Afshari, 426 F 3d 1150, 1156–57 (9th Cir. 2005), *cert. denied sub nom.* Rahmani v. United States, 549 U.S. 1110 (2007) (the Court ultimately addressed the issue this case presented in Holder v. Humanitarian Law Project, 130 S. Ct. 2705 (2010)); N. Jersey Media Group v. Ashcroft, 308 F.3d 198, 219–220 (3d Cir. 2002), *cert. denied*, 538 U.S. 1056 (2003); Edmonds v. Dep't of Justice, 161 Fed. Appx. 6 (D.C. Cir. 2005), *cert. denied*, 546 U.S. 1031 (2005); United States v. Awadallah, 349 F. 3d 42, 58 (2d Cir. 2003), *cert. denied*, 543 U.S. 1056 (2005); M.K.B. v. Warden, 540 U.S. 1213 (2004); Ctr. for Nat'l Sec. Studies, 331 F.3d at 932–33, *cert. denied*, 540 U.S. 1104 (2004); *In re* Sealed Case, 310 F. 3d 717,

736–37 (FISA Ct. Rev. 2002), *motion for leave to intervene to file petition for cert. denied*, ACLU v. United States, 538 U.S. 920 (2003).

15. *See, e.g.*, Edward J. Imwinkelried, *The New Wigmore: Evidentiary Privileges* (2002) § 6.12, 930–37.

16. 345 U.S. 1, 7–8, 9–10 (1953).

17. Reynolds v. United States, 192 F.2d 987, 996 (3d Cir. 1951), *rev'd*, 345 U.S. 1 (1953).

18. 345 U.S. at 11.

19. 92 U.S. 105 (1875).

20. 544 U.S. 1 (2005).

21. *Id.* at 2.

22. 345 U.S. at 9–10.

23. Garry Wills, "Why the Government Can Legally Lie," *New York Review of Books* 56:2 (Feb. 12, 2009), 32, 33.

24. *New York Times* v. United States, 403 U.S. 713, 723–24 (1971) (Douglas, J., concurring).

25. National Commission on Terrorist Attacks Upon the United States, The 9/11 Commission Report (2004), at 83–91.

26. These statutes are codified, respectively, at 5 U.S.C § 552; 50 U.S.C § 1801–1885; and 18 U.S.C App. III § 1–16 (2010). They were initially adopted in 1967, 1978, and 1982, respectively.

27. Mohamed v. Jeppesen Dataplan, Inc., 614 F.3d 1070 (9th Cir. 2010) (en banc), *petition for cert. filed*, 79 U.S.L.W. 3370 (U.S. Dec. 7, 2010) (No. 10–778).

28. ACLU v. Nat'l Sec. Agency, 493 F.3d 644 (6th Cir. 2007), *cert. denied*, 552 U.S. 1179 (2008); El-Masri v. United States, 479 F.3d 296 (4th Cir. 2007), *cert. denied*, 552 U.S. 947 (2007); Edmonds v. United States, 161 Fed. Appx. 6 (D.C. Cir. 2005), *cert. denied*, 546 U.S. 1031 (2005).

29. Mohamed v. Jeppesen Dataplan, Inc., 614 F.3d 1070, 1084 (9th Cir. 2010) (en banc).

30. *Id.* at 1093 (Hawkins, J., dissenting).

31. *Id.* at 1095 (Hawkins, J., dissenting).

32. Mohamed v. Jeppesen Dataplan, Inc., 614 F.3d 1070, 1091 (9th Cir. 2010).

THE GUANTÁNAMO MESS

1. Boumediene v. Bush, 553 U.S. 723, 787–88 (2008).

2. Benjamin Wittes, Robert Chesney, and Rabea Benhalim, *The Emerging Law of Detention: The Guantánamo Habeas Cases as Lawmaking* (Brookings, 2010), 1.

3. 1 William Blackstone, *Commentaries* *372.

4. Winston Churchill, *The Gathering Storm* (1948), 50.

5. Johnson v. Eisentrager, 339 U.S. 763 (1950).

6. Near the end of the war the Germans began training covert forces called "werewolves" to conduct terrorist activities during the Allied occupation.

7. Al Odah v. United States, 321 F.3d 1134, 1141–42 (D.C. Cir. 2003)

8. Rasul v. Bush, 542 U.S. 466, 480–81 (2004).

9. Hamdi v. Rumsfeld, 548 U.S. 557, 575–76 (2006) *rev'g* 415 F.3d 33 (D.C. Cir. 2005).

10. Boumediene v. Bush, 476 F.3d 981 (D.C. Cir. 2007).

11. Philip Hamburger, "Beyond Protection," *Columbia Law Review* 109 (2009), 1823–2001, at 1885–86.

12. Ex parte Quirin, 317 U.S. 1, 20–21 (1942).

13. John Hart Ely, "The Wages of Crying Wolf: A Comment on *Roe v. Wade*," *Yale Law Journal* 82 (1973), 920–949, at 947.

14. Al-Adahi v. Obama, 613 F.3d 1102, 1102–03 (2010).

15. Al Maqaleh v. Gates, 605 F.3d 84, 87 (D.C. Cir. 2010).

16. 625 F.3d 745, 746–47 (D.C. Cir. 2010).

OUR FIGHTING FAITH, TEN YEARS LATER

1. Charles R. Kesler, "The Moral Challenge," *National Review*, Sept. 11, 2001, http://www.claremont.org/publications/pubid.200/pub_detail.asp.

2. Newdow v. United States, 292 F.3d 597 (9th Cir. 2002).

3. Elk Grove United Sch. Dist. v. Newdow, 542 U.S. 1, 4 (2004).

4. Mike Glover, "Obama Stops Wearing Flag Pin," *Breibart*, Oct. 4, 2007, http://www.breitbart.com/article.php?id=D8S2K3UO0.

5. Jay Newton-Small, "Obama's Flag Pin Flip-Flop?" *Time*, May 14, 2008.

6. *Id.*

7. *Id.*

8. *Id.*

9. George W. Bush, President of the United States, Second Inaugural Address, Jan. 20, 2005.

10. George W. Bush, Address to the Nation, Sept. 11, 2006, reprinted in Aaron Hess and Z. S. Justus, "Re-Defining the Long War," in *Weapons of Mass Persuasion: Strategic Communication to Combat Violent Extremism*, ed. Steven R. Corman et al. (Peter Lang Publishing Group, 2008), 143.

CONCLUSION

1. Samuel Eliot Morison, *The Oxford History of the United States 1783–1917*, vol. 2 (Oxford University Press, 1927), 413.

2. Peter Baker and Scott Shane, "Obama Seeks to Reassure U.S. after Bombing Attempt," *New York Times*, Dec. 28, 2009, A1.

3. Office of the Director of National Intelligence, Summary of the Reengagement of Detainees Formerly Held at Guantanamo Bay, Cuba 1

(2010), http://dni.gov/electronic_reading_room/120710_Summary_of_the_Reengagement_of_Detainees_Formerly_Held_at_Guantanamo_Bay_Cuba.pdf.

4. Barack Obama, Remarks by the President in State of the Union Address, Jan. 27, 2010, http://www.whitehouse.gov/the-press-office/remarks-president-state-union-address.

5. Barack Obama, Remarks by the President in State of the Union Address, Jan. 25, 2011, http://www.whitehouse.gov/the-press-office/2011/01/25/remarks-president-state-union-address.

6. Max Lerner, *Thomas Jefferson: America's Philosopher-King*, ed. Robert Schmuhl (Transaction Publishers, 1996), 86.

7. Quoted in Edwin Corwin, *The President: Office and Powers, 1787–1984*, ed. Randall W. Bland et al., 5th ed. (1984), 18.

8. *The Federalist* No. 48 (James Madison), ed. Jacob E. Cooke (Wesleyan University Press, 1961), 334.

9. *The Federalist* No. 70 (Alexander Hamilton), ed. Cooke, 471.

10. *The Federalist* No. 73 (Alexander Hamilton), ed. Cooke, 494.

11. *Id.* 495.

12. *The Federalist* No. 71 (Alexander Hamilton).

13. *The Federalist* No. 70 (Alexander Hamilton), ed. Clinton Rossiter (New American Library, 1961), 472.

14. *The Federalist* No. 74 (Alexander Hamilton), ed. Cooke, 500.

15. Alexis de Tocqueville, *Democracy in America*, vol. 1 (1835), 8.

16. Barack Obama, President of the United States, Inaugural Address, Jan. 20, 2009.

17. Quoted in OnTheIssues.org, Barack Obama on Homeland Security, http://www.ontheissues.org/2008/Barack_Obama_Homeland_Security.htm (last visited on July 20, 2011).

18. Quoted in *The Presidents: A Reference History*, ed. Henry Franklin Graff, 3rd ed. (Thomson/Gale, 2002), 442.